School Administration as a Craft

Foundations of Practice

Arthur Blumberg
Syracuse University

Allyn and Bacon, Inc.
Boston   London   Sydney   Toronto

Copyright © 1989 by Allyn and Bacon, Inc.
A Division of Simon & Schuster
160 Gould Street
Needham Heights, Massachusetts 02194

Library of Congress Cataloging-in-Publication Data

Blumberg, Arthur, 1923–
    School administration as a craft : foundations of practice /
Arthur Blumberg.
        p.   cm.
    Bibliography: p.
    Includes index.
    ISBN 0-205-11674-4
    1. School management and organization–United States.   I. Title.
LB2805.B564   1988
371.2'00973–dc19   88-23085
                                                                        CIP

Printed in the United States of America
10 9 8 7 6 5 4 3 2 1 92 91 90 89 88

To the Memory
of
My friend and my Dean
Burton Blatt
A rare, rare person, indeed

Contents

Foreword

About 40,000 new nonfiction books are published in America each year. Clearly, most serve some useful purpose but only a small percentage make a unique contribution to a particular subject. Arthur Blumberg's book *School Administration as a Craft* is one of those few. Blumberg uses the metaphor *craft* to provide a refreshing and compelling view of the nature of administrative work. This view, I believe, can serve as the long missing bridge between what is known in the mind and experience of school administrators and the new practice situations they face.

The development of educational administration as a field of professional study and practice has long been stunted by its inability to link together theory and research and knowledge acquired from experience with the knowledge needed to solve the practical and immediate problems school leaders encounter. Heretofore, the metaphors *applied science* and *art* have been the candidates for helping both scholars and practitioners come to grips with this problem. Neither has worked very well. Applied science, for example, frames the way we think about educational administration in the direction of a tightly connected knowledge production chain that moves from theory and research to model building and from model building to practice prescriptions. But rarely do the models and prescriptions fit the specific problems and contents that administrators face. The verdict on applied science is that it reads well in books and sounds great in speeches but just doesn't work in practice.

The metaphor *art* leads us to think about the more implicit, tacit, and intuitive aspects of administrative work. But art is too difficult a concept to get a handle on and its qualities are often presumed to be well beyond the ordinary. This metaphor often causes us to lapse into mystical and transcendental images of educational administration, particularly when applied to leadership.

Before reading Blumberg's book, the promising alternative to applied science and art for me was to view educational administration as a form of reflective practice. This stance, borrowed from Donald A. Schon, acknowledged the dynamic and context-specific nature of administrative work and cast the role of the administrator as that of managing messes. In reflective practice the purpose of knowledge is to inform the administrator's judgment by helping to frame issues and to suggest new alternatives. The image of educational administration as reflective practice is helpful but leaves too much unanswered. Just how does all of this informing happen? How do administrators think about their work? What is the link between one's formal training, accumulated on-the-job experiences, and deciding what to do given the situation at hand? How do you coach reflective practice anyway? Blumberg's book takes a giant step toward answering these questions.

Readers will appreciate the style with which Blumberg writes. He tells his story in plain English, using his wit and charm on the one hand and the real-life thoughts and experiences of the administrators he studies on the other. He begins to explore the concept of craft by describing how the mind, heart, and head of the potter, working in tandem with the clay, are brought together to produce something useful. He then takes readers from the potter's wheel to the school, noting similarities. The craft of administration, Blumberg maintains, "is the exercise in individual fashion, of practical wisdom toward the end of making things in a school or a school system 'look' like one wants them to look." There are certain skills involved in any craft but the administrator-artisan develops certain kinds of know-how that go beyond just being able to employ these skills. Among them, according to Blumberg, are developing and refining "a nose for things"; having a sense of what constitutes an acceptable result as one works in a particular situation; an understanding of the nature of the "materials" one is working with; knowing administrative techniques and having the skill to employ them efficaciously; knowing what to do and when to do it; and having a keen sense of "process." By *process*, Blumberg means the administrator's ability to feel accurately what is happening while working with others, much as the potter senses or feels air bubbles in the clay.

In a series of delightfully written and well-argued chapters each of the know-hows of the administrative craft is described. Blumberg combines analogies from woodcarving, fishing, and other crafts with firsthand accounts of the work of principals and other school administrators. I learned a great deal about the nature of administrative work in reading these chapters and gained a far better understanding of how administrators think and act. Important for me was the concept of "rules of thumb" and the way they were used by administrator-artisans he studied. Rules of thumb don't tell school administrators what to do but inform their judgment as they make decisions.

I guarantee that practicing school administrators will like this book. It reflects the ways in which they think and act, and it can help them understand better the nature of their thoughts and practice. By contrast, many academics that align themselves with the notion of educational administration as applied science may well find Blumberg's words to be uncomfortable. To this audience I would plead: Give the book a chance. I read *School Administration as a Craft* as a skeptic. By the time I turned the leaf of the final page I became convinced that the book can provide the perspective needed to help us understand how theory and research might best be used and how professional practice might best be informed and improved.

Thomas J. Sergiovanni
Lillian Radford Professor
of Educational Administration
Trinity University

Preface

As I was in the midst of collecting data for this book, I was also involved in the not very exciting task of proofreading the galleys of the second edition of *The Effective Principal* (Blumberg and Greenfield, 1986). Fairly early in the proofreading, I recall remarking, with surprise, first to myself and then to my wife, that many of the thoughts about the practice of school administration that I was now starting to conceive of in craft terms were expressed in that book, but in a different language. In some way that I don't quite understand, what Greenfield and I wrote about the work and thinking of some out-of-the-ordinary school principals was foundational to developing the idea for this one.

I make note of that recollection for two reasons. First, it was important for me to understand that whatever it was that was happening to my own work and thinking was, itself, evolutionary. The idea of administration-as-craft did not just suddenly occur but apparently created a good conceptual link between the way I was starting to think and the way I had begun to understand that school administrators thought. And I found further, as I tested out the idea of their work as craftwork with school administrators, that we were very easily able to develop a common language about that work.

The second reason that recollection is important to me is the thought that the prior work was "foundational" to this one and has led to the use of the word *foundation* in the subtitle. A thought that is a foundation for something else provides, most importantly, a way to think about it. And that is the ultimate aim of this book—to provide a way of thinking about the practice of school administration that is in touch with that practice in a manner that neither the metaphors of administration-as-science nor art are.

To be "in touch" means the development and sharing of a common language; there can be no being "in touch" without it. I think this has been a major problem between the university and the field since school administrators began to professionalize early in this century. It is clear that the problem is with us today as the research of the professoriate has become ever more sophisticated and, in the process, resulted in findings that the practitioners seem to find ever more meaningless. It is not, incidentally, a matter of the practitioners not respecting the intelligence of those of us who live and work in the academy. They just think it is misdirected—and, I believe, with some justification.

This book, then, is intended partly as a way of bridging the language gap. I see it as a start and not the final word. I believe that the concept it proposes, administration-as-craft, will provide a vehicle for people interested in studying the field of administration and those engaged in practice to talk about common concerns.

I have been told that I write the way I talk. Most of my talk, whether it be in the classroom or my office, is aimed at getting students or colleagues to join me in a conversation. One way that the reader might treat this book would be as a continual invitation to join the conversation. In situations where the book is to be used as a text, a way to engage students in its study is to have them develop cases of administrative work and then analyze them in craft terms. I have tested that idea out and it seems to provide a provocative discussion and learning vehicle.

In the early chapters of the book, I take the notions of administrative science and traditional research that has been conducted in the name of that "science" to task, perhaps too harshly. I apologize in advance to any colleagues who may take umbrage at my suggestions that their efforts to make a science out of the study of school administration are apt to have little payoff. Rather, I think that their efforts, *like mine,* have been misguided.

Florence Toms is due my thanks for being my primary transcriber of tape-recorded interviews. She also learned much about school superintendents and principals through that process, as she told me on a number of occasions. Lindy Cirigliano has typed for me so well I scarcely know how to thank her. The accuracy with which she is able to interpret my scratching continues to amaze me.

Finally, I need to note my dedication of this book to the memory of Burton Blatt. He died much too young a man, leaving all of us poorer for the loss. But we are richer for the experience of having known him. Part of Burt, I'm sure, is in this book.

Arthur Blumberg

Chapter One

Introduction

It is my intent in this book to present and illustrate a way of understanding the field of school administration and the work of administrators as a craft and craftwork, respectively. This is not a book of prescriptions concerning effective administrative behavior, nor is it about the "nuts and bolts" side (important as that may be) of a superintendent's or principal's work. Neither is this a "how-to" book, whose aim is to help school administrators learn new techniques. I offer these caveats at the outset because, as the reader will discover, the data on which I draw have to do with the manner in which practicing administrators think about problems and what they do about them. And though some people may indeed get "how-to" ideas from reading this, my hope is that they will be considered as a value-added result beyond my central purpose.

On a somewhat different level, within the context of the daily work of school administrators, this book deals with the question posed by Wittgenstein in *Philosophical Investigations* (1958) and quoted by Howard (1982, p. 58), "Ask yourself: How does a man learn to get a 'nose' for something? And how can this nose be used?"

The phrase "has a nose for . . ." is one that communicates its intent unambiguously through every stratum of American society and probably of most others, at least in the Western world. It is applied to people who, in connection with their vocation or avocation, have somehow learned skills of understanding, insight, persuasion, or manipulation that enable them to do things that other people cannot. These skills may apply to incredibly complex and esoteric types of work or to work that may be considered by some (mistakenly, I believe) as requiring a relatively low level of intellectual activity. Thus, some physicians seem to have diagnostic noses that are acknowledged by colleagues to be

1

unusual; some research scientists have a nose for sensing more elegant questions than do others; and some automobile mechanics can listen to your car's engine and tell you what is or is not wrong whereas others must take the carburetor apart before they know the problem. Some people have learned in ways we are not sure about to have better noses for their work than others.

This book, however, is not about those unusual school administrators who seem to have a sort of sixth sense about the problems they confront and who are acknowledged to be masterful at their work. To the contrary, illustrations of having and using a nose for things will come from a variety of administrators, some of whom may be masters of their craft and some of whom may be considered to be apprentices. Nor does this book present a variant and, perhaps catchy, new twist on a well-established theme. Rather, it represents a search for a better, more functional way to think about school administration and what administrators do than what is reflected in the prevailing work ethos of university professors of administration, their students, and the literature they produce. For the most part, this ethos and the literature are based, first, on the view that there is something called an administrative science that professors teach, research, theorize, and write about. Second, this ethos suggests that the knowledge thus acquired and disseminated to field practitioners through journals or conferences and workshops will be used by them in their day-to-day work, much as a physician applies the results of medical science to his or her practice. One aim of this book is to persuade the reader that the idea of an administrative science, indeed, the idea that there even exists such a thing as an administrative science, is a fallacious one, and that the results of research in this nonscience have had little relevance for the work of school administrators.

Using a term that communicates most readily to people who have had anything to do with boating, and probably people who have not, this book's aim is to persuade the reader to "cast off" the lines that hold him or her to the idea of administrative science and research—at least, tentatively—and, along with the author, inquire into a less esoteric and more functional concept of the work and study of administration.

The title of this book and this chapter's first sentence suggest the replacement of the metaphor of administration as science with that of administration as craft, a concept that Howard (1982, pp. 70–71) defined in the following way: "Craft aims to produce a specific result be it a physical product or performing ability through the development of skills built up through practice." Howard, a philosopher of art, did not include what we might call the human crafts (dealing with people in problematic situations in order to achieve some end) in his definition. But as I hope will become evident, creating just such a metaphor does no violence to the concept. School administrators, after all, do what they do precisely "to produce a specific result" through the exercise of their skills that, deliberately or not, they have learned, practiced, and improved upon over time.

In the next several pages, I give attention to how thinking about school administration as a science developed in this country. I do this to set a backdrop for shedding that way of thinking and for suggesting that (1) what has been proposed as a science is no science at all, and (2) the most that can be said for this nonscience is that it has been nonharmful to the field, although that, too, can be disputed (Callahan, 1962).

The concern for establishing a scientific or research base for the field of education in this country, particularly with regard to matters of instruction, has a long history. It goes back at least to the early days of the organization of the common school system in New York state. For example, in his annual report to the New York State Superintendent of Common Schools, E. W. Curtis (1845), Superintendent of the Eastern District of Onondaga County, discussed the teaching innovation of the use of the blackboard combined with oral instruction without books—a method that he strongly supported. The closing sentence of his report was, "I doubt not that the Normal school at Albany will fully test the great utility of oral instruction in our common schools" (p. 258). This is not exactly an unbiased research proposal, but for our purposes, that is not the point. Besides taking note of this early concern with science and the scientific method, it is interesting to note that just before Curtis made that comment, he wrote of a teacher in Syracuse who "informed me that he taught it [grammar] to the whole school, in lectures, with explanations and examples on the blackboard; and that the pupils learned more in that way in one quarter, than they did with their books, in the common mode in one year" (p. 258). In the context of this book, what seems to have occurred is that the superintendent observed and talked with an innovative teacher who was good at his craft and then felt that the efficacy of the craftsman's work had to be etablished as a general principle through research. We don't know if research on oral instruction was ever carried out, but we can be quite sure that if it was, its results had little to do with what happened subsequently in schools. Innovations in human craftwork do not diffuse through research, best intentions to the contrary.

In the same volume in which Curtis's report appears, his colleague, Orson Barnes (1845), Superintendent of the Western District of Onondaga County, advocated what we take to be a craftwork view of improving instruction but, as we shall see, he sent a somewhat mixed message. Barnes wrote about the developing idea of teachers' institutes:

> Could the teachers of the several counties of this State assemble for two weeks during the vacations of their schools, [with reasonable financial inducements to attend] to compare the results of the various methods of teaching which they have reduced to practice, to cast their free-will offerings into a common reservoir for their mutual benefit, the effects would be seen and felt throughout the State (p. 261).

The implication of Barnes's thoughts are clear. The quality of teaching would be enhanced if teachers could be brought together to share their knowledge and know-how. The mixed message part came two sentences later: "We have also the benefit of lectures connected with educational science, and trust soon to have the assistance of teachers from the State normal school at Albany" (p. 262).

The issue is not, of course, whether or not teachers (or administrators) can benefit from listening to someone "from the outside" talk about problems of teaching (or administering). Rather, what is of interest is that (1) even so many years ago the idea of the existence of something called an "educational science" was beginning to be implanted in the field; (2) this science, its substance and its method, was the province of people who worked in what we now call institutions of higher education; and (3) the inference we make that somehow and in some way these people knew better what should occur in classrooms and in schools than the people who were in those classrooms and schools. In some ways, and perhaps particularly so in those long ago years, there is a kernel of truth in this last point. In the mid-1850s, after all, the training required to be a common school teacher was that one merely had to have completed that school's curriculum. We must presume that teachers on the faculty of the Normal school in Albany did indeed have some wisdom that could be shared with their compatriots in the "lower" schools. But that is less the point than the idea that whatever wisdom they had seemed to have been cloaked with the mystique of a science, though it is undoubtedly true that what passed for an "educational science" in those days bears little relationship to the same concept today. Nonetheless, the roots of the scientific tree were there. Nourished by generations of educators, those roots have proved to be remarkably hardy, despite doubts about whether or not the tree has borne fruit that is useful and used.

There seems to have been little professional writing about education, and certainly not about educational administration, in those early days. William Payne (1875) took note of this fact in the Preface of his book entitled *School Supervision,* which is a book about the superintendency as Payne had experienced it in a small city school district, Adrian, Michigan. Incidentally, he was careful to point out that "I do not presume to write for the instruction of those who superintend the school systems of our larger cities" (p. vii). That point, though, is less important for our purposes than others he makes.

Like his superintendent colleagues in New York of some years earlier, Payne sent mixed messages about the conceptual nature of his topic. Though he uses the term *profession,* he starts out with an eloquent statement of what can be thought of as a craftsperson's responsibility to his or her craft:

> Every man is a debtor to his profession. At the outset of his career, the current practice which he adopts is an inheritance left him by his professional ancestry; and this, in turn is to be transmitted to the next generation with such additions as his own industry, sagacity and thrift, have been able to accumulate through a life of toil (p. v).

His book, then, was to be Payne's repayment of his debt to his profession. He would transmit the results of his experience and know-how about superintending a small city school district to those who came after him—a most proper activity for a craftsperson, particularly in those times when such literature was notable by its absence.

But then Payne equates the transmission of his know-how of his craft (which he calls a profession) to the manner by which a science develops. Immediately following the quotation noted above, he writes, "Science grows by increments— insignificant, perhaps in themselves—which individual experience contributes to the common stock . . ." (p. v). In his next paragraph, he seems to include teaching as a profession comparable to law, medicine, and theology, and suggests that, relative to the latter three, "there are numerous treatises on the history and philosophy of the several sciences but practically no literature about education, at least as teachers might find it useful" (p. vi).

My point here is simply to reinforce the idea that, in an unplanned way, the concept of education as a science and now educational administration was one that seemed to receive acceptance by educators, particularly those few who wrote. To be sure, what were conceived to be the boundary lines or methodology of that science were not clear. But for our purposes that is not an issue of great import. Of more importance is that the notion of education and educational administration as sciences was planted and would soon become rather strongly entrenched on the scene as an ethos, which even today the field lives by (at least that part of the field that spends its career in universities).

Evidence can be found in the professional education literature of the early twentieth century that the idea of there being a scientific basis for education, in general, and educational administration, in particular, had achieved acceptance, aided as we shall see by the development of the idea of scientific management. Some of the examples of the nature of this early thought are taken from *Educational Literature* (Garland Publishing, 1979), which is an index of journal articles and books in education from 1907 to 1932. In addition to serving as an index, many of the items include a short summary of their substance. For example, in Volume 1, 1907, we have:

Magnus, P. "The Application of the Scientific Method to Education." *Nature, 22,* August, 76, 434–39.

Opening address before the educational science section of the British Association, April 1907. An argument to show that while education itself may not yet fulfill the condition which would justify its claims to be classified as a science, the scientific method is most effective in dealing with educational problems.

and

Allen, W.H. "School Efficiency" (In his *Efficient Democracy*). Dodd, Mead. pp. 113–141.

A study of the statistical method as the basis for intelligent progress in conducting the school. Shows what is lost in school efficiency by lack of proper methods of record keeping and later use of such records as correctives and guides.

The change from the general notion of "educational science" to a concern with scientific and statistical method certainly did not occur overnight. Precisely when the first ideas about these methods entered the thinking of educators is probably unknown. But we do know that by the early 1900s such thinking was not merely a glimmer in their eyes. Cubberley (1947) implies that it was Edward L. Thorndike who was the prime mover as "In 1904 [he] made the beginnings of a new method of attack by applying statistical procedures to social and educational problems . . ." (p. 692). At about the same time, scholars of administration, undoubtedly influenced by Thorndike's use of statistical procedures, commenced to study that field and publish books about it. The focus of most of their study was on fiscal problems. That they were mostly concerned with financial matters is less important than that they seemed to legitimize administration as a science. For example, Cubberley (1947) notes, "Those early studies marked the beginnings of a long train of related investigations . . . which have laid the basis of standard textbooks and for the scientific study of the problems of city and state school administration" (pp. 692–693).

Indeed, there seems to be little doubt that, by the second decade of the century, thinking about school administration had become "scientific" with a particular focus on statistical methodology. Strayer and Thorndike (1913), for example, published *Educational Administration: Quantitative Studies*. In the Preface, they state "The selections quoted or summarized in this volume are deliberately chosen from the work that has been done at Teachers College, Columbia University, in the application of quantitative methods to school problems." It must be noted that by 1913 Teachers College had started to assume its position as one of the foremost institutions in the country whose faculty was concerned with thinking about and conducting research in education. It must have been no small thing, then, to have two of its prestigious professors lend their names and reputations to the notion of developing a science of administration through the use of quantitative methodology.

Without a doubt a major force that gave impetus to the "administration as science" ethos of the time was the work of Frederick Taylor (1911) that was concerned with scientific management in industry. The idea made its way, for example, into the educational literature through a series of three articles (Levine, 1917) published in *Educational Foundations*. Each was entitled "Better Schools Through Scientific Management." Probably much more important, though, relative to its impact on promoting the idea of school administration as a science, was the work of Ellwood P. Cubberley.

Cubberley, a professor and later dean of the School of Education at Stanford University, was a most prolific and influential writer. He was also a missionary as far as the schools were concerned, as were numbers of other prominent educators of his time. It is also undoubtedly true that he, like many others, was influenced by the work of Frederick Taylor. Several of his books seemed to have been written most specifically as detailed texts for university classes in educational administration. Two comments made in the Preface of *The Principal and His School* (1923) have direct bearing on our discussion:

> The technique of school organization, administration, and supervision, from the point of view of the principal, has now been sufficiently worked out that there is a definite body of concrete experience and scientific information which should be taught to those who are looking forward to becoming principals of elementary schools . . . (p. vi).
>
> The organization of education during the past ten to fifteen years has gone forward by leaps and bounds, and there is every reason to think that the next ten to fifteen years will witness an even greater development in the scientific organization of the instructional process (p. vii).

The god of educational and social science was in his or her heaven. Cubberley had little doubt that in a few years all would be right in the world of the schools, particularly that part of the world that had to do with school administration. All that had to happen was for the social scientists to apply their quantitative methodology to problematic situations of school administration and organization and the generalized answers would soon make themselves evident. We may look back at Cubberley from our vantage point of sixty years or so and smile at what we might describe as his naivete. But that would be unkind. All of us are children of our times, and Cubberley's times, although not the "good old days," were certainly far more simple ones than those in which we currently live. And he certainly had no way of predicting the incredible changes and conflicts that have characterized American life in recent years. Why not, then, be confident on the sure and steady progress of scientific research that would make the schools more knowable, explainable, predictable, and manageable?

Cubberley, of course, was not a voice in the wilderness. His concern with a science of administration was shared by others, particularly his fellow academics. For example, in 1927, the Bureau of Publications at Teachers College, Columbia University, published a booklet by Alexander entitled *Educational Research: Suggestions and Sources of Data with Specific Reference to Educational Administration*. It is instructive to read the first two paragraphs of the booklet, as they are statements about the nature of research in educational administration and the way in which a researcher goes about his or her task of research.

> Research in educational administration seeks to discover, in the light of the purposes of education commonly acknowledged, the most efficient procedures in the organization, supervision, financing and evaluation of the program of educational

service. It results in the statement of principles or the description of procedures essential to the development of an efficient administration of schools.

The research worker in this field employs the methods common to all fields of scientific inquiry. He arrives at the solution of his problems through reflective thinking. In some of the steps in his thinking, he is assisted by more or less elaborate techniques. In others he relies solely upon the methods employed in everyday experience. In any case he inquires concerning the validity of any procedure which he proposes to use, accepting nothing solely upon the sanction of tradition or current practice. He tests the results obtained to determine whether they are consistent with all of the facts pertinent to the administrative procedure or principle under investigation. He favors objective measures and is satisfied with nothing less than competent evidence (p. 1).

There is little doubt, then, about the purposes of administrative research. It results in "the statement of principles" or the description of those procedures "essential to the development of efficient administration of schools." Further, the method of the administrative researcher is the same as that used in "all fields of scientific inquiry." Certainly, Alexander and Cubberley seemed to share a similar vision of what the future of school administration would look like. It would be a future in which science would reign and the totality of the school administration enterprise would be governed by the principles that evolved from the research undertaken. Some notion of this totality can be taken from the list of legitimate areas of administrative inquiry that Alexander went on to discuss.

Among the fields in which the scientific worker in educational administration will institute inquiries are:

1. The governmental control and arrangements for interpreting the desires of the community for education, involving the organization of public education in relation to national, state, and local governments and the financing of the program.

2. The methods employed in enumerating those persons who are subject to the compulsory education law and of securing their regular attendance at school.

3. The organization of schools and of classes with reference to the differences which exist among pupils in intelligence, in physical condition, and in vocational outlook.

4. The development of curricula and of courses of study in the light of individual differences, and on the bases of common factors.

5. The recruiting, assignment, supervision, and remuneration of the staff employed in the schools.

6. The cooperation of schools with other social agencies.

7. The provision of buildings and equipments suitable for the program of education to be conducted in them.

8. The conduct of business affairs of the school system.

9. Reporting to the public the results secured (pp. 1–2).

Very little was not amenable to the know-how and methodological skills of the researcher. Given this know-how and skill, it seems clear that administrative research would result in a codification of the world of school administration in a way that would make the unknown knowable. Questions ranging from school-community relations to curriculum to supervision to truancy would no longer be questions. Or, if they were, they could be answered through appropriate research. An unbounded faith indeed!

An additional, rather unobtrusive, point needs to be noted concerning Alexander's booklet. It was published at and used by faculty and graduate students at Teachers College. The thought is simply this: Building on my point about the Strayer and Thorndike book, from the mid-1920s, until about the late 1950s, Teachers College was a sort of "mother church" of educational administration in this country. At least, that was the lore. Its professors had national and international reputations and the number of its graduates was enormous. Its influence on thinking about school administration in this country was widespread. The faith was propagated and there were undoubtedly many willing converts who would continue to recruit and influence novitiates.

The intent here is certainly not to insult Teachers College. It is simply to note the fact that it was and still is a tremendously influential institution and that its commitment to the idea of a science of school administration was one that could not be ignored. This influence and commitment to the idea of administration as a science became reflected in the curricula of departments of educational administration in major research universities, the institutions with the most influence in any professional field. Not only did graduate students, particularly those who aspired to the doctorate, take courses in "administration," but they also took the traditional "stat" sequence of three or more courses plus at least one in quantitatively oriented research methodology. Indeed, as if to fulfill Cubberley's prediction, the universities were producing and continue to produce a corps of rather competent researchers who devote their time and energy to the continual refinement of the "scientific" principles governing the administration of the schools.

It is probably true that these efforts resulted in the theory movement in educational administration and the organization of the University Council on Educational Administration in 1956, a loose federation of major research university departments of school administration that were concerned with theory and research in administrative science.

Support for the administration-as-science idea came from another source as well. In 1956, the College of Business and Public Administration at Cornell University published the first issue of the *Administrative Science Quarterly*. Its introductory comment read as follows:

When we look back, in 1966, [ten years after its first issue was published][1] it may be obvious that administration was at a prescience stage in 1956. Yet if the name of this journal proves to have been premature, it was not lightly chosen. It expresses a belief in the possibility of developing an administrative science and a conviction that progress is being made and will continue . . . (p. 1).

If in ten years—or hopefully five—we can honestly conclude that we know better than we did in 1956, the belief and conviction upon which this journal is founded will be upheld (p. 2).

This is a refreshingly modest statement of purpose. It certainly contrasts sharply with Cubberley's statement in 1923, which left the reader with little reason to doubt that by the 1930s most of the answers to school administrative problems would be in hand, thanks to the science that the editors of the *Administrative Science Quarterly* hoped in 1956 it might be possible to develop.

If this last point leaves one a bit confused, that is not hard to understand. It is probably true that Cubberley's notion of a science of administration was of a much different order from that of the *ASQ* editors. Perhaps each was satisfied during the time spans they specified as important. One thing is abundantly clear, however: In no way could a practicing administrator of any stripe get much help concerning his or her job from reading the *ASQ*. Perhaps that was not its intent, in which case one might ask why bother calling it *Administrative Science?* One presumes, for example, that practicing physicians read and are helped in their practice by medical research journals. The same presumption cannot possibly hold in the case we are considering. If the reader doubts this, I invite him or her to pick up any copy of the *Administrative Science Quarterly*, read the table of contents, and speculate on its practical use for an administrator.

The same point can be made about the *Educational Administration Quarterly*, even though the editors in its first issue, Winter 1965, say, "Believing in the essential unity of theory and practice, the editors hold as major purposes of the *Quarterly* an increase in communication between and among professors and practitioners . . ." (p. iii). In the Spring issue of 1982 (Vol. 18, No. 2), the editors commented on the years of the *Quarterly's* publication:

Only with respect to the involvement of practitioners do concerns remain. We are aware, on the one hand, that practicing educational administrators are busy and perhaps beleaguered; on the other hand, we remain convinced that they should have a role in scholarly publication such as *EAQ* (p. iv).

One may sympathize with the editors of the *EAQ*—to a point. It certainly is not an unseemly aim to think about professors and practicing school administrators joining together in scholarly dialogue. But the point at which sympathy has to stop is reached when one considers the content of what the professors—the "scientists"—write about. For example, in the same issue of the *EAQ* just noted, the table of contents is as follows:

Methodological Rigor in Naturalistic Inquiry: Some Issues and Answers by R. Owens.

Do Political Ideologies Influence Education in the U.S.? by R. Kimbrough.

Two Images of School Organizations: An Explicative and Illustrative Text by W. Firestone and R. Herriott.

Educators' Illegal Behavior and Deterrance: A Response Allocation Approach to Malpractice in Education by F. Nelson.

Alternative Perceptions of Cost and the Resource Allocation Behavior of Teachers by D. Monk.

Religion and Employment: How Extensive is a Teacher's Religious Freedom? by B. Beezer.

Such a table of contents hardly seems capable of whetting the reading appetites of many practicing school administrators. The interests of professors of educational administration and those of the practitioner seem to be widely disparate. As many a superintendent or principal will tell a professor, for example, "If you want to know about school administration, come see us in the real world." I think they would not be inclined to say that, incidentally, if they could point to a piece of research about school administrators that had influenced their lives. I've not talked to any who can do that.

The phrase "Come see us in the real world" is a good point to leave this discussion of what I think is the nonscience of administration. My interest has been to suggest that an incredible amount of time, energy, thought, and financial resources have been poured into pretty much of a dry hole. It is time to move on and I hope this book will provide an avenue for that movement.

The book is organized into three parts. Part One, entitled, "The Argument," focuses in greater detail on the appropriateness of the concept of craft as a way of thinking about the work of school administrators. The several chapters of Part Two, "The Administrative Craft in Thought and Action," are concerned with school administrators and how they think about their work, all within the context of administration-as-craft. The two chapters that comprise Part Three, "Beyond the Craft," are discussions of questions I asked myself as I wrote what preceded them.

A few words need to be said about how I gathered the information that forms the basis for discussion, particularly in Part Two. Having the abstraction "administration-as-craft" clearly in mind and being convinced that it was a valid one to pursue, I was in need of a description and explanation of what it meant to engage in a craft. This thought led me first to talk with some people who are bona fide craftspeople. I visited and talked with a couple of potters, a woodcarver, and a cabinetmaker. I asked them to tell me about their work, how they went about it, what they thought about, where they learned how to do what they do, and so forth. My objective was to inform myself better about how craftspeople engage in their work and to find out what became important to them as they made things. In a very real way, these discussions became part of the basis for this book.

From working with a lump of clay to administering a school or a school district may seem like a quantum leap. I found out that this was not the case, though, if one is interested in the commonalities that exist when people think about their work as they are working or when they reflect on it. This became apparent to me as I spent days with school superintendents and principals, following them around and talking with them about what was going through their heads as they did things. I also talked with a number of those people outside their workplaces and I held several group interviews with administrators—again, always with the purpose of inquiring about what they had in mind as they confronted problematic situations on the job.

To repeat, my aim in all this was not to try and develop the concept of craft of administration. Somewhat arrogantly, I now think, that concept was already established as a viable one. Rather, what I wanted to do was to be able to understand and explain that concept in the context of the real-life world of the school administrator. Though my data come from superintendents and principals, the book is really about neither, except that what they do and think and say provides an explanation for the central idea of this book. My assumption is that this central idea—the practice of a craft—will generalize to all practical endeavors in or outside the schools.

• Endnote

1. Parentheses not in the original.

Part One

The Argument

Chapter One was not only an introduction to what this book is about, but an introduction to "The Argument." I think I have left little doubt in any reader's mind that I consider the metaphor of "administration-as-science" to be illusionary. In this sense, the notion of a scientific theory of administration is also illusionary, although, as we shall see in a later chapter, it is not a flight of fancy to think of administrative theory as a commonsensical and systematic general statement about the field.

So, there is an argument. It is a conceptual one. I am the protagonist whereas most of my university-based colleagues are on the other side of the fence. I am quite sure I can win the conceptual argument—administration-as-craft opposed by administration-as-science—but I am also certain that to win that battle will not win the war over the direction (content and process) in which thinking about administration and the preparation of administrators will take. This is because the point of view of administration-as-craft is at odds, and very strongly so, with the predominant attitude of most of those who study and write about school administration—the same university professors who study and write about it as if it were a science.

The craft idea is also at odds with the culture of the university and its emphasis on scientific research. Professors are children of the university culture in that its values become theirs if they wish to become respected members of its faculty. In a somewhat cynical reaction, which is not my usual bent, my sense is that for professors to study something conceived of as a craft would symbolize a less than academic endeavor and one to be avoided. Science, indeed, reigns supreme at the university, especially among its graduate faculties, and school administration is one of those. Though I do not wish to belabor the point, the position taken in this book is that no such thing as an administrative science exists, and thus the need for some thought to be given initially to "The Argument."

Part One has three chapters. Chapter Two, "Neither Science nor Art," sets out the broad base of what is to follow. For the most part, it consists of a rather lengthy quotation from the first paper I published on the notion that the practice of administration is a craft, not an applied science nor an art. In this chapter, I take the reader on a reflective journey with me as I tried to understand my uneasiness concerning my own work and thinking, as well as the direction the study of school administration has taken over the last twenty-five years or so.

Chapter Three, "The Touch of a Craft," takes "The Argument" further. Its initial concern is with metaphors and analogies and problems with their use, paying particular attention to the craft metaphor. It presents some thinking about how teaching is considered as a craft as a means of moving closer to our own concern with administration. It also deals with the thoughts of some writers who dismiss the idea of teaching as a craft because they see the concept of craft as symbolizing a rather low-level, almost anti-intellectual activity. The chapter closes with a comparison of the thoughts of a potter and a principal as they reflect on their work, the potter in a global way, and the principal with regard to a particular incident in school with which he had to deal. As becomes clear, the potter and the principal think in similar terms about very different kinds of work. Thus, "The Touch of a Craft" becomes apparent.

Chapter Four, entitled "From the Potter's Wheel to the Schools," contains a general definition of what the idea of craft means when used in connection with school administration. It provides an umbrella under which more specific elements of that craft are discussed. Most important, though, as its title implies, the chapter closes my conceptual argument and says, in effect, "If we choose to think about the practice of school administration as craftwork, here are some broad ideas to which we must attend."

A final point is in order: In a way, this entire book is "The Argument."

Chapter Two

Neither Science nor Art

The content of this chapter is a lengthy quote from a paper I wrote (Blumberg, 1984) that was entitled, in its manuscript form, "The Craft (Not Art, Not Science) of School Administration and Some Other Rambling Thoughts." The citation is included for three reasons. First, that paper was the genesis for this book, though I didn't know it at the time. That is, the idea of trying to study, understand, and explain the practice of school administration through the use of the metaphor "administration as craft" emerged in retrospect rather than as any carefully thought out plan that might use the paper as a springboard. Second, responses to the paper, mostly from practitioners in the field but even from a few professors, were very positive. It was as though I was being told that, on a conceptual level, at least, I had grasped the essence of what it means to "practice" in a way that made abundant sense. Third, because I think that the readers of a book are entitled to know something about how its author thinks—beyond what may be inferred from the text—and because the paper itself is somewhat of a reflection of the way I think, it seems appropriate to include it (with some minor editorial changes).*

I want to put into writing a sort of stream of consciousness that has been going through my head for some time concerning what I have been studying, teaching,

---

*Arthur Blumberg, "The Craft of School Administration and Some Other Rambling Thoughts," *Educational Administration Quarterly*, 20 (1984), pp. 24–40. Copyright © 1984 by the University Council for Educational Administration. Reprinted by permission of Sage Publications, Inc.

researching, and writing about since the mid-1950s. This "what" has generally been concerned with leadership and leadership behavior mostly, but not entirely, in school settings.

If I were to say that I want to call all of this work into question, that would not be true. To do so would be an expression of futility and I certainly don't feel that way about what I've done. It has been fun to write, and at least some of what I have written appears to have been helpful to school people. And certainly it has been fun and, I think, helpful to teach about schools and school leadership in ways that leave students asking more questions and maybe feeling less certain about the topic when a semester is over than when it started. Through it all, though, especially in recent years, I've had a sort of gnawing feeling that I may have been missing the point. And since I think that the general direction of my research and writing until relatively recently has not differed from that of most academics concerned with school administration, I would have to say that it is missing the point too. What follows, then, is an attempt to clarify what I think the point is.

Let me start with a personal anecdote. When I was in graduate school, I had occasion to read Ordway Tead's, *The Art of Administration* (1951). Being enamored with the newly developing field of applied behavioral science, I promptly rejected the idea of administration as an art. I even wrote a term paper (Grade = A) in which I argued that artists were born, not made; that there simply were not enough born artists–administrators to go around, in any event, and the answer to leadership problems in the schools rested in learning and applying more behavioral science. Humankind, thought I, is marked off (or so we believe) from other forms of animal life by its ability to think and then act rationally on its thoughts. Surely, we would soon be able to work out enough in the way of scientific principles about behavior to be able to train people in a fashion that would leave few questions about their performance as school organization leaders. I was ignorant enough of history so that I didn't know that Cubberly (1916), thirty-five years earlier, had suggested pretty much the same idea.

Nevertheless, I was off and running. I wrote about the skills of leadership; I researched and wrote about supervisory behavior; I taught about leadership behaviors. I became involved in the sensitivity training movement and researched and wrote about that. Becoming involved in the field of organizational development came naturally to me, and, once more, I taught, researched, and wrote about that. I did all this with a rather sublime confidence that things were working the way they should. All that had to happen was to get enough people skilled in the techniques that I *knew* would work and many of our problems in education would be solved. If this sounds simple-minded, let me quickly say that I was not totally naive. I also knew that we were in for a long haul, but I had abundant faith in the behavioral sciences and in the rationality of our kind. In time, I believed that intelligent people would apply to the school scientifically based ideas and methods of organizing and working and would assure motivated and productive people.

It's a little hard to say when I started to lose my innocence. There was no cataclysmic event. Rather . . . the process seems to have been a gradual one. Certainly it had some of its roots in the fact that whenever I walked into a school, I had a sense of having been there before. I don't mean to imply that my feelings of *deja vu* were negative. Nor does the sameness I felt imply that youngsters were not getting a good education—or *were* getting a poor one, for that matter. It just seemed to me that schools were operating in much the same way that they have been for a good number of years. For example, I recently served as a fourth grade teacher's aide for a week in a classroom of a very good teacher. I wanted to get in more direct touch with life in schools, and what better way to do that than by working in one, if only for a short time. The point, though, is that with a few exceptions that were idiosyncratically related to the physical structure of this school, my experience brought back complementary memories of my own "grammar" school time. And it was a good time.

The gradualness of the loss of my innocence, as I think about it, was also related to my own research and study. That is, for the last twenty years or so I have talked with supervisors and teachers about their experiences with one another. The language they use to describe these experiences today is practically the same as was used in the early 1960s. Further, in one study I had done on the language and thoughts of supervisors of the mid-nineteenth century, I found some incredible similarities in thinking about education, teachers, and the schools between that time and now. That discovery did, indeed, give me pause.

In any event, I found myself giving attention, as I wondered about schools and their leadership, less and less to whether or not there was a $p < .05$ relationship between this or that behavioral style and teacher satisfaction, for example. And I found myself thinking more and more about questions of the unquantifiable "somethings" of the person or people who administer schools that seem a bit out of the ordinary in their goodness. Of all things, I found myself starting to embrace a sort of modification of the great man (or woman) theory of leadership, a position that I had been taught to disregard and which I believed had no substance. A couple of important things influenced and supported the shift in my thinking.

First, a few years ago, a colleague (William Greenfield) and I decided to study the school principalship in a way that had not been done previously. Our initial focus, appropriately oriented to the behavioral sciences, was to be on the reference groups to which principals attended as they went about their business. It was to be an interview study. What we ended up with was not what we expected. Rather, the product was a book entitled *The Effective Principal* (Blumberg and Greenfield, 1986). For the most part, it is a description and analysis of the work-world views of eight principals who, by reputation among their peers, were considered out-of-the-ordinary educational leaders. Of course, we analyzed our data to find what commonalities emerged from all this. What developed was that these principals, though they were very different people, did indeed have some things in common. They all had a vision of what a school should be; they were clear about and oriented toward their goal; they were secure in themselves; they had high tolerance for ambiguity; they tended to test limits, to be sensitive to the dynamics of power, and to approach problems intuitively, it seemed, from a highly analytical perspective.

What occurred to me, only softly at the time, but more loudly now, was this: I thought I could make some sort of behavioral science case for the importance of most, but not all, of these factors in the exercise of school leadership. But, what we were really writing about were some characteristics these people seemed to have had long before they were exposed to "science" in their graduate education. They brought *themselves* with them to graduate school, so to speak—their visions, their security, their intuitions—and they took themselves back to their schools when they finished, knowing some new things, perhaps, but still basically themselves.

I note now that we dealt with the implications of this idea rather tentatively in a couple of paragraphs. We suggested that merely knowing some things and having some leadership "skills" may not be where the motherlode was. Now I think that was the understatement of the year.

Second, in preparation for teaching a course on the school principalship, I re-read Bridges' (1982) article that reviewed the research on the school administrator from 1967 to 1980. It is not a flattering review. In fact, he writes ". . . the research seemed to have little or no practical utility. In short, there is no compelling evidence to suggest that a major theoretical issue or practical problem relating to school administrators has been resolved by those toiling in the intellectual vineyards since 1967" (p. 25). I recall, on reading these sentences, smiling to myself and saying, "So what else is new?"

Bridges then goes on, somewhat apologetically it seemed to me, to suggest that other and more in-depth critical reviews of the research literature should be conducted. That should focus on six specific areas of research on school administrators that occurred with some frequency in his own review. My feelings here were, "Well, good luck!" What I am trying to say is that I had come around to the notion that efforts to conduct or review research in educational administration, if one approached them with the idea of trying to solve a problem or help administrators do a better job, might be better left undone. My bets are that one cannot point to a single administrative practice that has been influenced in any significant degree by research on the behavior of administrators.

This is not to say that we should stop doing research on schools or school administration. It is to say, though, that we ought to be clear about *why* we do it. I will settle for the goal of research being simply to produce relatively reliable and valid knowledge about what I call the psycho-social texture of schools. I should not try to kid myself into thinking that such knowledge will offer guidance on what administrators ought to do and how they ought to do it. I have already given my reason for taking this position. But to repeat, I believe that whatever it is that a person essentially is going to be as an administrator, that person already *is* before he or she finds out about our research. I do not mean, of course, that nothing useful may be learned from such research. I simply want to suggest that the extent to which an administrator has studied this research has, as I see it, little or no bearing on how he or she performs on the job. And I think this circumstance is not a function of the methodological rigor of the research.

My reading of Bridges' review, then, confirmed what I thought I already knew—that the practice of school administration and the results of research on schools or administration seem to have little relevance for each other and that there is good reason for this. And I'd be amazed if this condition changed. That same reading also stimulated some thinking about things of which I was much less sure. The question was, if being and functioning as a school administrator has so little to do with the results of research on that topic, what is a productive way to think of the practice of school administration? "Productive" meant for me a way of thinking I could be comfortable with and that might make sense to other people.

My thinking went back to the idea I had rejected many years ago—administration as an art. I browsed through Tead's (1951) book again only to be disappointed. The first chapter is entitled "Administration—A Fine Art?" The question was actually rhetorical:

If work with paints or clay, with combinations of sounds in music, with combinations of words and ideas in literature—if these are fine arts, we are certainly entitled to call that labor also a fine art which would bring closer together in purpose the organized relationships of individuals and groups to each other (p. 4).

Having said that, Tead was pretty much done. There is no discussion of how an artist's work may be different from other forms of human endeavor nor is there any notation of art or fine art in the Index. This is not to criticize the book itself which is a rather good discussion of administrative problems and functions. But *why* is administration an art? Because Tead said it was, as he so defined leadership (Tead, 1935) in an earlier book. Also my cynical side guesses that perhaps it gave the book a catchy title. Certainly if one had an intellectual curiosity about how the concept of art or a fine art does or doesn't fit with the activity of administration, *The Art of Administration* is not the book to satisfy that curiosity.

A quarter of a century after Tead's book was published seemed not to have made much difference in the art-administration realm. In what was an extremely thoughtful critique of research on the behavior of administrators, Griffiths (1979) makes the following comment, ". . . there is much in administration that lies outside the scope of theory. The practice of administration is largely an art that reflects the personal style of an administrator and the environment in which the person functions. Much of this lies beyond the reaches of theory as we know it" (p. 53). As with Tead, though, I was left with a statement of what purports to be fact and that is the end of that. How much is "largely" and how much is "much" is not made clear. But Griffiths goes on to suggest some new directions for explanatory and predictive theory development in educational administration (e.g., garbage can theory, loose coupling, environmental-situation). These, when tested through rigorous designs by competent researchers, would take the practice of administration ("largely an art") and make it more knowable as an applied science. Or, perhaps, by working on these new directions, it may become possible to put boundaries around the art of administration so that, at the least, we will be able to say that so much is science and so much is art. Needless to say, that thought left me with an uncomfortable feeling.

More discomfort came from reading Bogue and Saunders' book, *The Educational Manager: Artist and Practitioner* (1976). Similar to Tead, the terms "art" and "artist" are used early on—in the Preface. There is no notation of them in the Index. Bogue and Saunders do give a couple of brief, and I must say platitudinous, definitions. The manager as artist is conceived as "an organizer of talents" and the art of management "involves righting wrongs and healing wounds." There is a chapter in the book entitled "Organizing as a Management Art" in which the term "organizational artistry" is used twice, but I was left wondering just what that meant. Further reading did not enlighten me.

The dilemma I found myself with, then, went something like this: On the one hand, the idea of administration as a science, despite the fact that we have an *Administrative Science Quarterly* which might be more appropriately entitled "Organizational Behavior Quarterly," doesn't appear to hold water. If science implies the discovery of cause-effect relationships, whatever "scientific" knowledge we have about school administration is jelly-like to say the least. In a recent article, Rosenberg (1983) makes my critique seem like child's play. This is not to say that descriptive studies or those that seek to explain individual or organizational behavior may not be helpful to an administrator. But surely, for example, no research needs to be conducted to know that you have a better chance of getting adults to behave like adults at work if you treat them like adults than if you treat them like children. On the other hand, to hang one's hat on administration as an art, while appealing, seems to be symbolic of a position that suggests, "Well, we don't know what we're talking about, anyway, so we might as well call it an art and we won't get too many arguments." This would not be too difficult a position for me to accept. For one thing, by accepting this, I could go along my merry way doing what I have been doing for a number of years. I would have fun. No one would be terribly worse off and no one would be terribly better off.

Another part of me, though, took over at this point. It is that part of me that I call my "sniffer" tendency. The label comes from a classroom exercise in which I once asked my students to think of a metaphor that might describe a dominant part of their work style. I joined in and characterized myself as a beagle, a dog whose nose is close to the ground and simply seems to spend a lot of time just sniffing around until it finds something that will occupy its attention for a while.

I became involved in a "sniffing around" activity aimed at learning more about how the concept of art could be used to understand administration. It involved trying to understand what art is—and what it isn't—from the point of view of people whose life is devoted to the study of that topic, philosophers of art.

As I write about what I learned from my brief study of the philosophy of art, I do so with some uneasiness for the obvious reason that I am not a philosopher of art. It is a field with a long scholarly tradition and one in which there is much controversy. Nonetheless, as the old truisms tell us, "Nothing ventured . . ." and "Fools rush in. . . ."

I had two conversations. One was with a graduate student in art history and the other with a philosopher colleague of mine who, while not a specialist in the philosophy of art, is most knowledgeable in that field. Both conversations led to further thought and study.

If I understood my art historian friend to whom I put the question, "How do you define what is art?", the key to the answer does not rest in the finished product—the painting or sculpture, for example—but rather in the expression of something called "lyrical intuition." The term, coined apparently by Croce (1976), refers to a sort of pureness of expression of the imagination that reflects the apprehension of "the pure throb of life in its ideality" (p. 557). That was pretty heavy stuff for a behavioral scientist. For one thing, one would be hard put to think of the idea in empirical terms. How does one measure, for example, the ability of a person to convey in his or her work "the pure throb of life"? The answer is, of course, one doesn't. One simply accepts, quite gratefully, the nondefined and nonmeasureable ability of another to do so.

I was convinced that I was on the right track. Croce's ideas were taking me beyond the bland and rather meaningless "administration is an art" statements. At least I thought they were. I thought, for example, I had known an administrator or two who could apprehend and express "the pure throb of life" and if I did, then I might come to understand more fully the idea of the art of administration. That was exciting.

As I continued to read Croce's paper, however, I was soon disabused of the thought that there could ever be an art of administration. Because, it seemed to me, of the difficulty that attaches to defining art as the expression of lyrical intuition in other than philosophical terms, Croce went on to write about art in terms of what it *is not*. The last two of seven "is not's" struck directly at the problem with which I was dealing and set it in a new light. They were:

> *Art is not instruction or oratory:* it is not circumscribed and limited by service to any practical purpose whatever, whether this be the inculcation of a particular philosophical, historical or scientific truth, or the advocacy of a particular way of feeling and the action corresponding to it. . . .
>
> As art is not to be confused with the form of practical action most akin to it, namely instruction and oratory, so *a fortiori*, it must not be confused with other forms directed to the production of certain effects, whether these consist in pleasure, enjoyment and utility, or in goodness or righteousness. We must exclude from art not only meretricious works, but also those inspired by a desire for goodness . . . (p. 561).

Clearly, if one is to agree with Croce's thinking, administration is immediately removed from the realm of thought that conceives of it as an art. If art excludes practical actions which are directed at having utility, then it most certainly excludes school administration, the activities of which are *always* concerned with utility, with a concern for means and ends.

If administration is neither an art nor a science, what then? My conversation with my philosopher friend and colleague helped fill in the gap. Our discussion, as with many of our previous ones, went back to the Ancient Greeks, the words they used to describe certain aspects of life and their views on life. A brief paraphrase of part of our conversation went something like this:

He: For the Greeks, just about all of living of life was an art. From carpentry to sailing a boat. But they didn't give "art" the aesthetic meaning we do now. Rather, they meant a craft, some form of specialized skill. A craft and an art were undifferentiated. The word they used to describe what they had in mind was "phronesis." It means practical judgment, perhaps a form of prudence, and it involves understanding how things work.

I: But how, with this idea, can you differentiate between someone who merely does things adequately, a sort of run-of-the-mill behavior, and someone who does things in ways that defy prosaic description? For example, between an ordinary sailor and one whose boat-handling is a marvelous thing to watch, almost a work of art?

He: What the answer is is that beauty of boat-handling involves an *exquisite* understanding of how things work.

Things were starting to fall together. If the living of life, which includes engaging in some form of work, involves exercising practical judgment based on an understanding of how things work, an exquisite understanding might somehow, in some undefineable way, partially account for the behavior of some administrators who have that *je ne sais quoi* something; that something that makes what they do things at which to marvel. It is necessary to include the "partially" because in addition to an exquisite understanding of how things work, the behavior of these administrators needs to be congruent with their understanding. In a way, it must complement that understanding with an exquisiteness of its own.

As always, though, my philosopher friend enabled me to go further in my thinking by suggesting I read R. G. Collingwood's *The Principles of Art* (1938). Book I of this volume is entitled "Art and Craft." It seemed to me that I was closing in on my quarry and I recall now the excitement I felt when I started my reading. I was not disappointed. In a more readable fashion than Croce (whom I found helpful, but heavy), Collingwood enabled me to start separating out the art and craft ideas with clarity and in ways that made sense. A number of his comments focused so directly on the problem with which I was dealing that I quote them below as a means of sharing my own sense of where I was being led.

> Craft always involves a distinction between means and end, each clearly conceived as something distinct from the other but related to it (p. 15).

> In a craft the end is thought out first, and afterwards the means are thought out (p. 16).

> . . . art proper cannot be any kind of craft (p. 26).

> The artist must have a certain specialized form of skill, which is called technique. He acquires his skill just as a craftsman does, partly through his experience and partly through sharing in the experience of others who thus become his teachers. The technical skill which he thus acquires does not by itself make him an artist, for a technician is made, but an artist is born (p. 26).

> . . . however necessary it may be that a poet should have technical skill, he is a poet insofar as this skill is not identified with art, but with something used in the service of art (p. 27).

> The craftsman's skill in his knowledge of the means necessary to realize a given end, and his mastery of these means (p. 28).

> . . . a joiner knows the specification of a table he is about to make. This is always true of a craftsman; it is therefore true of an artist in those cases where the work of art is also a work of craft (pp. 28–29).

> . . . what makes Ben Jonson a poet, and a great one, is not his skill . . . but his imaginative vision of the goddess and her attendants, for whose expression it was worth while to use that skill . . . (p. 27).

The bits and pieces started to coalesce. A craft may not be an art, but a work of art may also be a work of craft. Being merely skillful, no matter how highly developed the skills, does not imply that one is an artist. Having skills may make one a technician or craftsperson, but to be an artist implies at its roots an inborn something, imaginative vision, or, as what I think is Croce's parallel concept, lyrical intuition. It cannot be taught. It is something that is there. I suspect it is a rare quality—and I think that a rarer condition still is to possess it and be able to express it in a way that draws people toward the work of art.

Collingwood had taken care of most of my intellectual curiosity about the art and craft business. I write that, knowing a student of the philosophy of art will probably be appalled at the brevity of my study. Nevertheless, the philosophers of art have their interests and I have mine. And I was comfortable with the way things were fitting together. The metaphor of administration as a craft made much more sense than administration as a science and it was ruled out as being an art.

I must take a slight parenthetical detour here. I can picture at least some readers reacting to what I have just written with an attitude of "He's just nitpicking. It is of little consequence whether we call administration a science, an art, or a craft as along as we do the things we know how to do." I disagree, of course, with the straw-man I have just set up. It is important that we name things, particularly if those names carry implications for behavior and the hoped for results of behavior. Thus, while "a rose by any other name . . ." suggests that what a flower is called would not take away from its visual and fragrant beauty, a "rose" does not imply any particular kind of behavior. Being a scientist or applied scientist, artist, or a craftsperson does, however. What a scientist does is to try and explain phenomena and predict causality; an artist to express creative imagination; and a craftsperson to produce something. The issue, then, is one of being intellectually honest concerning what we are about. I think it is intellectually dishonest to conceive of school administration as an applied science. I think it is misguided and possibly less a matter of intellectual dishonesty than one of ignorance to call it an art. I think it is intellectually honest and appropriate to think of it as a craft, as the use of skills and techniques in the service of some definable and useful end. At least for me, it has been freeing to rid myself of the idea that I was preparing practitioners of a science that I somehow knew didn't exist. Likewise, understanding the difference between a work of art and a work of craft enables me to be honest with myself, with my colleagues, and with my students.

By no means do I mean to imply that the notion of administration as craft suggests a necessarily pedestrian level of intellectual activity or behavioral skill. I am not speaking strictly of the nuts and bolts of administration functioning, though they are certainly part of the craft and, at times, very important to it. Rather, I think the administration-as-craft idea implies, centrally, a mix of social diagnostic and behavioral skills that when exercised by the administrator somehow have the effect of maintaining both the system's balance and its goal orientation. I don't at all think this is a scientific act, although something we call the scientific method may somehow be mixed up in it. But a method does not make something a science any more than skills of painting make a picture of work of art.

After some further discussion in the paper concerning the possibility of there being such a thing as administrators who could be thought of as artists and some implications of the craft notion for administrative preparation programs, I ended it with the following paragraph.

I think that what I have written reflects a sense of the realism of the school administration world. Also, as I noted earlier, it also reflects my own loss of innocence, a loss that has occurred incrementally over a long period of time and which I find to be quite liberating.

Chapter Three

The Touch of a Craft

In Chapter Two, I asked the reader, in effect, to take my word for it that it made sense conceptually to think of administration as a craft and to reject the idea that it was a science or an art. In this chapter the argument is extended, but it becomes more specific.

There is one *caveat* that we must attend to at the outset, however. It stems from the obvious fact that as we use the idea administration-as-craft, we are thinking metaphorically (much as is the case with administration as a science or an art). The *Oxford English Dictionary* explains that to think metaphorically is to use a "figure of speech in which a name or descriptive term is transferred to some object that is different from, but analogous to, that to which it is properly applied." Thus, throughout the book it is important to bear in mind that we are dealing with a figure of speech—an analogy—and not a literal thing. A school is not a lump of clay. As we shall see, however, the way in which an administrator thinks about his or her work in any of its variant forms bears a close relationship, in analogic fashion, to the way potters, for example, think as they work with clay.

This last point is most important, for as Scheffler (1960, p. 48) tells us in *The Language of Education*, "If a given metaphorical statement is to be judged worthwhile or apt, the analogy suggested must be important with respect to criteria relevant to the context of its utterance." The metaphor of administration-as-craft, then, will be of value to the extent that the analogy it presents throughout this book makes sense to the reader as a way of understanding and ultimately studying the work of administrators. Scheffler makes another point in this regard. He says, "Further, the metaphorical statement does not actually state the analogy, even when a relevantly important one exists. It is rather in the nature of an

26

invitation to search for one and is in part judged by how well the search is rewarded" (p. 48). So, while knowing that there will be times when the analogy will break down, this book may be seen partly as an invitation to the reader to join me in the search and see what we find.

Despite the risks inherent in the unpreciseness of thinking analogically, two important practical functions are served by use of the craft metaphor of administration. First, it creates an image of administrative work to which all of us can relate, and may even provide a sense of the complexity and sometimes elegance of that work. For example, think of situations in which a school principal or superintendent engages in shaping and molding, as potters do; cutting and chiseling, as woodcarvers do; hammering and bending, as metalsmiths do; or interlacing patterned threads together, as weavers do.[1] Further, one can imagine a variety of adverbs associated with these activities that imply skill. For example, *gently, precisely, forcefully,* and *delicately* come to mind.

The second important function stems directly from the first. It is that the metaphor of administration-as-craft provides us with both a language and a way of thinking about the work of administrators that is widely understood, thus enabling conversation about that work to take place in ways that brush away its arcaneness, its knowability only to those who somehow have the key to it all. This is not to suggest that the use of the metaphor reduces the work to thinking in simplistic terms. To the contrary, its use enables its complexity to be discussed intelligently and in practical ways.

• What Is in a Craft?

Most of the thinking and the arguments about the meaning and use of the idea of craft have taken place among scholars of the philosophy of art. Collingwood, whom we referred to in Chapter Two, is thought of as representing the purist school of thought. That is, he drew sharp lines between an art and a craft. For example, the work of a craft is seen as being something produced that has intrinsic worth. As such, it certainly cannot be considered a work of art which, by definition, has no intrinsic worth.

Howard (1982), in his book *Artistry: The Work of Artists,* takes strong issue with what he sees to be the purist separation of the ideas of art and craft. The lines are blurred, according to Howard, and the theme of his book is that the work of artists—what they do—is craftwork. Howard's prototypical example of his point is, of all things, the process of learning to sing.[2] Learning to sing means to learn a craft, which, in his case, means to learn how to use one's physiology, anatomy, and intelligence in order to produce a desired sound—to develop a certain "know-how."

The idea of "know-how" brings us close to the heart of things. That is, we use the term *know-how* to denote the ability of someone to provide or make a specific something. We observe how a cabinetmaker joins wood so as to produce just the desired angle and we say, "Now there's an example of 'know-how.'" Or we are in a meeting where a school principal guides a group toward the resolution of some conflict. Though we may say, "That principal sure runs a good meeting," what we are really saying is that he or she somehow has developed the "know-how" to be able to apply certain techniques and skills that enables him or her to help a group overcome problems.

It all sounds deceptively simple and, to be sure, putting it the way we have it *is* too simple. However, if we attend to a number of Howard's comments, we start to get an inkling of how complex the idea of engaging in a craft really is. Here are some examples:

- *On a definition of craft:* "Craft aims to produce a specific result be it a physical product or performing ability through the development of skills built up through practice" (pp. 70–71).

- *On craftsmanship:* ". . . requires a constant and often mutual adjustment of means and ends that in turn requires extending creative possibilities to the fabrication phases of craft" (p. 130).

- *On skill:* ". . . comprises at the very least both certain habits and their intelligent deployment in situations demanding continuous means-ends adjustments across a wide range of sensory-motor, symbolic, and evaluative frontiers" (p. 176).

- *On critical skills:* ". . . involve an irreducible element of critical judgment as opposed to routinized competencies" (p. 178).

- *On being a master rather than a journeyman:* "The former's idea of a schedule of ends and means *is* that of a plan revisable under the stress of unforeseen difficulties. In effect, the master knows when to be doubtful—and creative" (p. 134).

- *On imagination in craft:* "In effect, it is imagination that enables us to adjust our know-how to particular cases and even to revise it radically or transfer it to new realms of application" (p. 135).

Howard, of course, did not have administration-as-craft in mind as he wrote. He was thinking about a "physical product" or a "performing ability." Yet I'm sure that any thoughtful administrator will be able to relate to and understand the comments he made as being applicable to his or her work—as a starting point, at least. The ideas of producing specific results, of skills developed through practice, of the constant adjustment of means and ends, of the intelligent deployment of one's abilities, of judgment in making one move or the other, of knowing and planning that things must be revised because unforeseen difficulties *will* occur, of letting one's imagination help one know what to do—these elements of conceiving of what a craft is and what a craftsperson does are all part and parcel of an administrator's daily life, even if they are not articulated in that form.

All that one has to do to test this thought out, as I did, is to ask a superintendent or a principal what he or she is currently working on, listen to the response, and then gently probe the person's thought processes about what he or she is doing and why. Or, in a more time-consuming way, but one that is incredibly illuminating, one can accompany a superintendent or a principal through a day's work and then talk about one or more incidents that occurred during the day. Again, through careful listening and probing, one will find out that the individual will be talking the "language-of-craft" even though he or she will undoubtedly not have read Howard's book. The metaphor of administration-as-craft, then, is a very productive one for our concerns here; however, as I indicated earlier and will elaborate on next, the analogy it implies will break down. But then, all analogies do.

• Breakdowns in the Analogy

There are four important places where the analogy breaks down, but none of them, in my judgment, invalidates the metaphor itself or its importance. The first has to do with what is produced as the end of craftwork. In the case of what we conceive to be the work of traditional craftspeople (for example, woodcarvers or cabinetmakers) a tangible product is produced. It is seeable and touchable and, as such, the quality of the skill that went into its making can be judged by others. One can literally take note of the finer and less than fine points of the finished product and evaluate it accordingly. Furthermore, the materials with which the craftsperson works, though they may and frequently do have idiosyncratic characteristics, are inanimate. They have no mind of their own (although a piece of wood may "talk back" to the woodcarver, certainly it does so without intentionality).

The end product in administrative work, on the other hand, is not tangible, seeable, or touchable. This point certainly holds true, without much argument, for most of the things that occur in the daily school world. The satisfaction of a parent who has had problems with a school's treatment of a child and has had those problems resolved by the principal is not a tangible, seeable, or touchable thing for others to observe and admire. Nor is the community support that a superintendent has been able to mobilize in an effort to win passage of a hotly contested school budget. In a very real way, then, the administrator has to be content with a private sense of accomplishment concerning his or her craftwork, although there are occasional accolades for work well done. But there is no permanency to the results of the work. Fellow craftspeople cannot inspect or critique the product because, in fact, it isn't there. (It is true, of course, that failure to produce a desired end can result in a retrospective critique of an administrator's work, but this critique is usually conducted by those who were involved and not by other craftspeople who are inspecting the end result because, in the sense that I noted, there is nothing to inspect.)

Another place the analogy breaks down has to do with the learning, development, and practice of the skills of the administrative craft. Learning the skills of a traditional craft is or can be a much more precise enterprise than learning the skills of the administrative craft. Potters, for example, usually start out in a class, or possibly with individual instruction, where they learn the basic techniques and skills of making things out of clay. They can practice these skills over and over again until they "get it." The same learning conditions do not hold for administrators. When a practicing administrator is asked where he or she learned particular skills, the answer, almost universally, is "through experience." This is not to say that administrators think they did not learn anything in graduate school or by having engaged in an administrative internship. However, it does say that the skills of administrative craftwork seem to be learned more through a process of socialization, perhaps having a good model, and experiential trial-and-error than they are through any conscious teaching, learning, practicing, and critiquing process.

There is one further point that confounds efforts to make the learning of the craft skills of administration more programmable and teachable. The way each administrator confronts a problem, how he or she analyzes and diagnoses it, and what judgments are made relative to what skills are employed to resolve it reflect distinctly idiosyncratic predispositions. That is, what a person brings with himself or herself in terms of personalized learning or "baggage" has a much greater impact on the way that person practices his or her craft than particular skills that the person may have learned somewhere along the line. How else can we account for the highly effective work of some administrators who never took a course in administration or were never administrative interns?

The third way the craft analogy breaks down is that a traditional craftsperson has a choice of the materials with which he or she wishes to work. A potter selects a clay appropriate for a particular project, and this selection depends on his or her knowledge of the characteristics of the clay and previous experience working with it. A woodcarver selects particular wood for the same reasons. Administrators have no choice over the "materials" with which they must work. There is no way for a principal to predict the character of the next discipline case that arrives at his or her doorstep, or what will be the character of the next teacher who has a problem, or the character of the problem itself. The administrator must work with "materials" of all intellectual and emotional sizes, shapes, and forms. Thus, administrators often find themselves working with a "type of clay" with which they don't feel comfortable or whose demands on their skill make them feel incompetent.

There is one more way that the craft analogy breaks down. It needs little elaboration beyond the fact that when one of our traditional craftspeople sees that things are not turning out well with what is being crafted, several options become available: the project can be started all over again, the materials can be thrown away because of their inferiority, or time can be taken to learn new skills. None of these options is available to the practicing administrator.

As I noted earlier, though the analogy implicit in the craft metaphor would break down, I did not believe these breakdowns would invalidate the metaphor;

that is, make it less important or not useful for thinking about the practice and study of the work of administrators. My opinion remains the same after the foregoing discussion. The major points of breakdown occur in matters external to the individual and not, as our discussion will lead us to understand, in the *thinking* about what one is doing or making.

• Teaching as a Craft

The idea of a craft as a description of the work of school people has been almost exclusively associated with the practice of teaching rather than with the practice of administration. Why this is so is a matter of speculation and not germane to our argument, and, as we shall see later, the use of such description has not been without controversy. Nevertheless, discussing the idea of teaching as a craft will provide us with an entree to the idea of thinking explicitly about administration in a similar light.

The literature on teaching as a craft, with a couple of exceptions that I will discuss, does not delve very deeply into the implications of that term for the activity of teaching. Mostly, the word is used in passing as simply a generic descriptor for that activity. For example, Bolster (1983, p. 296), in the context of an article proposing a more effective model for research on teaching, writes that "the most important influence on teachers' knowledge of their *craft*[3] is that it is formulated and determined in a classroom." And in a different context, that of raising questions about the effective school movement, Cuban (1984, p. 149) suggests that "there is a danger in smothering the *craft*[4] and rewards of teaching in the rush to make instruction scientific and efficient." So we have the use of the craft metaphor of teaching by two professors (Bolster at Harvard and Cuban at Stanford) but without any exploration of the meaning of that metaphor. This is not to criticize, but simply to say that it apparently made more sense to both of these scholars to describe the activity of teaching as a craft than as either an art or a science. And, this leads one to ask, "If teaching, why not administering?"

Greene's (1984) paper, "How Do We Think About Our Craft?" treats its subject in much more than a passing manner. It is concerned with teaching and Greene makes several points pertinent to our concern. I quote them as a way of indicating something about the character of thought that necessarily accompanies the idea of craft as it applies to the field of education:

> To speak of craft is to presume a knowledge of and a certain range of skills and proficiencies. It is to imagine an educated capacity to attain a desired end-in-view or to bring about a desired result (p. 55).
>
> To reach back, even for a moment, into our life stories may be to find the sources of our craft (p. 58).
>
> The way we think about our craft must be influenced to some degree at least by the models with whom we came in contact . . . (p. 59).

> We may find ourselves reconstructing familiar techniques, honing a set of unused skills, and—significantly—using our imaginations in what turns out to be an effort to improve our craft. . . . This is in many ways an example of personal knowledge at work; it is also a reminder that mastering a craft goes far beyond repetitions and routines (p. 61).

Though these comments do not detail the depth of Greene's thinking about teaching as a craft, they do provide a glimpse of the richness of the concept with which we are dealing. Note, for example (and substitute in your mind the idea of "administering" instead of teaching), some of the things that she includes under the topic of "How Do We Think About Our Craft?" We need to think about skills and proficiencies, about imagination, about what it is that is good to achieve, about our personal history, about how we learned what we learned, about improving our skills and understandings, and about the idea that becoming a master of one's craft suggests the need to stretch far beyond simply being able to repeat a behavior that seems to have worked in the past.

Indeed, to think about teaching (administering) as a craft is no exercise in the merely prosaic. It involves knowing what to do and being able to do it, and this means the ability to make judgments that are appropriate to each situation. It involves the ability to see beyond the immediate and to think about ends in moral terms (i.e., what is desirable). It means becoming conversant with our own personal and social world so that we can become aware of the ways in which those worlds influence the choices we make as teachers (or administrators). And finally, perhaps the key idea involves the ability to develop a sort of tempered dissatisfaction with one's work that serves as the energy source for becoming better.

So, if we follow Greene's thoughts, indeed we are not led to think about the ordinary. To the contrary, we are led to think about the craft of teaching (administering) in terms that are highly complex, imaginative, and exciting—if one takes them seriously, as I do.

In *Teaching as a Moral Craft,* Tom (1984) approaches the complexity, imagination, and excitement of the craft of teaching by use of the imagery that is conjured up by the metaphor of teaching as fishing. He says, "Fishing, I argue, has three components: mechanical skill (e.g., accurate casting of lures), analytical knowledge (on how to find and tempt fish), and the ability to apply analytical knowledge to specific situations (e.g., the locating of spawning blue gills on lake 38 at Busch Wildlife Preserve on May 16, 1982)" (p. 89).

Of course, teaching or administering is not the same thing as fishing, any more than it is the same thing as weaving or potting. Indeed, teaching or administering is a much more complex activity. Nevertheless, the montage that emerges from the teaching-as-fishing metaphor is a rich one and has import for our argument here. In order to be successful at fishing, one must have three kinds of "know-how." The first is mechanical and skill oriented. One must know how to cast a line with accuracy. This is a teachable skill, although certainly some people are better at it than others. Second, one must have a sort of conceptual know-how concerning the general lore of the craft. What needs to be done in general, for example, in order to find and tempt fish, and particular kinds of fish, at that? In a way, the conceptual question is, If you want to catch fish, how must you think about that activity? Further, when a highly skilled fisherman or woman scans a lake, he or she would be likely to see and think about the lake in different terms than would a novice. And this know-how would come from experience on the particular lake or one similar to it. Third, to catch a particular kind of fish, one must be able to take the skills and conceptual knowledge and apply them to a specific situation. What kind of bait does one use? Does one troll or still-fish? How does one "play" a particular fish? How does one sense a fish is only nibbling at the bait or has actually taken it and is hooked? Everything comes down to specifics, and how well one performs these specifics is a function of experience, coaching, success, and failure.

Even though this analogy also breaks down at several points, the metaphor is a delightful one. It presents us with a mental image of the work of a teacher in a classroom (or of a superintendent in a school district or a principal in a school). Two final points about the metaphor need to be made, however. First, note that the adjective Tom uses in the title of his book is that teaching is a *moral* craft. By this he means that it is concerned with making decisions about desired ends. And when the word *desired* is used, it implies that some ends are better than others. Thus, in fishing, the decision about what is the end product to be attained is not an issue for thought or discussion. It is simply to catch the fish. The same cannot be said for teaching or administering. Choices about ends abound and they all involve some deeper value.

The second point is that the use of the craft metaphor (fishing, potting, woodcarving), because of the vividness of the imagery it conveys, may tend to oversimplify the nature of the know-how that is integral to the kind of work that is the concern of this book. Tom puts it well when he says, "The very complexity of teaching (administering),[5] which makes craft knowledge even more critical for success in teaching than in fishing, also makes the conceptualization and codification of craft knowledge on teaching an extraordinarily difficult task" (p. 99). One can hardly doubt that statement or its transfer to the activity of administering. And, in a way, what this book is about is making a start on that transfer but with the foreknowledge that it can only be a start.

• The Other Side of the Argument

In several places in this chapter and in Chapter Two, I have suggested that I was presenting or extending my "argument" for the idea that the work of administrators is most profitably thought of as a craft, not an art or a science. No one

argues in a vacuum. There is always another view of things, even if one is argu-
ing with oneself. This section discusses what appears to be the major argument
for not characterizing teachers (or administrators) as craftspeople—and my
counterargument.

What appears to lie at the heart of the position that we are ill-advised to
think of the work of school people as craftwork is that to do so diminishes the
chances of that work being thought of as a profession. That is, the argument is
more of a political-economic-social status one than it is having to do with the
substance or processes of the work itself. What seems to be the issue, according
to Broudy (1956), is that professionals know the theoretical why's of their actions whereas an everyday craftsperson does not. He writes:

> A craftsman is guided by knowledge, but it is likely to be the kind of knowledge
> that has been gleaned through long trial-and-error experience. A carpenter makes
> a joint in a certain way. Why? Because that is the way good carpenters have made
> it for a long time. . . .
>
> Our carpenter may defend his methods by arguing that they produce joints
> that work well—better than any other sort. If some hair-splitting professor persists
> in asking *why* this method of making joints works better, the carpenter will prob-
> ably shrug his shoulders and go on making perfectly good joints (p. 178).

In other words, Broudy tells us (1) that craft knowledge differs from professional knowledge in that the former is gleaned through trial-and-error, and
(2) even very good craftspeople know only that their method works, but not why
it works.

I've had a couple of recent experiences that permit me to demur somewhat
from Broudy's argument. Some months ago I was in a dentist's chair, mouth open,
while my friend Seymour was working on my teeth. When he finally got his
fingers and tools out of my mouth and I had a chance to speak, I said, "Seymour,
do you think of yourself as an applied scientist (a professional, in Broudy's terms)
or a craftsman?" Quickly and unequivocally, he responded, "Craftsman." So
a week or two later, we had an interview. At one point, I asked him what he
thought he did particularly well in his work and how he had learned to do it.
"Tapering teeth," he answered, "and I learned to do it through trial-and-error."
There may be some readers who will chuckle at this with the thought that "That
dentist is not for me. I don't want to be practiced on." Seymour, though, is an
excellent dentist, and my hunch is that we are all continually being practiced
on when we sit in the dentist's chair.

The second experience is this: My wife and I were having the kitchen in
our house remodeled, most of the work being done by two young carpenters.
Shortly after reading Broudy's paper, I asked them if they know why they do
things in a certain way or was it that they had simply learned, in an uncritical
way, that "this was the way you do things." As one might expect, the response
was of a yes and no variety. That is, some of the things they did were matter-of-fact

"This is the way it is done" behavior, unthinking in the sense of only knowing that it works. Other things, however, were different in the sense that not only did they know how, or learn to know how on the job because some things didn't work initially, but they also knew why.

I think the issue here is somewhat similar to the one that forms the basis of Howard's thinking, discussed earlier, about the work of artists. Recall his point that the *work* of artists is craftwork. My thinking, as should be obvious, is that the work of administrators is craft-like and the issues of professionalism present problems of a different order. I am sure, for example, that my dentist sees himself as a member of the dental profession. But he also sees his work as the practice of a craft. That is, his professional *practice* is the practice of a craft.

The issue of professionalism, then, is pretty much of a straw man, at least as far as understanding the work of administrators (and teachers) is concerned. It is more related to matters that are political, economic, and social status in orientation than it is to anything else. Let me illustrate this point briefly by reference to comments of two other professors. What is important to attend to in reading them is to think about the language that is used and what it implies. First, Tom (1984, p. 98) quotes Howsam et al. (1976, p. 11): "Professionals cannot exist without an undergirding science. *To fail to develop* principles, concepts, and theories, and to validate practice is to restrict the occupation to the level of a craft." Second, Shulman (1986, p. 43) in an article entitled, "Those Who Understand," writes, "What distinguishes mere craft from profession is the indeterminacy of rules when applied to particular cases."

The key phrases are "to restrict the occupation to the level of a craft" and "What distinguishes mere craft from profession." I don't think I am being out of line when I interpret these remarks as suggesting that it is somehow better to be an educational professional than it is to be an educational craftsperson. Maybe it is, but if it is, my thinking is that it has nothing to do with how well one does one's work. Indeed, the most frequent use of the term *professional* by administrators or teachers of my acquaintance has to do with rules of conduct and not matters of skillful work. And on those occasions when I hear one administrator say of another, "She did a real professional job," what is being referred to is the craft skill (my interpretation) that the person referred to used to accomplish a certain end and not that person's knowledge of theory that she applied to practice.

I don't wish to be misinterpreted as suggesting an anti-intellectual approach to understanding and explaining the work of school administrators. To the contrary, I think their work has an almost exquisitely complex character to which a great deal of thought and intellectual know-how must be given if it is to be performed with even a modicum of success. What I do reject, though, is the idea that seems to be implicit in the comments I have cited that unless an administrator (or a teacher) knows the whys and wherefores of their work *in terms prescribed by professors and other researchers* he or she is somehow not quite worthy. That is, he or she is engaged in mere craftwork. I am moved to this position, at least in part, by my experience with two exceptionally fine university administrators who never took a course in administration, never read a book on administrative theory, could never cite a piece of administrative research, but absolutely knew why they did what they did. And they could talk about it in terms that conveyed a high degree of sensitivity to both the personal and organizational factors involved.

• The Touch of Craft

This final section of this chapter has the same title as the chapter itself. We will now move away from the conceptual arguments and get down to cases as a means of setting both the tone and content for the remainder of the book. What follows presents the flavor of the administration-as-craft metaphor through a comparison of the thinking of a potter as she talked about working at her craft with that of a middle school principal as he reflected on a particular situation that had occurred during the day. What the reader should attend to while reading is the character of the "thinking about doing" in which the potter and the principal engage as they talk about their work. Here are the potter's comments,[6] responding to my request to "Talk with me a bit about what you think as you go about making something out of clay."

When I first started, I would put the clay on the wheel and then when it began to resemble something I decided what it was that I was making. That was many years ago. Now I sit down and decide exactly or pretty exactly what I want to make. Then you have to decide how much and what kind of clay you're going to use—whether you want it to be out of stoneware, which is more durable and can go into an oven, or if you want it to be of finer clay like porcelain, which doesn't have the same properties and can't go into an oven. Some operations are much more delicate than others. What kind of clay you use and how you work it depends on what you want the finished product to look like. Your tools are your head and your hands, for the most part.

There are huge differences in clay, going from the crude stuff you can find in a clay-pit up to porcelain which is like working with talcum powder. Stoneware can take a lot more abuse. It's rougher, more solid, fires better, has less distortion in it. Porcelain is more fluid. It wants to do what it wants to do. It sinks and collapses. You have to work much slower with it because it's much more delicate. A lot of people just don't work with porcelain because it's so delicate.

There can be problems every step of the way. It can be in the clay itself—impurities. You have to watch out for air bubbles. Sometimes you sense that something's wrong and sometimes you see it. Sometimes you feel it in the clay. You can feel how things are going and you simply learn to make judgments about what's going on through experience. You continually make adjustments in what you're doing according to the way you sense things are turning out.

The interview with the principal of a middle school was held at the end of a school day. I had spent that day with him, following him around and observing him deal with any number of situations. The particular circumstance to which we attend involved a girl who had been referred to him for cutting classes the previous school day and spending most of the time hiding in one girls' lavatory after another. There is a tragic background to the incident. A classmate of this girl's committed suicide, and it was the day after the funeral when she cut her classes. She had then been referred to the principal. The reason she gave was that she had been grieving over the suicide and had not been able to attend to her school work. The discussion—the principal's work—between the two of them lasted for about twenty minutes. Here are the principal's comments, reflecting on that discussion:

> One of the things that's important is the time of year. We're starting June and she had been in the office several times during the year. So I know her. But it was difficult because of the suicide. You just don't know whether kids are playing that there's a lot of grief or if there really is. Her mother said she wasn't particularly close to the girl. There were two things I was trying to get to. One, what was the appropriate way to deal with the situation and, also, what was the consequence that fits what she did. What I wanted her to walk out of here knowing is that she's responsible for the decisions she makes. When she makes a choice to miss class there are consequences. The classes are worthwhile and she has to make them up. And I also wanted her to know that the system will provide help for her if she's truly grieving. I gave her a pass so that she could come down and see a counselor any time she wanted to. Part of it is calling her bluff and the other part is, if she's sincere, she can go ahead and get help. You never know for sure about the bluffing. So you let them know that you're listening to them so that they know what their feelings sound like. From there, you can pretty much get an indication of what's going on. It's a matter of covering every base. I pretty much focus on dealing with the here-and-now with kids so that they start to understand the logic of the consequences of their behavior. Kids have to feel like they have their time to be listened to. I think I know when I've been good at what I do when I sense a kid has started to understand what I have on my mind.

As I noted earlier, the case for thinking about administration as a craft does not rest on the resemblance between the nature of the work of administrators and that of traditional craftspeople. To watch a potter shaping clay is not to watch a school principal talking over a problem with a youngster. Where the resemblance exists, and I believe it to be a very striking one, is in the way each *thinks* about what he or she does. Note the parallelism in the thinking in the two examples just given—and note the differences.

The potter thinks about and has an image of what she wants her end product to look like, including what function it might serve. What she does and how and with what she works depends on that image. The same holds true for the principal. He had two things in mind as he worked with the student as hoped-for outcomes, but he will never be as sure as the potter that he produced what he wanted to. The potter gives thought to the type of clay she will use to craft her product. Her sense of the characteristics of different clays is finely honed. One gets a feel for her knowledge, for example, when she said, "Porcelain is more fluid. It wants to do what it wants to do. It sinks and collapses." The principal, of course, cannot choose his "clay." He must work with whatever raw material presents itself at his door. Nevertheless, in this particular case, because of the school history of the youngster involved, he knows about the character of the material with which he is working. And he also knows that there is a broader context (the time of year) that he has to consider as possibly influencing his work. In other words, the work environment of the principal varies and may well influence the material with which he is working, whereas the potter's studio is a relatively invariant environment and, for most purposes, has little effect on the clay.

Both the potter and the principal need tools in order to work at their craft. "Your tools are your head and your hands, for the most part," said the potter. One's "head" enables one to see and "feel" how things are turning out, and one's hands function as the means of shaping the work or, perhaps, probing the clay for imperfections in it. The principal's head functions similarly, but his "hands" are his ability to listen and to use himself in ways that will make the problem he is working on take the shape of the image he had in mind. Both have a sense of the "needs" of the materials with which they are working; they are aware that circumstances may occur that will necessitate a shift in what they are doing; both have a "nose" for the cues that will tell them how things are going; and both have ways of knowing when they have done a good—or not so good—job.

All this, of course, has been much too brief for the reader to develop a sense of the richness and complexity of thought of these two craftspeople as they reflected on their work and the way they go about it. But it has not been too brief to enable the reader to join me in seeing that the conceptual argument for the validity of thinking about the practice of administration as a craft holds up in the light of experience, as well. To be sure, I have only used one example to make my point but the balance of the book will reinforce it in a number of ways.

"So," one is entitled to say, "it all seems pretty simple. Is this all there is to it?" The answer, of course, is no. As I have learned in my own study of the work of administrators, if one would really understand how administrators go about doing what they do, one must be prepared to cast aside traditional and deliberate rational-technical ways of thinking and enter a world in which the action is almost always fast and fragmented; things are rarely tied neatly into small, manageable packages; problems are practically never "solved" in the sense of finding lasting solutions; and what it is that an administrator does is so much a function of idiosyncratic predispositions that, unless an observer understands that, what one sees happening can be somewhat bewildering.

Perhaps, though, the best way to sum things up is by recalling my earlier reference to Scheffler's (1960) discussion of metaphors. What he said was that the use of a metaphorical statement was really an invitation to search for the analogy in the metaphor. And so, the invitation is given to the reader to join me in that search.

• Endnotes

1. Barbara Wood and I (1986) reported a study in which we asked principals to describe their behavior in precisely these craft terms in different problematic situations. Their descriptions were abundantly clear and validated the metaphor nicely.
2. Besides being a professor of philosophy, Howard was also a professional singer.
3. Emphasis added.
4. Emphasis added.
5. Parentheses added.
6. All interview excerpts have been edited.

Chapter Four

From the Potter's Wheel to the Schools

I use the term *potter's wheel* in the title of this chapter as a generic descriptor for all traditional crafts. Thus, as its title implies, the concern of this chapter is to leave the philosophical, metaphorical, and conceptual arguments behind and lay out some general ideas about what is involved if we choose to think of school administration as a craft.

First, though, there are two prior considerations that have to do with the setting in which the administrative craft is practiced and the content of the work it involves. Potters' studios are the settings for their work. The content of their work is to make something out of clay. The "studios" in which school administrators work are schools, school districts, and communities. The work to which they direct their craft skills involves "making something" out of a variety of problematic situations with which they must deal, mostly reactively but also proactively. In a manner much more profound than is the case with the potter, both the setting and the nature of the work of administrators have a critical influence on the way their craft is exercised. Thus, our concern will be directed to these variables at the outset.

• The Setting

The term *setting* refers to the physical, sociological, and psychological stage on which or from which administrators ply their craft. Each setting, of course, is part of a broader culture—the system of beliefs, values, expectations, and attitudes—in which it is situated. Further, each setting develops its own subculture with its own system of beliefs and so forth.

It simply is not true that "once you've seen one, you've seen them all." The truth is that "a school is not a school is not a school," meaning that although schools and school districts are similar to each other in many ways, there is a great deal of variability among them that affects the work of administrators and their practice. Let us take what, on the face of it, is a simple example: the way in which the physical setting affects the information-gathering behavior of superintendents and principals. Administrators in every setting will be concerned, in some fashion, with gathering information about the general state of the system—an individual school or a school district—on any given day. It is the basic ingredient of their work diet. But the setting will be highly influential relative to how such information is gathered. Superintendents, for example, use the telephone much more than principals. Principals gather a lot of information by walking around their schools. A statement of the obvious? Perhaps, but it is only the tip of the iceberg.

The setting also influences the tempo of administrative work. The pace at which a superintendent works, though it may well belie the potential stress inherent in that position, seems almost to be leisurely compared to that of either secondary or elementary school principals. To watch a superintendent perform his or her job is sometimes akin to watching someone play chess. Slowness and deliberateness seem best to describe the action, for the most part. In no way can the tempo of work of a principal be described as slow and deliberate, except perhaps in some quite unusual cases. Things happen quickly and, for most intents and purposes, in a quite unpredictable way. Superintendents can typically plan what they are going to do on any particular day; that plan has a pretty good chance of being carried out, even though unexpected events can certainly occur that will upset things. Principals can rarely expect to plan a day's work; at the end of the day seldom will they have a sense of having worked their way, in any deliberate fashion, through their plan.

There are also, of course, differences between settings within the same organizational category. Being a high school principal in an affluent suburb means something very different with regard to one's practice than being a high school principal in the inner city or in a rural area. An elementary principal whose parent population is largely professional-managerial faces a much different work setting than one whose parent population is mostly working class—not better or worse, just different.

And certainly, to take things a bit further, the craft of administration requires different kinds of sensitivities and skills—and, perhaps, predispositions—if one thinks about working with a school population of teenagers, some of them young adults, compared with a population of young children. And this is only a starter, because it also makes a difference in the practice of one's administrative craft whether the young boys and girls, for example, come from families who live in single-family homes that are surrounded by well-manicured lawns and in which they have their own bedrooms or those who live in multi-family dwellings where there is a lot of crowding.

The point of this brief discussion concerning the setting and the practice of administration is not to provide any startlingly new information. Rather, it is to suggest that each school setting is idiosyncratic in some ways, and that characteristic calls for idiosyncratic craft skills on the part of its administrator. Although this statement may seem obvious to the reader, its implications are anything but obvious and they only become more clear as one starts to inquire, by observing and talking, into what administrators do and why. Putting the idea back into metaphorical terms, the setting influences what one does because it plays a large part in determining the characteristics of the material one has to work with in exercising one's craft. To forget that is to live in a dream world.

• The Content of the Work That Administrators Do

In two earlier papers (Blumberg, 1985, 1986), I suggested that the job descriptions of superintendents and principals have little relevance for their work behavior. This is not to suggest, however, that they have no meaning for the things to which administrators must attend. They do spell out the expectations a school board has for the performance of a particular job in functional terms and they may well serve as sort of vague criteria documents for evaluation purposes. But the job descriptions leave unsaid, because there is no way they can say it that would have any meaning, how a principal, for example, should go about his or her work, how he or she should think about that work, what skills should be used, what theoretical or philosophical stances should be taken toward conflictual situations, and so forth. In short, job descriptions have little to do with how administrators practice their craft, though, in very global terms, they do talk about the kinds of things the administrative craftsperson should be "making." They speak to ends and not means. Realistically, this is all they can do.

We must inquire, then, about what it is that school administrators actually do. What is their work? As we start to deal with that question, we enable ourselves to poke beneath the level of generality of global function and to think about the very demanding understandings and skills that every administrator must employ in the course of a work day.

Over the last several years, a number of studies have been conducted that move in the direction of trying to answer questions relating to what administrators do. Their methodology is that of naturalistic inquiry (implying the study of the human condition in any of its forms in the natural setting where whatever it is one wants to study takes place). For the most part, these studies have focused on trying to make sense of the administrative world by observing the relative amount of time that administrators gave to categories of observable activities. These categories, though, were without content. Mintzberg (1973), for example, in his study of five organizational chief executive officers, one of whom was a school superintendent, identified categories of time use as scheduled and unscheduled meetings, telephoning, desk work, and tours. Martin and Willower (1981) and Kmetz and Willower (1982), in their studies of five high school and five elementary school principals, showed that these same five general categories of "doing something" accounted for a little more than 70 percent of the way their subjects spent their working day. Each of the studies also noted that the tempo of administrative activity was fast; that the day was fragmented in the sense that a great many activities took place; that frequent interruptions of work occurred; and that the work life of an administrator was, for the most part, a verbal one. Talk was the stock-in-trade. But what the talk was about was mostly left unstudied.

The question then becomes, What is administrative talk about? This is another way of asking, What is the content of the work of administrators? Certainly, there is more than one answer to this question, such answers being probably as much a function of what is on the question-asker's mind as anything else. That is, I don't believe any observer approaches a situation with a completely *tabula rasa* mindset, having no pre-formed notions about what he or she will find, or having no categories or theoretical constructs into which data from observations may fit. In our own case, different observers of administrators at work will draw different inferences about what that work is all about, and those differences will be a function of what the particular observer brings with him or her in terms of a theoretical or philosophical background, for example.[1] "Believing is seeing," Weick (1980) has said, and I agree with him.

Thus, when I approached the question of, "What is the content of the work of administrators?" I did so with a particular frame of reference in mind. As I observed superintendents and principals at work and talked with them about my observations, or as I interviewed them in their offices or mine, it was always with the intent of studying their work as it might be conceived of as the practice of a craft.

There was, of course, more to it than that, because in order to study any craft one has to know what it is that is being worked on. So the questions became somewhat clinical as I observed and probed. They were of the nature of "What's going on? What were you trying to do?"

Given these thoughts, then—What *was* going on? and What *were* you trying to do?—the content of the craft of school administration seems to involve the following kinds of things:

- Keeping things running as peacefully as possible
- Healing wounds
- Dealing with conflicts or working to avoid them
- Supervising the work of others
- Developing the organization
- Implementing or reinforcing educational ideas

There are several important comments to make concerning this categorization of administrative work. First, it represents my inferences and interpretations. A different observer with a different concept guiding his or her observations might well develop a different listing. However, I have tested these ideas with several different groups of administrators and there seemed to be some agreement that these activities, for the most part, were what they spent their days doing.

Second, having said that, I must note one activity that is not on the list. It has to do with the paperwork, the reports of one kind or another, with which administrators must deal either during the day or at home in the evening or on weekends. The decision not to include this type of activity as craftwork was deliberate and based on the idea, stemming from Green (1968), that the concept of work is associated with producing something but that not everything one does on a job results in the production of something in the craft sense, which is our focus here. And though it is true that a school principal might think of herself or himself as crafting a particular report to produce a desired effect on the superintendent, this type of job-related activity usually falls outside our concern with the practice of the craft of administration. This is not to say that it is unimportant in the grand scheme of things or even that some skills do not come into play when one does paperwork. Rather, it is to say that doing that kind of activity and even exercising some skills that might accompany it is not generally conceived of as craftwork. To take an activity from another type of job as an example, when a typist exercises skills at typing, it is not an instance of craftwork even though something—a letter—results. Or, when a carpenter hammers a nail skillfully, it is not a craft that is being enacted, even though the result is two pieces of wood being joined.

Third, it should be obvious that the time devoted to the activities of administrative craftwork I have noted varies greatly depending on the predispositions of the individual involved and the demands of the particular school situation. Some administrators pay more attention to maintaining a smooth and peaceful system than others; some are scarcely aware of wounds that need healing; some devote a great deal of time and energy to matters of instruction; and others, for whatever reason, avoid becoming involved in such matters.

Fourth, and perhaps not quite so obvious, is the thought that it is not easy to be discrete in isolating these work activities from each other so that one can say, "Now I am doing this" and "Now I am doing that." Things mix with each other. A school superintendent may visit a school primarily to learn about it and, in the process, find that he or she runs into a situation that requires healing, for example. Or a principal, while engaged with instructional matters, may become involved in resolving an unanticipated conflict. The overall point here is that though it is my intention to discuss the administrative craft in relatively discrete ways, it is also necessary to understand that its discreteness is artificial. In fact, the work of school administrators is a messy and mixed-up business which requires that one be able to shift one's attention from one situation, or within one situation, to another quickly and frequently with no foreknowledge of the new problem that is presented.

Fifth, it should be obvious that when we talk of the craft of administration we are not speaking of a unitary set of techniques or skills. The variety of things to be worked on or produced is too wide to permit that idea. Keeping things running smoothly, healing wounds, and supervising teachers demand that an administrator know and be able to do different things. And everyone is not good at doing everything, just as some potters are good at making functional pieces but not so good at making delicate vases.

Finally, there is an issue that is related to the practice of administration that seems to be ignored, but which, in my judgment, is crucial to understanding how and why administrators do what they do—the way they practice their craft. What I have in mind here is a parallel to both Tom's (1984) and Greene's (1984) thoughts (Chapter Three) about the morality of teaching as a craft. That is, it seems inescapable that if one is to understand the practice of school administration, one must consider it a type of work in which the question of what any particular administrator holds to be of value comes into play almost incessantly throughout a day of work. I think this is true with regard to those parts of administrative work that may seem to be mundane or routine as well as those parts that almost publicly present a value-oriented problem.

For example, consider this question that a school principal might ask himself or herself: "Shall I do this paperwork that is on my desk now or should I see how things are going with the kids in the cafeteria?" On the face of it, that question is rather matter-of-fact, involving what appears to be a simple decision about how to use one's time. But implicit in that question is another, "Will I or perhaps the school be *better off* if I do my paperwork now or check the cafeteria?" In other words, the essence of the time allotment question is found in the words *better off* and these words imply issues of desirability or values, even if they are not obvious on the face of things.

In a chapter written by Greenfield (Blumberg and Greenfield, 1986, p. 226), the problem is set within a larger context, and in rather elegant fashion. In discussing the impact that a principal may have on a school, he wrote:

> The moral component to action and decision-making requires that a judgment be made. It thus carries with it the possibility, often a high probability, that one standard of goodness may be sacrificed for another. We cannot always have our cake and eat it, so to speak. The world of the school principal (and, of course, the school superintendent)[2] . . . is characterized by many a moral dilemma—that is, the necessity to make a judgment that one set of valued alternatives is to be preferred over another.
>
> . . . A principal had to decide whether to support a teacher against a student—and thus validate and reinforce a criterion of goodness central to the ethos of teachers as a group ("principals support teachers, right or wrong")—or to subscribe to a criterion of goodness held central by the normative community of educators

as to what constitutes good teaching or good educational practice; and by this standard support the child against the teacher. . . .

Thus, not only do decisions require assigning values to facts and making judgments regarding courses of action, but also often include a moral component involving the application of *competing* standards of goodness.

To come back to our concern with the practice of the administrative craft, then, it needs to be borne in mind that throughout our discussion there will always be underlying components of the valuing process. Sometimes they will be explicit and sometimes implicit. Regardless, they will be there.

• The Craft of Administration— A Definition and Its Elements

So far, I have used the term *craft* in an undefined way, relying on the reader to supply his or her own definition. Here I wish to become more definitive, starting with a general idea and then working down to the more specific, with a discussion of the elements of the administrative craft.

The starting point is to go back briefly to Collingwood (1938) and his discussion of craft as different from art. He defined craft in terms that are deceptively simple and even seductive. He states that craft is "the power to produce a preconceived result by means of consciously controlled and direct action" (p. 15). That is pretty cut-and-dried—almost either-or. You either know what you're going to produce and you have the power (the skill) to do it or you don't. Further, you do all this in a preplanned, deliberate fashion in which you have control of the situation. Any school administrator, though, will tell you that if there is one thing schools are not it is cut-and-dried or either-or; that what they want to produce may vary while they're in the process of producing it; and that with some exceptions the setting and content of their work do not permit a great deal of preplanning and deliberateness. This last point holds particularly true for principals and somewhat less so, I suspect, for superintendents.

These demurers notwithstanding, Collingwood's definition contains enough of the general idea so that the following can be offered as a starting point for thinking about the craft of administering the schools. As I have observed and talked with school administrators, their behavior and how they think about what they do suggests that their craft is defined as the idiosyncratic use of self to make prudent decisions concerning problematic situations in school life. As in the case of Collingwood, this, too, is a deceptively simple and even seductive statement. What it implies, on a very gross level, is that the craft of administration is the exercise of practical wisdom toward the end of making things in a school or a school system "look" like one wants them to look. Before moving into more detail, I need to reinforce a point that has to do with my observations and discussions that formed the basis of how the craft of administration might be defined. The behavior and talk of administrators told me how to define what they do. It wasn't so much that they said, "Here's how I define my craft" as it was that what emerged was a statement of "Here is what my work is all about."

Elaboration of this rather broad statement is needed if we wish to develop a more finely honed view of its implications for the way administrators work at their craft. What seems to be involved, as they move from one circumstance to another, are the following types of know-how, a term whose use in this context goes beyond being able to employ particular skills:

- Being able to develop and refine "a nose for things."
- Having a sense of what constitutes an acceptable result in any particular problematic situation.
- Understanding the nature of the "materials" with which one is working. This includes oneself as a "material" that needs to be understood, as well as others. It also includes understanding the way other parts of the environment may affect the materials and the acceptableness of the solution at a particular point in time. (Recall how the principal in Chapter Three made reference to the particular time of the school year as important to his understanding the situation.)
- Knowing administrative techniques and having the skill to employ them in the most efficacious way possible.
- Knowing what to do and when to do it. This involves not only pragmatic decisions—what behavior or procedure is called for at a particular time— but also implies issues of right and wrong. Much as Tom's (1984) description of teaching is that of a "moral" craft, so too is the practice of administration one in which there are moral dimensions to every action taken, with the possible exception of those that are simply mundane. This is not to suggest that administrators are aware of these moral dimensions at all times; it is simply to suggest that they are present.
- Having a sense of "process," that is, being able to diagnose and interpret the meaning of what is occurring as people interact in any problematic situation. As our potter in the last chapter noted the necessary ability to sense or feel air bubbles in clay, for example, so an administrator needs to be able to "feel" accurately what is happening in the process of working with others. The process is a type of material he or she must understand and employ.

On the surface, all this seems not to be exceedingly complex. But if we poke and inquire into subsurface matters it all becomes very complex indeed. Two facets of this complexity, because I see them as heavy contributors to it, will be discussed briefly here. A chapter is devoted to each later in the book. The first is concerned with the phrase with which the general definition of the administrative craft started, "the idiosyncratic use of self." The second deals with the question of how administrators learn to do what they do.

It all starts with that idiosyncratic self and it is related to what I have referred to elsewhere (Blumberg, 1984) as the "baggage" that an administrator brings with him or her to the role. "Baggage" refers to the various values, predispositions, attitudes, perspectives, preferred ways of relating to others, and so forth that have their roots in the personal history of one's biological, psychological, and social life and which are carried by a person into adult work life. It is the baggage that largely defines the self and it is the self that confronts, defines, interprets, and acts on the situation. Thus we have the idea of the idiosyncratic use of self as the prepotent starting place to think about the administrative craft.

We can clarify this idea in fairly simple terms, although their simplicity cloaks a very complex social psychological phenomenon. For example, take the problem of what constitutes an acceptable solution to a problem. In the brief anecdote in Chapter Three, a principal told us about dealing with a young girl who had cut classes the previous day with the excuse that she was grieving over a classmate who had died. An acceptable solution to the problem for him was (1) to have her make up her work, (2) to have her understand her responsibility as a student to go to class, and (3) to have her understand that counseling services were available to her should she want them. His work with the student was guided accordingly.

The point is that it was an acceptable solution *for him.* Certainly, another principal might conceive of a different solution that would be acceptable for him or her. He or she might have focused much more heavily on the grieving of the student, paid less attention to the fact that she cut classes, engaged in a counseling session with her, and had as an acceptable solution helping the student feel better about herself in that situation. This other principal might have said, in effect, "Forget about the classes, think a bit about yourself, and then go back and do the best you can."

Which is the better solution of the two? No one can say, of course. What we can say, though, and with some confidence, is that each would be a reflection of the principal's baggage; that predisposition to analyze, think about, and judge problems in idiosyncratic ways.

We will have much more to say about the idea of administrative baggage in a later chapter. Suffice it to say at this time that a similar analysis could be made relative to each element of the administrative craft. This is another way of saying that we cannot understand what administrators do and why they do it without attending, on some level, to thoughts about what it is that each individual brings to his or her position and role.

Quite related to the idea of idiosyncratic use of self (thus sharing its complexity) as a starting point for understanding the way administrators work at their craft is the question of how they learned to do what they do. And how did they learn to know what they know? If you query principals about *why* they dealt with a problem in a particular way, the chances are good that you will get an answer that makes sense in terms of their understanding of the problem. But if you ask the principals *where* they learned to do what they did, the chances are very good that the response will be "experience." There will be occasional times when a person, if pressed, will be able to point to a situation in his or her experience from which the person learned and was able to articulate a new and different way of doing things. Much of the time, as we shall see later, such a recollection has its roots in a failure. But for the most part, when an administrator says, for example, "Experience taught me to do X in situation Y," the experience he or she is referring to is a rather undifferentiated thing.

An elementary school principal once told me about how, in a meeting, she had manipulated her superintendent into delaying plans to change a program that was just getting off the ground and that she thought had a good prospect for success if given a chance. She did this by agreeing to the change if he would agree to pay for summer work of teachers who would be involved in the change he proposed. She knew that the budget was very tight and that it would not accommodate summer salaries, and that he would have to delay his proposal—which he did. She had carried the day not on the basis of an educational argument, but on an economic one. When I asked her where and when she had learned to do this, her answer, quite expected, was, "Experience, I guess."

What needs to be understood at the outset, then, is that a very large part of the question of how administrators learn the techniques, procedures, and skills of their craft is a difficult thing to discern and lends to the complexity of trying to understand it. My initial hunch about it all, though, hinges on two points: First, to be an administrator involves, above all, dealing with and relating to people in a variety of problem-oriented contexts. Second, our learning to deal with and relate to people is a function of our long and quite personal social history—a history which, for the most part, is buried beyond recall.

We have made the transfer "From the Potter's Wheel to the Schools," at least conceptually. The image of that craft in action is still a vague one, though, and most of what follows in the book is an attempt to fill in the details so that the image becomes more clear.

• Endnotes

1. We see this phenomenon operating in many sectors of life. Most obviously, it seems to me, it can be observed in courtroms when two psychiatrists will make polar opposite interpretations concerning the sanity of a defendant.
2. Parenthetical expression not in the original.

The Administrative Craft in Action and Thought

The aim of the chapters that comprise Part Two is to explain and elaborate on the work activity of school administrators in order to understand it as a craft. In a sense, it is a task of separating the inseparable. That is, although it is not difficult to engage administrators in more or less clinical discussions of their work, the actual work behavior itself, particularly in school buildings and less so in the superintendent's office, frequently appears to be a jumble of activities. And many times it is just that.

Observing a school administrator at work is observing action, sometimes such rapid action that one wonders what kind, if any, thinking takes place while it is occurring. But, indeed, thinking does take place and it is the explication of the thought that enables us to separate and write about that which appears to be unseparable.

There is another problem that makes the separating task somewhat difficult. It has to do with the idea of action just noted, but is more centrally related to the thought that upon observing an administrator engaged in one activity, it soon becomes apparent that he or she may be engaging in several activities at the same time. This experience can be vividly seen when following a school principal, as I did, on such a seemingly simple thing as a trip to the lunchroom in order to get a sandwich and bring it back to her office. Within a space of no more than five minutes, this principal made a quick in-and-out trip to the girls' lavatory "to flush it out," as she said; asked a teacher how things were going in a particular program; got lunch; chatted for a couple of moments with a cafeteria worker; checked with another teacher about a discipline case; complimented a youngster on some work that he had done; picked up some pieces of paper from the floor in the hall; and hustled some lingering students off to class.

Automatic behavior? Yes and no. Purposeless? Definitely no. During those five minutes, the central purpose of which was to get lunch and return to her office with it, this principal was also engaged in the work of the school. She was plying her craft as she kept things going ("flushing out" the lavatory and hustling students off to class), evincing interest in a particular instructional program, getting information about a particular student, and even picking up pieces of paper from the floor. In a very subtle, perhaps miniscule way—and certainly unintentional as our later discussion revealed—she was communicating to those to whom she talked and to those who observed her, a symbol of what she thought the school should be all about. It should, for example, go about its business in an orderly fashion, not tolerate "goofing off," be clean, and be concerned with program development and appropriate student behavior.

There is another point to which we need to attend in all this. A different principal confronted with the same five minutes in the same school with the same objective of getting lunch would have done different things. Not better, not worse—just different. Recall that the general definition of the administrative craft that was offered in Chapter Four started with the words "the idiosyncratic use of self." Those five words say a great deal about the subject of our inquiry. A different principal, using himself or herself idiosyncratically, would have seen different things on the way to the lunchroom and back, talked with different people about different things, and so forth. And, in all likelihood, his or her behavior would have communicated a different symbol, perhaps not widely divergent, of what the school was all about.

Part Two will create a type of generality out of idiosyncracy. That is, though each administrator practices her or his craft in an individual sort of way, there are general categories of activity and thought under which whatever they do and think are subsumed. These categories are the focus of Part Two, and their description and elaboration are the subject of individual chapters.

There is an extremely important caveat about these chapters that needs to be noted by the reader. Although the chapters deal with the things that administrators do—how they think about and practice their craft—they are not intended to be prescriptive as to how things should be done. The illustrations used are highly particularistic to each individual, and their main purpose is to clarify the craft element that is the focus of each chapter.

Finally, the focus of Chapter Five, "Getting and Using a 'Nose' for Things," though indispensable to the administrative craft, seems to have no clear parallel in the lore of traditional craftspeople. One thing is evident, though. Without that "nose," any school administrator risks forever staying a naive apprentice.

Chapter Five

Getting and Using a "Nose" for Things

In his book *Artistry,* in which Howard (1982) characterizes the work that artists do as craftwork, he devotes two rather detailed chapters to a discussion of "the language of craft." He sets the stage for his discussion with a brief question that Wittgenstein (1958) raised in his book *Philosophical Investigations:* "Ask yourself: How does a man learn to get a nose for something? And how can this nose be used?" Interestingly, Wittgenstein makes no effort to answer the question. It is simply posed without comment as a sort of invitation to the reader to reflect on it.

The phrase, "getting or having a nose for something," as we might suspect and as the Oxford English Dictionary tells us, came from the sniffing activity of animals, dogs in particular, as they were observed trying to organize their environment (or so we infer) by the use of their nose. The image of "nosing around," though, was apparently attractive enough to us humans so that we appropriated it as a way of referring to activities that enable us to get an overall sense of the setting in which our work takes place. At the least, it was attractive enough so that, in this study, the use of the "nose" idea communicated readily to everyone involved. We know what it means to "have a nose," and with very little trouble we seem able to talk about its meaning for us, in particular, and how we go about getting our own special one. It all sounds simple, but, as we shall see, getting a nose for things in a school district or a school can be an activity that has many components, some of which can be elegant in their subtlety.

This chapter is about the reflections of a number of school administrators as they responded to my invitation to think about how they got and used their nose for things in their schools or school districts. The point of it all is both simple and crucially important to engaging in the administrative craft. Without a highly developed nose, an administrator has no basis for understanding what is happening around him or her. Or, as one school principal put it, "If you don't work on your nose for things, the whole architecture of the school can tumble down and you wouldn't know it." First things first, then, as the story begins with a discussion of what the craft of administration is about. The focus is on that which seems to be most basic to it—the activity of sensing and understanding one's work environment.

Here is how a central office administrator reflected on how he gets his nose for things:

> Mostly I get it from just being around and from consciously telling myself not to take anything for granted, and from telling myself time and again not to make assumptions. I get it from being aware that not only is the world stranger than we would imagine, but it is stranger than we could possibly imagine and some of the things I uncover are the strangest. I move around a lot from school to school and, you know, I think I focus on the commonplace perhaps more than things that seem strange. If I don't focus on the commonplace, I may be missing the most important thing.
>
> I'll tell you a joke about that. There was a man who worked in a factory and every night he left work pushing a wheelbarrow full of sawdust. The guards at the gate became suspicious that he might be stealing something and so they started sifting through the sawdust each night, but could never find anything. One day one of the guards said, "Okay, you're getting away with whatever it is you're stealing and we can't catch you. We won't stop you, but tell us what it is that you're stealing." The guy said, "Wheelbarrows." It had become so commonplace for him to leave with a wheelbarrow full of sawdust that they simply took it for granted that he was trying to hide something. They were looking for the wrong thing.
>
> So what's really important for me is to try and understand what may be strange about the commonplace or to sense out what it is that the commonplace is not telling me about itself.

As a start, then, it seems fair to say that getting a nose for things in a school or school district can be a highly complex activity and one that involves, perhaps, a strong sense of the obvious and what the obvious may communicate to the interested observer. To place the problem on a more abstract level, what this administrator seems to have uppermost in his mind when he visits, observes, and listens to people is to make some valid inferences about what Schein (1985) has called "the nature of the organizational culture." Schein defines this concept as

> a pattern of basic assumptions—invented, discovered or developed by a given group as it learns to cope with its problems of external adaptation and internal integration—that has worked well enough to be considered valid and, therefore, to be taught to new members as the correct way to perceive, think, and feel in relation to those problems (p. 9).

Little could be more basic to the practice of the administrative craft than getting a nose for the culture of the particular organization in which one is functioning. That is, knowing the particular culture of a school or a system forms the basis upon which the behavior of that system, the people who work in it, and the students becomes intelligible. But getting to know and understand a system's culture is no simple matter. It is not, for example, a one-shot deal. Even an extremely keen observer cannot spend a few hours in a school and come away with any type of valid sense of what are the basic assumptions upon which the behavior of the various subgroups in it rest. Although it is true that teachers, for example, may talk about the culture of the school if asked, the issue is not talk but behavior. What they *do* speaks much more loudly than what they *say* about these assumptions. This is not to say that they are dishonest, but only that what is involved in understanding a school's culture is an ability to observe and make sense of what may be, and frequently are, very subtle behavioral nuances.

So we have the administrator just quoted getting his nose, or a good part of it, by focusing his observations on the commonplace and trying to learn from it. This focus seems to make abundant sense, for if we think of Schein's notion of culture as "a pattern of basic assumptions" then it is also reasonable to think that people don't deliberate about them as they act them out. For example, if, as I think it is, one of the basic assumptions of the culture of my university is that professors will write and publish books and articles, when I sit down to write I certainly don't think to myself, "I am now acting on a basic assumption of my university's culture." I just do it and, indeed, it is a commonplace activity for me—but it is not necessarily so for others in my university nor is it necessarily commonplace for professors in other types of institutions. Perhaps that example is too simple-minded, but I think it makes the point that getting a nose for an organization's culture involves observing the behavior of its members engaged in their everyday activity over a period of time—and thinking long and hard about what that behavior means.[1]

There is another and very fundamental point that needs discussion here. Recall that the administrator who told the wheelbarrow story started his comment with "from just being around and from consciously telling myself not to take anything for granted, and from telling myself time and again not to make any assumptions." This thought takes us back to the derivation of "getting or having a nose for something" as coming from the manner in which many animals seem to get a sense of what their immediate environment holds for them. If you watch a dog sniffing around a piece of ground, even one that it may be familiar with, you will note that it frequently goes back to a spot that it has previously sniffed. At the risk of being somewhat playfully anthropomorphic, it almost seems as though the dog, through its second or third sniffing, is not taking anything for granted or making untested assumptions about its first sniff. The dog's message is a clear one—before you act on your assumptions of what the environment is like, check them out.

Checking out one's assumptions is a good rule of thumb but it is easier to hold that rule than it is to act on it. The administrator we quoted, for example, had to tell himself "time and again not to make any assumptions." A key to the survival and effectiveness of administrators is for them to be able to develop as clear and unambiguous sense as possible of the meaning of both the obtrusive and unobtrusive behaviors that occur in their work environment. Without this sense, what they do and the decisions they make are quite apt to be faulty. People new to the job of administration, or those who take on a position in a new school or district, consciously try to "psyche out" the system. After a while, though, they come to feel at home with it. Their understanding of it creates a foundation for the work they want to do. And herein lies the pitfall that needs to be avoided by "telling myself time and again not to make any assumptions." It is a comfortable feeling to sense that one knows the ins and outs of a system— what behavior signifies a green light and what a yellow one, and so forth. It is so comfortable, in fact, that one can easily take familiar signals for granted and then find out that the signal was something other than what one had first seen or thought to have seen. In this sense, the caution not to make any assumptions as one "works on one's nose" is another way of saying "caveat emptor"—things are not always what they appear to be. This is not so much because people consciously create scenarios of deception (although at times they do) as the thought that the same behavior an administrator observes on Monday may have a different meaning on Tuesday.

This same theme came into a discussion with another central office administrator, a person charged with overall responsibility for a district's program of curriculum and instruction.

Quite often it happens that you believe something was going on because you were told that it was. You act on that information and then you find out it wasn't going on. At least not the image of it that you have. So consequently without having that nose to the ground all of the time you may think certain things are happening but, in fact, they are not. It could be little things and it could be big things.

And I think if you don't have your nose to the ground what you find is that you have an image of what's going on out there that doesn't match reality. It can be an extremely wide gap. And when the gap becomes public, as it always seems to do, you lose your credibility both with the public and, even worse, with your staff. They sense you don't know what's going on and they think you're really out of it. They say, "Man, you don't know what's going on. You're really got your head in the sand." So for me, I've got to keep my thumb on the pulse of things. If I don't do that, forget it, because what they'll do is to sidestep you. They'll play games with you.

The thing that has been most effective for us is getting into those school buildings on a regular basis. But even more important than that is cultivating a group of people that you know darn well are going to be up front and honest with you. I think there are about 30 people in the District that talk with me that way.

An additional factor, then, is entered into the equation of why a central office administrator needs to have a sensitive and accurate nose and how to go about getting one. It has to do with the fact that, though school systems have the essential mission of providing a quality education for youngsters, part (sometimes a substantial part) of their character as social systems is their politicalness. This politicalness can be observed both in the system's relation to its external community and with regard to its internal operations. Externally, its political problem is to get and maintain the community's support for the educational program. Central office people tend to be rather open in their discussions of the problem. Superintendents, for example, freely acknowledge the strong political nature of their very central role as the system's institutional representative to the community-at-large.

Internally, though, the problem is of a different nature. It is not dissimilar to the organizational dynamics of any system in which authority and responsibility are delegated; in which those to whom authority and responsibility are delegated thus have needs to convince their supraordinates that they are doing a good job; and, in which they may have needs to protect their organizational territory, and so forth. The point is, as the person we just quoted understood quite well, that this constellation of factors can and does produce information that cannot always be trusted. Zurner (1986), for example, interviewed principals with a specific focus on their illusion-creating activities. Even though there was an initial denial by some of them that they engaged in creating illusions about their school, all of them eventually admitted that they did. And the strongest focus of the illusions they created was directed at their central office superiors. None of this was done, incidentally, with malicious intent. Rather, the idea was to create a variety of believable impressions—of the worth of innovative programs, of the need for additional resources, of the morale of the faculty, or what have you—so that the school and its principal would be viewed favorably by relevant others.

And so we have our central office administrator, a wise one, we might add, understanding that if he wants really to know what's going on in the schools, he must have "that nose to the ground all the time." He can't afford to take for granted, as was the case with the man we discussed previously, that which is told him in the ordinary course of the day. If he does, he risks making inappropriate public statements and decisions. But much worse, he risks making a fool of himself in the eyes of the instructional staff and losing credibility with them. Having a reliable nose for things serves both an educational and political function, or so it seems.

This man keeps his nose to the ground in two ways. First, he has a regular schedule of visiting schools during which time he sniffs around. But it is more than simply a random, untutored sniffing, and this is the critical second point. It is a goal-oriented activity aimed at surfacing the problems being encountered by teachers and administrators and—crucially important—having at its base an understanding of the particular language that is used by school personnel to indicate the nature of a problem they are confronting. That language is a subtle one and, as he suggests in the following, seemingly designed to let him know that something is wrong or that somebody is not doing things the way they are expected to do.

> Our staff is such that they won't comment directly on something they're having a problem with. They're indirect. They'll talk about something they're interested in or struggling with. I find that there are very few times when they are very straightforward with me, and I think that in the back of their minds they think they might be getting somebody in trouble, but they want the problem solved. It's almost like they're dropping things for you and you're going to pick them up. I think they also have a sense of the things they can drop for me that I will understand as opposed to the things I will not understand—that I will not pick up on.
>
> It's the little cues that make the difference and, again, they're rarely straightforward. For example, there's a teacher whom I know very well. One day he said, "Our high school principal, he's probably the best you can get." Interpretation: There are some things he screws up on. And my knowing this teacher and him knowing me, he's telling me that there is some communications lag taking place in the school, and there was.

Though in many ways schools and the people who work in them share surface similarities, they also develop their own idiosyncratic ways of thinking and talking about things that concern them. Something said in one school setting may not at all have the same meaning in another. Slightly different, perhaps, but very important meanings become associated with the slightly different cultures and the language that is used in them. To go back to the point made earlier, part of getting a nose for things means much more than simply visiting a school, observing what is going on, and asking questions. If all this walking around activity is to yield a feel for the environment that will help an administrator understand what he or she needs to attend to, then it most centrally involves a sense of the subtleties of the language that is used so that one will know when someone is "dropping things" with the expectation that "you're going to pick them up."

There is another type of language that becomes important when one is nosing around. It has to do less with the subtleties of understanding what a particular message may mean and more with sensing, from a wide range of cues, what life may be like in a school on any particular day. Principals, more than central office people, seem to have this language as a concern and quite naturally so. That is, for a superintendent, getting a nose for things has as its purpose finding out how things are going in general, as a rule. His or her responsibilities tend to be of the long-range variety and not with the day-to-day or minute-by-minute operation of any particular school. Occasionally, of course, an "of the moment" decision is required that depends on the adequacy of some central office nose, but for the most part this is not the case. Not so for the building principal for whom getting a nose for the school each day, and most frequently several times each day, seems to be an absolute necessity—for that day and not beyond it. One high school principal, who walks around his school three or four times a day, put it this way:

> I can sense when things are going right or wrong on any particular day. When I walk around, I listen for the level of noise in the building and I look for the amount of debris or litter. If it seems to be more than normal, it's a signal that some vandalism may be creeping in. I need to be out sensing things because if I'm not, I find myself operating in a vacuum and I don't know how anybody can do that. And I watch how the kids are behaving, not so much what they say to me but that, too. But how they're behaving with each other is a pretty good cue for me of how things are going on any particular day. They tell me things even though they don't come out and tell me.

Two things become important, then. The first is understanding the unspoken messages that get communicated, not through words, but through behavior. What does a lot of litter mean on any particular day or what does it mean when there appears to be more jostling of each other by students on Wednesday than there was on Tuesday? Answers to these questions are school specific, of course, and the validity of the answer is related to how "refined" the principal's nose is. This idea of a refined nose for things leads to a second important thought. Not only does the idea mean a skilled sensing ability for the meaning of unspoken messages but also an acute ability to sense the variability of school life on a day-to-day, week-to-week, or season-to-season basis (Burlingame, 1979).

To an eye or an ear that is not aware of the subtle changes that take place constantly in a school's human environment, what is seen or heard from one day to the next may appear relatively invariable. But to an eye or an ear that is aware of these changes, the school environment may present an image of high variability with its consequent change in meaning. For example, a one-time visitor to a high school may hear what he or she interprets to be an inordinate amount of loud talking in the halls while students are going from one class to another. To the school's principal with a refined nose, however, because he or she has a sense of the variability of the tone of that school, the same volume of loud talk may be indicative of a rather quiet day. That is, the principal knows what life was like in the school the day before and the day before that and, thus, has a basis for comparison. He or she is not only in the school every day, but is also *of* the school and from a particular vantage point, at that.

These ideas, the vantage point from which a principal views a school (or a superintendent views a school district) and being not only in but *of* the school, are critically important if we are to understand having a nose for things. What is meant by vantage point is that being a principal means, first, that the total school is one's domain of primary concern. It also means that being a principal implies a sort of potential psychological advantage in the sense that a person has the opportunity to become aware of the subtleties of school life that others may not see or hear—or simply ignore if they do. To put it simply, the chances are good that, while walking around a school at various times during the day, a principal will attend to and understand what is seen or heard in ways that an outsider will not—even if that outsider happens to be a teacher in the school. Events take on different meanings for the person who has responsibility for a particular domain than for one who does not. This is certainly not a startling insight, but it seems to be one to which not enough attention is paid. (This same reasoning, incidentally, probably accounts for a common complaint of teachers that their supervisors frequently don't understand the complex conditions that prevail in their classroom.) These thoughts do not mean, however, that outsiders cannot provide help to a principal interested in increasing his or her sensitivity to what is occurring in a school. Indeed, they can help by calling attention to conditions or events that the principal, on reflection, may take for granted but which, perhaps, shouldn't be. But the essential point remains. Being a principal almost forces an alertness to particular cues about what is going on in a school that others will either miss or interpret differently.

Merely being a principal does not connote that one is of the school as well as in it. Being "of the school" refers to the ability of a school administrator (superintendent, principal, or whatever) to communicate not only a presence in his or her domain but an empathic presence. That is, the administrator is able by words and behavior not only to let people know that he or she is "there" but that "there" means sensing the deeper meaning of the events that occur daily in the life of the schools. At issue, then, is not only being able to get a highly refined nose for things but to be able to act on it in ways that communicate a sort of "oneness" with the organizational and interpersonal environment.

Here are a couple of examples that elaborate on that idea. The first has to do with an elementary school principal who has a deep concern both for keeping in touch with the daily climate of his school and for conveying to his teachers that he is in touch with that climate and with them as people.

I visit every classroom every morning, just to walk in and say "Hello." But a lot happens there. And they know I'm there. They know things are okay or not okay. We talk about that. You can just feel it when you walk in in the morning. It's almost a collection of cues coming at you.

Sometimes it's a day—sort of—when the cues say, "This is going to be a day that you'd better stay in the building and spend a lot of time in the hall." And the teachers feel it, too. And the cafeteria people will come in, roll their eyes and say, "There's a storm coming." A favorite expression.

With my teachers, I try to get to know them in kind of a personal way. I think it's extremely important to be able to have some tie, some cord, some string with every member of the staff. You don't have to know them intimately but you have to know what makes them feel good in the morning. I'm not going to function well unless I know what's going on and I'm talking about the subliminal stuff. Problems don't necessarily get communicated through talk. It may be a quick hello instead of the usual leisurely one. Or it may be the flicker of an eye. I'm always alert for responses that aren't usual for a person. I know what's going on and I use what I know to help teachers. When I do a good job at this kind of thing, I find that I shape the kind of relationship that I want with the staff and this means that they trust me. That's what I want.

The important message in this reinforces the idea that being "in" is not the same thing as being "of," and that having a refined nose for things can be a powerful way to become "of." But it must be used for that purpose and its use needs to rest on philosophy of principal-teacher relationships that is functional for both. In this case, note the language: ". . . some tie, some cord, some string with every member of the staff." There is a subtleness to it, for not only to the words suggest a binding together but also distance. And this point speaks to the idea of using one's nose to shape relationships. It appears to be this principal's awareness of that which enables him to deal with teachers in a way that communicates his knowing them as individuals and as professionals, and to create that delicate balance between personal and professional relationships—closeness on the one hand, and distance on the other.

A second bit of subtleness may be found, although we may doubt that the principal would conceptualize it this way. It is that, at their heart, schools are interpersonal systems particularly with regard to the relationships between principals and faculty. For the most part, principals deal with and foster relationships with their teachers as individuals and not as a group, and it is of this fact that this principal's nose continually seems to remind him even though he may not be aware of it. Thus he becomes "of" the school as teachers sense he is interested, in some way, in being bound to them by the simple fact that he is the principal and they are the teachers.

Getting and using one's nose and being of the school had a somewhat different meaning for another elementary school principal. She, too, established ties to individual teachers but what was on her mind continually was what was going on in the instructional program.

Sure, you have to be visible, but you also have to experience the school in ways other experience it. I want to see my school. What I mean by that is that I want to experience it as a student, a teacher, a parent, or some person who is not part of the institution sees it. Sometimes I will simply go into the kindergarten or another classroom and just pretend I'm a pupil on the receiving end of what the teacher is doing. Sometimes I will go and teach a PE class and see how that feels. I want to be able to sense what's going on, what my school is like. What I'm trying to say is that there is a life to a school that a child experiences and that a teacher experiences that is quite different than the view that the public has. And if I'm going to do my job the way I think it should be done, I want to be able to experience that life as close as I can to the way kids and teachers do.

The idea of getting a nose for a school by trying to experience it as teachers and students do, then, becomes very complex, indeed. Clearly, it involves a different attitude about the school, and perhaps a different set of skills from those required for the very important activity of walking around and observing what a school is like on any particular day. First of all, one must *want* to experience the school in the way this principal talked about. That is, it has to be important to a principal's concept of self-in-role before he or she can enact the behaviors associated with that type of experiencing in a believable way. Teachers as well as youngsters spot phony behavior quite quickly, and merely for a principal to tell a teacher that he or she wants to sit in a class to try to understand what kids are experiencing will probably not ring true. Similarly, the request of a principal to teach a class in order not to forget what it means to understand being a teacher is likely to be greeted with doubt, even if the doubt remains unspoken. Teachers have had too much experience with principals as inspectors and evaluators to react with other than suspicion—initially, at least.

What is required to get a nose for the school in the way this principal conceives it is to build a type of relationship with teachers such that they believe—really believe—that what the principal has in mind is to refine his or her understanding of the experience both teachers and students are having in the school. This is not a short-term proposition. Rather, because teachers seem to have ample reason to distrust the presence of their principal in their classroom (Blumberg, 1980), it can be only a result of a long-term effort to build such a relationship. It is a very demanding task and one, I think, that some principals, perhaps most, are incapable of performing.

A second requirement of the principal who would experience the school in the manner that has been described is the ability not only to *assume* the role of the other (a teacher or a student) but to *be* that other as closely as possible. As an example, I once quite accidentally had the opportunity to observe a type of work very much unrelated to the work of school administration. I had taken my car to a local garage for some needed minor repair. While there I wandered around and was startled to see a mechanic listening to the running motor of another car with a stethoscope! My first reaction was to smile with amusement. When I asked him why he used the instrument, he responded, "Because it lets me get as close as possible to what's going on inside." My smile changed from one of amusement to one of appreciation for a highly developed skill. The mechanic could not only hear better with the stethoscope, but he could understand better.

So it is, then, with the principal's ability to "be" the other in a desire to experience the same thoughts and feelings of that other. In a way, the principal becomes the human stethoscope (with eyes): listening, seeing, sensing, and feeling what the other does (or as close to it as possible) and thus, becoming of the school.

There are undoubtedly many principals (and superintendents) who will be forever *in* their schools (or school districts), but never *of* them. And what this means is that their nose will be developed to that kind of understanding—perhaps limited and somewhat distant—that enables them to do their job in the way they conceive it best, a pure managerial way, I suspect. And this is not to criticize but simply to say "different strokes for different folks."

• Surrogate Noses

Walking around a school, talking with people, observing the behavior of youngsters during the course of the day seems to be the most prevalent way that school administrators and principals get their sense of what is going on, of what the school is like on any particular day. It is nose-developing activity primarily, but as we shall see later in the book, other purposes are served as well. But for high school principals, and very particularly for superintendents and other central office staff, this type of sensing activity, while very important, is not sufficient for their needs. They need to develop and use what I have called "surrogate noses"—people who will provide them with information about what is going on that, for whatever reason, they cannot obtain firsthand.

It is not hard to divine the reasons that administrators whose responsibility is either on the school district or secondary school level need to develop such an information-providing network. They involve organizational size, both in terms of number of people involved and physical setting, and complexity, the way the organization is structured to perform its tasks. Or, to put it simply, elementary schools, by their size and structure, lend themselves more easily to the type of nose-getting activities associated with walking around the school than do secondary schools or, certainly, school districts. Things are closer at hand, and furthermore there is no organizational hierarchy that might present a barrier to an administrator as he or she tries to find out what's going on. And though this is not to say that elementary principals do not develop individual sources of information among their faculty, it is to say that the character of the organization they head is not nearly so demanding of that need as that held by their colleagues in other school work settings. At least, that is the impression one is most apt to gain if one spends time observing these people at work.

When one observes a superintendent at work, for example, an impression that develops is that one is at the nerve center of an intelligence network much of the time. For obvious reasons, the telephone serves as a major instrument for information-gathering as he or she stays in touch with a number of surrogate noses throughout the school district—principals, school board members, the head of transportation, the personnel director, the district's lawyer, and so forth. For the most part, it seems that what superintendents do on the telephone is to ask questions. They poke, they test, they ask what alternatives the other is considering, they seek information, they ask for advice. It is all done with the aim of deepening their understanding of particular problematic situations or of simply getting a sense of what is going on in one school-related setting or another.

The telephone is not the only instrument superintendents use to gather information, of course. They have a staff (in all but very small districts) with whom they consult regularly and who serve, as one superintendent put it, "as my eyes and ears for what's going on in the district." People ask to see them; they ask people to see them; they convene and chair meetings; and they visit schools. But dominantly, what they do in this variety of settings is to seek information, but it should be abundantly clear, it is not just for the sake of knowing more. The information is sought so that the decisions they must eventually make, in either the short- or long-term, will be based on as much reliable data as possible.

It is this last point, the gathering of reliable data, that is critical to the whole process. Its importance is related to the need for a superintendent to develop, quite consciously, his or her network of surrogate noses. Put rather baldly, some people can be trusted to give a more accurate picture of things than others. Superintendents know this, as do their assistants, and they also know that if they don't develop this network both their survival on the job and the effectiveness of their decisions (quite related) are at risk. So it is not surprising to learn that they or their central office colleagues will be able to respond to the question, "Whom do you trust to give you reliable information?" quite readily. They are aware of whose data are straightforward, whose are biased, and whose tend to be incomplete. And, of course, they choose to rely on the first. Here is what one superintendent, relatively new to a small district, said as he addressed this point, unprompted by me:

> When I first came to the district [his second superintendency], I wandered around a lot, trying to get a sense of the place and the people in it. I like to talk to people about their particular program and, in an informal way, get a sense of what's happening. Sometimes people try to lobby me. I hear them out as best as I can and I try to pigeonhole what they tell me. But they aren't the ones I use—they're good people—because their views are too narrow and biased. So what's happened is that there are three or four people I use as sounding boards, you know, that I have particular confidence in, not only because they make sound decisions but because they seem to have their finger on the pulse of what's happening.

This developing of a reliable network of surrogate noses, then, all seems rather simple. In reality, of course, the process is anything but simple. It involves sensing a compatibility of interpersonal styles, sensing who has an axe to grind, sensing who has developed reliable information networks, and sensing who will be willing to talk about what they know. How this sensing ability is learned and developed is a matter of conjecture and probably unknowable in any precise kind of way. That it must be developed seems to be without question, for as superintendents will frequently tell you about situations concerning their colleagues who didn't deal with deeply troubling circumstances or who perhaps permitted these circumstances to arise, "They simply didn't know what was going on. They didn't know about them."

As we have suggested, in a district's central office, the need to have surrogate noses who can be trusted is not only the superintendent's need. A person with the responsibility for a district's instructional program reflected this way:

I consciously cultivate that relationship because I need feedback about programs from people. But it's almost like one of these undiscussable things. If someone were to say to me, "Do you cultivate certain people in your district?" I'd say, "No, not really." But, in fact, I do. They know I do it, but would deny it just as well. It's kind of just like one of those informal kinds of agreements that people have with each other. And they will protect their anonymity to the point where sometimes at staff meetings with teachers, they will constantly take me on so that they can demonstrate to the rest of the staff that "I'm not his boy or girl."

I've got to be able to trust the people with whom I deal. I look at an awful lot of central office people and I don't think they've been able to develop that trusting relationship because they haven't had or taken the time to interact with people. You can't develop a trusting relationship with someone you interact with rarely.

Several points become important. There is the deliberateness implied in the use of the term *cultivate*. Cultivating, be it a garden or surrogate noses, is a thoughtful matter. Not a haphazard enterprise, it involves an ability to sense who can be trusted to provide an accurate description of what is going on. And, with this purpose in mind, the cultivation of people takes both time and much interaction with them over matters of mutual concern. It is through this interaction that both administrator and the people with whom he or she is working get the opportunity to test each other out to see if they are *mutually* trustworthy.

Though it is not fair to say that central office administrators need to recruit and cultivate a cadre of central office spies, there does appear to be a bit of a spy-novel flavor to it all. After all, the system is a political one, at least as far as its organizational relationships are concerned. Additionally, the notion of cultivating people who will provide reliable information has an odious undertone to it. Thus, we see the need of the administrator to deny his or her efforts to cultivate surrogate noses and, once cultivated, to protect their anonymity. It is a delicate situation in which to be. One might dream of the best of all possible school worlds where such imperatives did not have to be met. But it is only a dream, and perhaps that's all right, too.

The work of secondary school principals requires the use of surrogate noses just as does that of central office administrators. Whereas the concept involved is a similar one, getting a nose for things through other people, there is a major difference that affects the way the activity is played out. That difference has to do with the physical and, thus, social proximity that the people involved have to where the action takes place. School district offices, even if they are located in a school building, tend to be somewhat physically distant from where the action of school life takes place. Physical distance tends to create social distance, which is made even larger in this case because of the symbol of authority and power that attaches to the "superintendent's office." The basic point is that a secondary principal is almost literally surrounded by the information that he or she needs; and the people needed to provide that information, also surrounded by it, are close at hand. The following high school principal talks about getting his nose for things, in addition to being visible around his rather large and rambling building, by using his staff:

> I sound out everybody, but Joe is one of my primary sources. He's all over the place, knows all the kids, and really knows what's going on. Every high school needs a Joe. And then there's my other vice principal. I sound these guys out a lot. I try to meet with them at least weekly, see what their impressions of things are, what problems we've got, what did we do, who needs to be seen—all that stuff. And I use my guidance counselors a lot. They're the first ones to spot trouble with a teacher 'cause the kids will go first to them when there's trouble in a classroom. The storm flags go up and they let me know about it.

The principal's surrogate noses are built into the structure of the school, so to speak. One might suggest that the same holds true for a superintendent's staff and, indeed, the formal structure would confirm that. There is a difference, though, and it is that a building-based staff doesn't have to go very far to get the information they need to be a good nose for the principal. It confronts them day-by-day, hour-by-hour, and not infrequently, minute-by-minute. This is not so for the central office staff who often have to make a distinct physical effort to get information that is important to them.

There is another factor that suggests a difference between the ability of a superintendent to get the kind of information he or she needs from the central office compared with the high school principal. As was discussed earlier, it is related to the social distance that is created merely by the fact that one's office is "downtown," whether or not that location is really downtown or somewhere else. It is almost as if a district director of elementary education, for example, carries with him or her a sign that says, "Central Office Spy. Be Careful of What You Say." The information that gets provided to this person tends to be limited and guarded. On the other hand, staff people in a school are "there" all the time and may be seen as one of "us" and not one of "them." They tend not carry the symbolism of distance or threat that accompanies their downtown colleagues. Thus, the information they get is more valid and focused. They can serve as a principal's surrogate nose in a way that an assistant superintendent can't for the superintendent, for example, unless he or she has developed an informal system the likes of which has been discussed earlier.

There is one further point that needs addressing. Despite the fact that a principal's staff may function very well in helping him or her understand the nooks and crannies of the school, there is a line that the principal is not permitted to cross by teachers, in particular, during the ordinary course of events. It is the type of line with which all of us have had experience. Put simply, much as principals do with central office personnel, teachers screen out or cover up certain types of information which, for whatever reason, they judge the principal should not have. One middle school principal described the circumstances by saying, "You never know what you used to know as a teacher. The day you become an administrator, the door is closed. You're simply deprived of the access that you used to have to all kinds of things."

Access does tend to develop, at least partially, through informal means and in much the same way that it develops for administrators in the central office. Over a period of time, most principals strike up relationships with one or more teachers whom they can trust and who trust them. And these teachers, surrogate noses, help a principal become aware of and understand some, but not all, of these nooks and crannies in a school's life.

Interestingly, it is quite likely that there's a good bit of reciprocity present in relationships of this sort—an experience familiar to most of us. A high school principal, speaking about a teacher who is an important source of information for him, said rather simply, "She confides in me and I confide in her." When a person gives something to another, he or she usually expects something in return—friendship, confidence, favors, or whatever. And it is probably true that the surest way a principal can deprive himself or herself of help received from surrogate noses is not to reciprocate.

• Endnote

1. Somewhat tangent to the discussion of administrators "getting a nose" for the organizational culture, but critically important to the basis upon which principals, in particular, practice their craft is the question, How do teachers "get their nose" for the school? They start to get it on the first day of school, or before, by the subtle messages that are sent to them by the principal, other teachers, and the students. In formal orientation sessions what is left unsaid is often more important than what is said. For example, one teacher I know described her orientation session as a situation in which stress was placed on monitoring absenteeism, discipline, and the lavatories. No mention was made of what the school was all about or about what was expected of the teacher in the classroom. Except, of course, it was. The school was about keeping things orderly, and teachers were on their own unless they could get help from other teachers. Another teacher, recalling his first conversation with his principal, said, "He asked me two questions. First, how I felt about teaching a racially mixed class and, second, he asked me if I could start the next day." Once more, and quote obviously, what was left unsaid was more important than what was said. What was important in that school, as it turned out, was simply to have enough teachers.

    I make these points simply to suggest that administrators, by their behavior, are extremely important cultural norm setters and they need to attend to this.

Chapter Six

In the Beginning—
An Image of the End

Biblical scholars will forgive me, I hope, as in somewhat of a playful manner
I use the story of Creation to start this chapter, which discusses how having an
image of the hoped-for result of one's work plays a role in the practice of the
administrative craft. The creation of the world, as it is described in the Book
of Genesis, can be seen, not irreverently, as a work of craft. "In the beginning,"
we are told, "the earth was unformed and void." And then God went to work.
He "made" things and He "created" things, it seems, with a rather clear image
of what the result would look like. I infer that because seven times in Genesis
I reference is made to God reflecting on his work: He "saw that it was good."
The result of His work was apparently subjected to His evaluation of it against
the original image He had of what it would look like when finished.

For obvious reasons, it would be risky of me to push my biblical exogesis
any further, but I think the point has been made. God was crafting the world
("on the seventh day God finished His work which He had made," Genesis
II). He seemed to know what He wanted to happen and it also seems that this
image was functional for Him. At least, so we are told, though the reader, of
course, can make of it whatever she or he will.

Back down to earth we return, as it were, and closer to our task of understanding the craft of administration. Here are a few examples of how having an
image of what they want to make comes into play as traditional craftspeople
work. Recall, for example, the words of the potter in Chapter Three:

When I first started, I would put the clay on the wheel and then when it began
to resemble something, I decided what it was that I was making. That was many
years ago. Now, I sit down and decide exactly or pretty exactly what I want to make.

70

The potter then goes on to say that the decision of what is to be affects what kind of clay should be used, how much of it should be used, whether or not it can go in the oven, and so on. Everything, though, depends first on what it is you want to make. The image that is held serves as the prepotent guide for one's work.

Another potter echoes the first:

> First, you think about what you want to be your end product, in general terms. Is it going to be practical, nonusable, a fun project, or is it just going to be an experiment? I think you structure it that way. Then you think about the materials, what kind of clay you want to use and this depends on what you want to make. Some clays are high fire and some are low fire; some are very sturdy and some are very delicate. And the character of the clay you use affects the tools you use.

And now a woodcarver who specializes in carving likenesses of birds:

> When I see a block of wood on which I'm going to work, I see the bird in the wood. And it's important to visualize it in all its perspectives—depth, height, width, and so forth. That way I have a feel for what I have to do and for how I'm going to work on it.

When one is crafting some *thing*, then, the image that is held "in the beginning" of what is to result from one's work with some essentially formless material (but with substance, thus differing from the Creation story) becomes an overriding factor in pursuing the work itself. If you don't know what you want to make, you can't start making it. It's as simple as that. It is possible that one might play with clay or wood, for example, and see where the play leads. Once the image develops, though, other elements of the craftsperson's work begin to emerge—the materials to be used, techniques to be followed, tools to be employed, and so on. The initial image, which may change as the work proceeds, perhaps depending on the idiosyncracies of the particular material, provides the criterion against which the results may be evaluated. And though this all seems rather noncomplex and straightforward, it is hardly that. Most important, I think, what all this involves is an interaction between the self of the craftsperson and the image he or she has of the work itself. Certainly, that is not a simple thing to understand.[1]

We don't need to be reminded that school administrators don't craft things. What they craft, for the most part, are workable solutions to problematic situations. Nor do we have to be reminded that the nature and tempo of their work, particularly that of school principals, does not often permit them the luxury of slow contemplation of an acceptable image of what a workable solution might be. To elaborate, a high school principal, responding to the question of the nature of the images he forms of solutions to problematic situations, put both a practical and philosophical perspective on the issue this way:

> Normally, you perceive that because of the time factor, most situations that might possibly have an ideal conclusion would take considerably more time than anybody has. There are simply few situations that you can process on either a personal or mechanical level well. You have to think, act, do something and, in a sense, you kind of sit back with the expectation that it will work out. In my case, I think my instincts, my feelings, my perceptions, and my resolutions are successful in calming the waters. Often that's all that's necessary. You're not going to change a mindset or a lifeset that somebody has. That's not going to happen. It's getting beyond the moment and moving to the next moment which will be different with the hope that your work in the first has made life somewhat more liveable.

In one form or another, I have tested out this perspective with many administrators. I have no reason to doubt its validity as it applies to the day-to-day work of administrators, particularly those whose work is at the school building level. It is not so much that images of solutions are not formed for specific problem resolution, but that there is an overriding image that sets boundaries around what one might expect or hope for as a result of one's work. And that overriding image, hoping that your work "has made life somewhat more liveable," is a function of some of the facts of school organizational life, which means, in the words of this principal, "getting beyond the moment and moving to the next moment which will be different."

Lest the reader interprets these remarks as an expression of pessimism or depression, let me say that I don't see them that way. Rather, it seems that this principal had a finely honed and articulated insight into the demands of everyday school work and the way in which these demands set limits on what one could hope to achieve in the course of a day. It is a statement of the conditions of school life and is not in itself a statement of depression or pessimism, though some people might interpret it that way. And, to repeat, those conditions suggest that the governing image of a school principal's daily practice of his or her craft is that work has the aim of making the school a more liveable place to be. Not everything falls in that category, of course, but as I have observed principals at work and talked with them about their work, their focus on making the school more liveable becomes abundantly obvious, though they may not use that term in their thinking or talking. They seem to understand very well that they can't change people in any substantive way, but they can help them to live together better. That is really not a bad image to hold.

There is one further and unexpressed thought in all of this. It is what appears to be an underlying assumption about the effects of creating and maintaining a satisfactory state of daily school liveability on the quality of teaching and learning that takes place in a school. The better that state, the thinking goes, the better will be the teaching and learning. That assumption is certainly arguable, but it is also not without merit. One thing, though, does appear to be certain. When the level of liveability in a school is not satisfactory, quality teaching and learning will not take place. So, the plethora of recent reports that tell us what to do to make the schools better notwithstanding, principals seem to know where it all starts.

Superintendents also seem to know where it all starts. As one observes them at work and talks with them about their work, even though they may speak of their very real concern about curricular and instructional quality, there is little doubt of their awareness, usually unarticulated, of the same kind of overriding image that governs the work of principals. That is, by the things they attend to and the way they attend to them, superintendents seem to focus their energies on creating and maintaining a satisfactory state of organizational liveability at the district level.

There are differences, of course, as we have noted earlier, between the work setting of superintendents (and other central office staff) and building principals. The one difference that seems to take primacy in the present context is that of work tempo—the pace at which work goes on, at which problems develop, and at which they have to be resolved. The moment-to-moment situational focus of a school principal's life is precisely that. Things occur quickly and need to be dealt with quickly and very frequently in bandaid fashion so that the life of the school goes on in as satisficing (March and Simon, 1958) a manner as possible. In the superintendent's office, things move at a slower pace, which is not to say that there is not a continual flow of problems into that office. It is to say, though, that the need to create a quick "liveability" solution to a problem is not one that tends to characterize a superintendent's work as is the case with the work of the principal.

One can picture this difference in other, more colorful ways. As I sat watching superintendents work, it was as though I was watching an unending chess match. Action was slow, deliberate, thoughtful. The "board" was looked at carefully, and I could almost feel the superintendent calculating her or his own moves in anticipation of the move that would be made by the other—who was not, incidentally, necessarily an opponent. The ultimate goal of these moves, though, was not a checkmate, but to play to a draw so that the game would continue. My picture of the work of a principal, however, was that of watching a ping-pong game. The ball goes back and forth over the net very quickly, creating a new situation with each return, and the objective of the principal is to keep the volley and the game going as long as possible, not to win a point.

It is an odd game that one plays not to win, not to lose, but to "play to a draw" or "to keep the volley going." And this takes us back to the overriding image of creating and maintaining organizational liveability that I suggest is always in the mind of school administrators. It is probably below the level of their consciousness and articulated only when someone else asks about it. Nevertheless, "first things first," an old rule of thumb, is so deeply ingrained in administrators that its activation is automatic and perhaps non-sensed in each situation that arises in their work. Other images of work and work problems are created within the context of this one's primacy, even though an administrator may not be aware of it on a moment-to-moment basis.

Another important thought to consider about this overriding image of creating and maintaining a state of school liveability is that it is vague and nonspecific. Liveability varies with the culture of each school and school district, and with the preferences and expectations of the various constituencies involved. It means different things depending on the level of the school involved, its community setting, its faculty, and the characteristics of its student body, for example. And most certainly, different school districts define what it means for themselves as evidenced by teacher union contracts, personnel policies, and student discipline policies.

If this were all there is to the problem of understanding the role that image formation plays in the practice of the administrative craft, this chapter might well end here. We could provide a few illustrations to make our point and that would be that. Administrative life, though, is much more variable. In rather general terms, what seems to happen is that images of what one wants to produce develop in three separate but frequently related areas. That is, school administrators develop pictures in their minds, sometimes very clear and sometimes vague, of (1) what they would like their district or school to look like as a result of their work, (2) what would be an acceptable outcome for each problematic situation that confronts them or which they may initiate, and (3) how they would like to be perceived as a person in a role. The balance of the chapter is devoted to elaborating on these ideas. The reader should bear in mind two things. First, my aim is only to be illustrative of the concept of "In the Beginning—An Image of the End." The incredible number and type of events that occur in the life of the schools, combined with the idiosyncratic tendencies and values of the people involved, make other than an illustrative goal unrealistic. Second, though we will deal separately with each of the three categories, as we shall see there will be circumstances in which they come together.

• Images of School Districts and Schools

I recently asked a superintendent what it was that he had on his mind for his district. What were to be the fruits of his labor? A hard question to answer, perhaps, for a person who himself was in the process of learning about what it might be possible to do. He started out with a very general statement and then became more specific.

> My job, as I see it, is to have some anticipated outcome and, very generally, I want a figure, I want a painting, to use the analogy, that will be pleasing to the eye and also give some inherent value to the object.

> What I inherited when I came here was a district with a highly centralized decision-making structure. About 90 percent of the decisions were made at the district level. That didn't fit me, personally or professionally. It simply became apparent to me, from my own experience and from my reading of the literature, that, first, I would be personally more comfortable and, second, the district would be better off if I started to broaden the base of decision making.
>
> Well, I must admit I didn't know just what that meant. I just knew I had to do it. So I established a District Planning Committee to address four or five particular needs that its members saw as important for the district to address. It's been new, it's exciting, risky—but all on the positive side.
>
> The real exciting part is that I didn't have the plan completely conceptualized when I started talking about it. I knew what I wanted as an outcome—grassroots recommendations based on a reasoned process. But I also knew that I work best when I create a basic design for something and then talk it through and have it developed through people that either I trust or I think should be involved. I develop the structure and when it works well, I literally view myself and act as a staff person.

In the context of the type of work with which this book is concerned, it is a bit difficult to react to this man's initial concept of the aesthetics of the image of the school district he had in mind. School administrators don't usually talk about something "pleasing to the eye" when they talk about their work. Yet, there is an attractiveness to the idea. Perhaps it refers to the results of some sort of goodness of fit between self and work or, to put it another way, a feeling of comfort with creating procedures and processes of work that match well with some preconceived notion of how things ought to operate.

This thought takes on more validity as we note the superintendent's comment about his image of developing plans, and a vehicle for broadening the base for decision-making in the district. Although, of course, problems had to be addressed, note that the substance of the problems was not mentioned. That would develop, and probably with a vengeance, as people learned and trusted their learning that he was really interested in "grassroots recommendations." It was no democratic "game" he was playing. Nor was it simply a free-for-all brainstorming kind of thing, for as he said at another point in our interview, "My control over the Committee is to make sure that while they identify the issues, the process they use is a valid one."

But note, as well, that when things started, he didn't know exactly where they would lead and that the exciting part of the enterprise was to be part of it and watch it develop, changing to meet changing circumstances but always, one suspects, with the overall target in mind. And when everything works well, "I literally view myself and act as a staff person." There, I think, is the aesthetic element with which we started combined with "something of value." As I read and studied this man's interview, I was reminded of the closing line of a recently popular television series, "The A-Team": "I love it when a plan comes together." There is that sense of having planned and accomplished something that works out nicely, even elegantly, as well as the sense that others will view it in a similar light.

That is not all there was to it, however. Just as knowing what a craftsperson wants to make is related to the materials, tools, and techniques that a potter or woodcarver will use, so does knowing what one wants to happen provide guides for adminsitrative craftwork. For this superintendent, having the image of developing a district that would be characterized by a broadened base of decision making meant thinking about who should initially be involved, what kind of group should be formed and how it should be used, what role he should play, how he should use his control and for what purposes, and so on. It also meant that he would know through some personal means when things were going the way he wanted them to. Recall that he said, ". . . and when [things work] well, I literally view myself and act as a staff person." At least in this situation, then, the extent to which he could play that role and feel comfortable about it was the measure of how well his image of what he wanted to have happen had been matched by events.

I hasten to add what is perhaps a statement of the obvious connected with this set of circumstances as well as to all others that will be discussed. It is, as any administrator knows, that there is no aura of permanency. Temporariness characterizes the results of what one does, for the most part. In the present case, for example, there is no particular reason to suppose that once established, a broadened base of decision making will remain inviolate. Things change and images of what should be along with them—which, one suspects, is about the only inviolate thought one can have.

Another type of image a superintendent may hold for a district came to light as I visited and observed a man while he was working. The district was a large suburban one. Its superintendent, publicly acknowledged as a highly successful one, had been in his position almost twenty years. At one point in the morning he told me that he wanted to visit an elementary school to which a new principal who was also new to the district had recently been appointed. The school had been a troubled spot for the superintendent in that its reputation was one of relative mediocrity of performance (thus, the new principal).

The visit itself seemed to be relatively routine. We walked around with the principal, stopped in many classrooms for a moment or two, and chatted with teachers and youngsters. Finally, we arrived at the teachers' lounge and the principal pointed out that the teachers had complained to him, as apparently they had to the previous principal, that some of the furniture in the lounge was distasteful and in a state of disrepair. "How much will it cost to get a new lunch table and chairs?" asked the superintendent. "About $1000," was the reply. "Go ahead and order them" came the response.

A rather simple bit of talk, it would seem. But as my discussion with the superintendent late in the afternoon revealed, it was anything but simple in its inner meaning. What was the bottom of it, as it turned out, was this superintendent's image that the route to developing and maintaining successful school programs and instruction was lined with successful school principals. Being a successful principal is, in part, a political phenomenon in the sense that in addition to having expertise in matters educational, one must be able to have one's ideas and influence accepted or, at the very least, considered on such matters. That is, one must be paid attention to, and at least part of getting oneself paid attention to as an administrator involves gaining a reputation for being able to get things done and as having influence with organizational supraordinates (Pelz, 1952). The superintendent in this case, a very skilled and insightful manager of school politics, realized this very well as he said:

> One of the reasons I try to get there as often as I can is to reinforce the good things he is doing so that he gets a feeling of being successful. You reinforce him whenever he needs help and you also help create the idea that he's got clout. He needs to show his teachers that he's the kind of person who gets things done. So, one way you build him up is by doing reasonable things that indicate to his faculty that he has influence in the system. And once they start to get that idea, they will also know that he's considered to be of value by us. It will simply make it easier for him to work with them on the things we want him to do, improve the quality of instruction. Getting a couple of new tables and chairs for the teachers' lounge is a small price to pay for that, though, of course, it isn't all that simple in the long run. But it helps.

There is an interesting difference between this example and the previous one of how the images a superintendent holds for his or her district may be related to the behavior of that superintendent. In the first instance, "to broaden the base of decision making" functioned as the impetus for deliberate planning and action. In the second, the idea of creating a system whose hallmark was a group of very good and respected principals seemed to serve as a means of alerting the superintendent to opportunities to use himself and, in this case, his control of the school budget to further that aim. It is not hard to imagine a superintendent, for whom the "successful principal" image is not salient, not letting go of the $1000, commenting, "The table and chairs look as though they'll be okay for another year. Tell the teachers we'll try to build the item into next year's budget." Such was not the case, though, as we have seen. His antennae were out, as they always seem to be, helping him sense on-the-spot chances to build another successful principal. Buying a new table and chairs for the teachers' lounge was most certainly not a part of his plan for visiting the school that day.

All this is not to say, of course, that holding one image of what a district should look like excludes the holding of another. It would be foolish to suggest, for instance, that in the first situation the superintendent was not concerned that his building principals should be productive ones. Situations change and points of view change along with them. For example, the images that guide the behavior of a superintendent new to a district are quite likely to be different than those of one who has been in a district a number of years. To think otherwise would be to hold the view that the life of a school administrator and of the schools themselves are static ones, and this view is about as far from reality as can be imagined.

Building principals, of course, hold images of what they want their schools to look like, much as do superintendents of their districts. There are differences, though, and they are to be expected. Of necessity, the latter must take a broad view of things whereas the work circumstances of the former mandate a somewhat narrower concept of what ought to be. Administering a school building is a more focused enterprise certainly than administering a school district if for no other reason than the difference in the physical boundaries of one's domain. And, though some principals might argue the point, the opportunities to control and influence the direction in which one wishes a school to go are much more available to the principal than to a superintendent. The reason for this is that principals are "there" all the time—if they choose to be. They are in continual interaction with teachers and students and thus have the opportunity, through their words and behavior, to foster the image they hold for their school hour-by-hour, if not minute-by-minute. What this suggests is that the potential for a school to take on the image that a principal holds for it is greater than might be the case with the school district and the superintendent. In any event, what follows is a sample of the variety of images held by some principals concerning what they want their schools to be:

A woman with a strong academic orientation, new to her first principalship in a junior-senior high school which was in disarray, states:

> I want the school to be a 7–12 school where teachers at both levels are very con-sistent in their discipline, in their approach to dealing with kids outside the classroom, that they are objective-based, and they're all on the same wavelength and heading in the same direction. Previous to my coming here, the two levels, junior and senior high, operated on entirely different wavelengths because they had two different principals who were competitive and uncooperative.

A long-time high school principal in a community with high expectations for its schools says,

> I'd like it always to be thought of as a school where people care, as a school where kids achieve well, as a school where kids are successful and come back and talk to us about their success. I relish it when a kid comes back and says, "Gee, I got a great education in those four years." That's what I'd like to keep going. We have that image, I think and obviously I want us to sustain it.

An elementary school principal engaged with his teachers in examining the curriculum of the school claims:

> The big thing, not only for this project but for everything we do, is to develop in the teachers a sense of ownership of the school and everything that takes place in it.

> They have to feel like it belongs to them. The more you throw into the ring, the more they turn to you and by the end of whatever it is you're working on, they'll say, "Well, it's not my idea in the first place." It's not a problem for me to give direction on routine things—I'm comfortable with that—but on things that affect the whole school, I just refuse to take ownership.

Words, words, words. That is what they are, after all. And we might well be inclined to pass them off as just that—the right thing to say. To do so, though, would be to miss the point because the words and the images of the school they convey provide, once more, the organizing theme for action. Thus, the principal concerned with inconsistency of discipline in her junior-senior high school, and realizing that before her academic aspirations for the school could be achieved consistency had to be developed, held meeting upon meeting with the teachers to work precisely on that problem. The school had to become more liveable and, as most teachers will tell you, inconsistency of discipline is one thing that makes a school hard for them to live in, to say nothing of the problem that it creates for students. By all her actions, then, the principal had to communicate the need, as she put it, for people to operate on the same "wavelength." First things first. She had to change things and, at least at the times that I talked with her, this was just what was happening as she talked about her feeling that the time was at hand for her to go to work on matters of curriculum and teaching.

The matter of the principal who had the image of his school as being a place where there was a sense of caring for its students and where students achieve well might seem to be a simple matter. All that he has to do is monitor things, one might think. Yes and no. Aiding and abetting would be a better way to put it. That is, as I observed this man, it seemed that he was always on the prowl in his school but not, it appeared, with the primary motive of detecting things that might be going awry. Rather, the purpose of his prowling became evident in the question he continually asked, in one form or another, of students and teachers: "How are things going?" The image of the school, then, was constantly being reinforced by not mentioning that image. But what is perhaps most important is that not only did he know the words but he also knew and could sing the music. What got communicated when he asked "How are things going?" was that he really wanted to know. His behavior became the believable symbol of what he wanted to the school to be.

Making a fact out of an image of a school that teachers "own" may be as difficult an idea to put into action as can confront any principal. First of all, the idea of owning as it is used here is an intangible sort of thing. There is no solid measure of "Now we own. Before we didn't." Second, the concept of teachers "owning" a school and its programs seems not to be a part of what is involved in the education of teachers nor of the socialization processes that they encounter in a school. The more prevalent lore is one of avoidance of activities that might result in a feeling of ownership even if they are not so named. And perhaps with good reason, at that, as teachers can recount numerous times when they have been asked by their principal to consult and plan, only to finish their experience with a feeling of having been used. Third, the very idea of ownership of such an intangible thing as a school (not the building, of course) is very delicate. It can "break" very quickly. A joking slip of the tongue can do it all in rather nicely, for example, if that slip conveys that a particular activity is just an exercise, after all.

Nevertheless, the image of developing a school that teachers "own" seems to guide our elementary school principal. In our talk, he acknowledged both the difficulty of the task and its worthiness. It was his answer to making a school over into a place where good teaching would take place in an atmosphere of general commitment to what the school was all about. What was required of him, besides highly developed skills in working with groups, was an ability to tolerate the frustration that accompanies the slow pace of the growth of such commitment.

• Images of Problem Solutions

Picture a continuum, one end of which is labeled "number of daily problems that require immediate solutions" and the other "number of daily problems that do not require immediate solutions." If one were to ask a sample of central office administrators and principals to indicate what their job demanded of them, in all likelihood, one would find the principals clustered at the "require immediate solution" end and their central office colleagues at the other. We have noted this difference between the two administrative job settings before. The daily craftwork of a principal typically involves confronting a large number of problems or predicaments that require immediate attention and, hopefully, resolution. People who work at the administrative craft in the central office confront a large number of problems or predicaments daily that typically do not need such immediate resolution though, indeed, they may be more vexing. Regardless, in each setting resolution images need to be formed, however, as we shall see from the illustrations to be presented, these images may develop in different ways.

Here is an example of the requirements of immediacy at work in a high school principal's office. It was close to the end of the school year and a girl who was to be graduating had committed an infraction of school rules that required a three-day suspension.

> I opened my office door and there was the girl's mother. She wasn't irate or demanding but she made it clear that she didn't want her daughter suspended. It had been touch and go all through school and she was afraid the girl would not graduate and that would be devastating for everyone. I was on the hook because my concept of fairness and consistency didn't allow me to forget about it. I had to resolve my own dilemma and the mother's problem. All of a sudden it hit me. It was something I had done once before and it involved requiring the girl to be in school for three days, just there, after classes and exams were over. The mother bought the idea completely. She was happy with it.

> I knew how I wanted the conference to end. It was that the mother would be pleased with what we decided and that she would feel good about the school; that the school was here for educational purposes and is not here to punish her daughter. But I also wanted her to know that the problem had to be dealt with.

If one reads this anecdote casually, it may seem a rather simple, even elementary, type of situation. However, it is complicated, involving as it does three problems and three associated resolution images. There was the question of the presenting problem, a school infraction and appropriate discipline; the problem of the mother and the image that the principal had of wanting her to leave thinking of the school in positive ways; and the principal's problem of maintaining an image of herself as someone who was consistent and fair. And this had to be attended to in a short period of time.

Things that seem simple, then, if we would learn from them, have a way of becoming complicated as they are subjected to analysis. What started out as a relatively straightforward situation, the assessing of a penalty for breaking a school rule and this assessment to be guided by the principal's image of being consistent and fair, became a much more complex affair. The unexpected appearance of the girl's mother changed the whole complexion of things and, in fact, created another problem with which the principal had to deal and quickly, at that. There simply wasn't time for the luxury of slow contemplation of possible solutions. Further, the entrance of the mother changed the focus of the situation in that her concerns forced the principal to rethink the nature of her original decision if she wanted (another image) the parent to feel good about the school and the way it dealt with students, which, indeed, she did. Notice, then, how memory (about which we will have much more to say in a later chapter) came into play. A similar situation had occurred once before in the principal's experience and she tested a different image of the problem resolution with the mother who "bought the idea completely. She was happy with it." And, it must be remembered, the principal was able to maintain the image of consistency and fairness she had of herself and wished to be known for.

I think, with regard to this incident in the work life of a principal, it would pay the interested reader to go back to Greene's (1984) comments in Chapter Three where I quoted from her paper, "How Do We Think About Our Craft?" Note the phrases "to imagine an educated capacity to attain an end-in-view or to bring about a desired result," "we may find ourselves reconstructing familiar techniques," and "an example of personal knowledge at work." The point is that it becomes possible to see and understand, even with reference to very brief moments in a school principal's work, the way in which the concept of administration as craft unfolds and plays itself out.

Here is another example of how the images one has of the hoped-for result of a problematic situation enters into what a principal does and how he or she behaves. I was spending a day with an elementary school principal, trying to understand her work and to see how well what she did fitted the craft idea. At one point during the day a young boy came to see her at her request. He was new to the school and she had become aware that he was having a bit of trouble with his arithmetic work and with being comfortable in the school. She talked with him for three or four minutes, during which time she quietly asked him questions and also gently reminded him how important it was to attend to his work. He left with a promise to come back and show her the results of his next arithmetic exercise. At the end of the day we talked about the situation and she said:

> What I had in mind was hoping he would have a better understanding of why he is here and I think that was accomplished, though I know I'll have to keep after him. I felt better about the conversation even though I know he wanted to leave or maybe didn't want to be here in the first place. He kept saying, "Yes" when I asked him questions and he opened up, "Fractions I can do, but division I can't do," he said. I need to keep on top of it.

But that was not all there was to it, as we had talked a bit earlier about the image she had of herself and wished to communicate in her work with youngsters. It was that of a "loving and demanding teacher and mother," and that was precisely what got communicated to me as I observed what happened. There was warmth and gentleness but there was also no doubt that the school existed for young people to learn. She was not going to let him "off the hook" of doing his school work but she also wanted him to know that people cared for him. She cared enough to ask him to come back with a sample of his work so that he could be helped, reinforced, and feel more comfortable at school. It was as though that in the back of her mind this image of self was in constant interplay with the conversation she was having with the boy.

A different situation in the same school on the same day caught my attention. This one had to do with the instructional program and an early morning meeting with a new instructional specialist, a helping teacher, who had been assigned to the school. Establishing this person's credibility by having her assume important responsibilities so she could display her competence was what was on the principal's mind. At one point in our discussion of the meeting, the image of the role she wanted this person to be able to assume emerged as a metaphor:

> I want to make her my right arm as far as instruction is concerned. I wanted to give her a really important job of trying to figure out the fifth grade team. They're kind of mixed up. They don't understand their strengths and weaknesses like the sixth grade team. So I wanted to give her some responsibility to help them as a team, even though they probably don't know they need help, so that, if she can pull it off, she will become a leader in their eyes. I'll have to keep my finger on it and support her.

Crafting someone into one's "right arm" is an interesting image. It conveys the impression of a person performing important functions for another, but not being separate from that other. Note, as well, that this type of administrative craftwork involves a longer time perspective than most of the problematic situations that a principal must deal with in the course of a day. The latter, as we suggested earlier, have mostly to do with maintaining organizational liveability. The time perspective they involve is relatively short as the administrator deals with one situation, patches it up, and moves on to the next. Making someone into one's "right arm," though, is a developmental project that will take time and necessitates accompanying images of what one will have to do in order for things to turn out well. "I'll have to keep my finger on it and support her" was what the principal said as she visualized what would have to be done if her "right arm" was to be crafted the way she wanted it to look at some point in time. Further, though it may seem a bit fanciful, the use of another metaphorical phrase, "I'll have to keep my finger on it," is somehow congruent with the "right arm" image. Right arms and left ones, too, do have fingers at the end of them. Perhaps this is too playful of me, but what I want to note is what I think is an example of the way an image of what one wants to happen is connected to the image of what one will have to do in order to make it happen.

• Images in Process

Though we don't need to be reminded, because everyday experience confirms it, an administrator's work life is not a neat, packaged deal. And though innumerable circumstances arise that have a short life span and whose resolution requires the quick formulation of a desired end result, there are also large numbers of conditions in which the image of what will or should be produced emerges over time. That is, though our woodcarver told us that he could "see the bird in the wood" before he started carving it, there are situations that administrators confront in which the "bird" is not seeable at the outset and in which its outline becomes evident over time and then, perhaps, only vaguely. Here is the way a director of elementary school programs in a medium-sized city described such a set of circumstances:

> One of my responsibilities was to organize and implement a program to improve basic schools and overall student achievement. The development and implementation of it is supposed to take three years. Having been an elementary principal and teacher before that, this was a project that was near and dear to my heart. I started out as I normally do. I tried to see the big picture and that kind of stuff and what would be the details. But as I got into it, it's been about six months now, it's gotten bigger and bigger and it sort of gets more like a weird octopus with eighty-five arms coming out in all directions. But what makes me feel good is to be able to identify this big, somewhat enormous goal. Really, what does it mean?

I suspect that the thoughts and feelings expressed here are not unfamiliar ones to any school administrator. What they imply is the need to be tentative about one's image in those situations that are long term and involve large numbers of people. This is curious, in a way, because tentativeness is not taken to be an admirable characteristic of administrative behavior. Rather, decisiveness is thought of as the thing to be admired. Nevertheless, this person seemed to sense, as would most others, I believe, the need to be open to the kaleidoscope of cues and conflicting forces that continually mandated the reformulation of the initial image she had.

This point brings us back to our woodcarver who could "see the bird in the wood." True, but the internal character of the wood may bring some surprises. A knot, an unexpected shift in the grain, of necessity shifts the image of the outcome. Wood does talk back, so to speak, and the woodcarver needs to be aware of its "language." And so the administrator needs to be aware of the shifting languages that she or he hears because of the way these languages may bear on the nature of the image of the product that finally develops. This is not to suggest the advisability of a pawn-like stance as administrators engage their craft, bending with every breeze that blows. But it most certainly does suggest the need to be aware and understand the variety of tongues that are spoken in a school district as a project gets underway, coupled with the skill and willingness to revise images of outcomes as the scenario unfolds.

Sometimes, though, the boat is missed. Here is the case of an elementary school principal in a rural district who had decided that it was important to bring her school into the computer age. This would involve getting funds to equip a computer lab, developing the support of the teachers, and providing some initial training for the teachers in the use of computers for classroom purposes. All this she was able to do with a lot of hard work and not a little wheeling and dealing as far as the funding was concerned. But the story here involves the training program and its outcomes for which she had the image of teachers becoming comfortable with and able to use the technology. She observed and took part in the training, and toward the end of it, she became aware that it provided a real-life laboratory setting for them to learn about learning by using themselves as the object of study.

> It dawned on me at one point toward the end of the course that the one thing missing in their discussions of it were their thoughts on the teaching-learning process that was used and what was making it successful or unsuccessful for them as learners. I thought, "I wish they could hear themselves talk as they express frustration over the homework assignments or a pop quiz." They were concerned because they thought it was unfair, even though there were no grades involved. The thing I wish they had focused on was their own reactions to what was happening and how they may cause the same thing to happen in their own classrooms with their own students.
>
> I tried at the last session to have a conversation about it. And I've since referred to it on several occasions but I didn't hang on the way I wish I had. It was a real opportunity that I let pass.

And so these are at least some of the facts of administrative life. Indeed, this principal became aware of the language that was spoken—or unspoken—that helped her develop a new image of a possible outcome, one that may have been more important in the long run than the straightforward goal of becoming somewhat computer literate. But the awareness came too late. It may have been that this new image of what could or should happen was too much at variance with the original to permit that it be given serious consideration by the teachers. Whatever the reasons, the boat was missed.

There is, though, possibly a positive side to it all. As we shall see in a later chapter on how people learn their craft, failures play an important role in future behavior. One might suspect, and indeed I do, that the memory of this missed opportunity will highly influence this principal's awareness and behavior down the line.

• Three-Quarters of a Loaf

There is a caveat to this discussion of the role that image formation plays in the exercise of the administrative craft. It has to do with the common wisdom notion that much of life is concerned with seeking out workable compromise in problematic situations. It also has to do with the thought that to compromise on one's image of what ought to be is not a sign of weakness but an acknowledgment of one's sense of the possible. Here is the way one administrator expressed the thought:

> The problem is you always have this mental image as to how you expect this project to come out and your mental image isn't someone else's mental image. It may come out 75 percent of what you thought and then the other 25 percent is stuck on the side, while you would have put it on the other side or the top or the bottom or whatever.
>
> It was very difficult for me to let that situation alone, to let that 25 percent just sit there. In fact, to figure out some way to praise it. If what you want a project to look like when it's finished is the only thing that counts, then don't bother trying to get others to work with you because they won't or they'll simply go through the motions. I know because I got burnt a couple of times when I didn't leave that 25 percent alone. They felt I devalued what they had done.

The ability to compromise on one's image of the ideal, to settle for that three-quarters of a loaf, then, is more than a matter of finding solutions that will work and to which people will commit themselves. What may be at issue, perhaps most importantly, is the idea that the essence of excellence in the practice of the craft of school administration is to work so that the people with whom you work sense that they and their ideas are held to be of worth. And this is true even if what they produce doesn't quite coincide with what the administrator thought should eventuate. If the beak of a carved wooden bird somehow looks out of place, the carving won't be entered in a craft show much less win a prize. Contrariwise, if the "beak" of a curriculum project is a bit at variance with the administrator's original idea, this may not at all be a reason not to implement the project and to see if it needs to be shifted over time.

• Images of Self in Role

What has been left largely but not entirely unsaid in our discussion thus far has been the way that the image that one holds of oneself comes into play in administration craftwork. On a few occasions, because they were part of the story that was told, that image was made very explicit—the principal whose desire was to be seen as consistent and fair, for example. Another example, not included previously, concerned a superintendent whose specific purpose in meeting with a community group that had a problem it wished to discuss was "to build an image of myself as a person who would listen." For the most part, though, things were left in rather subtle form and with rather explicit intent. That intent was to say to the reader, "If you go back and reread the various anecdotes that were presented, you will be able to tease out the image of self that applied to and affected the particular situation described. Further, your inference may be somewhat different than that drawn by others."

The point is that the specific and differing content of the image one holds of oneself in the incredibly wide variety of situations one confronts as an administrator is less important than is the knowledge of what it is and how it influences what happens in that situation. For example, I have a different image of myself as a classroom teacher than I do as a dissertation advisor. And these different images—the former as a person whose interest is to promote wide-ranging and, sometimes, loose thought and who will tolerate mistakes, and the latter as a person whose interest is promoting tightness of thought and who will not tolerate mistakes—clearly affect what I do in each situation. Further, these images are bound up in yet a more subtle one in that, by my behavior, I want my students to know that I consider myself to be an adult, working in adult ways with other adults. The tale could undoubtedly be spun out in highly refined detail, but I think the point has been made: In everything we do and everything we say, we tell a story about ourselves and, in fact, this story influences what we do and what we say.

Sometimes we are aware of this very complex process as it develops. Most times we are not and, in a peculiar sort of way, it may be as well that we are not. It leaves open the possibility of being pleasantly—or rudely—surprised from time to time.

In the previous chapter the idea was to suggest that one's "nose" constitutes a sort of psychological ground upon which one is enabled to ply his or her craft. Not developing a nose or developing an inadequate one can lead to error and sometimes gross error. The concern of this chapter with images that are formed as the basis for craftwork on any particular problem is not a concern with potential error. And while it is true that one may misconstrue the requirements of a situation and thus form a flawed image of how it should turn out, my suspicion is that most judgments made in this regard are idiosyncratic ones. There are few rights and wrongs in school administration, and the range in between is a very large one, thus accommodating many shades of gray. What seems to me to be inescapable, though, is the idea that what one is is largely related to the images one forms about one's work and the ways in which one goes about trying to make those images into reality.

• Endnote

1. If the reader is interested, for example, in some rather profound thoughts about the relationship between working at a craft and the development of self-knowledge, Carla Needleman's book, *The Work of Craft* (1979), takes its reader on an unanticipated and delightful journey into that territory.

Chapter Seven

The Materials of Work—
Self and Others

In Chapter Three, our potter said the decision about what it was she wanted to make had a very direct and causal relationship to the type of clay that was to be used. To repeat, her words were:

> Whether you want it to be out of stoneware, which is more durable and can go in the oven, or if you want it to be of finer clay like porcelain, which doesn't have the same properties and can't go in the oven. . . . What kind of clay you use and how you work on it depends on what you want the finished product to look like. . . .
>
> There are huge differences in clay, going from the crude stuff you find in a clay pit up to porcelain which is like working with talcum powder. Stoneware can take a lot more abuse. It's rougher, more solid, fires better, has less distortion in it. Porcelain is more fluid. It wants to do what it wants to do. It sinks and collapses. You have to work much slower with it because it's much more delicate.

Metaphorically, then, our potter has set out the focus of this chapter and in vivid imagery, at that. Its concern is with the thinking of school administrators with the "materials" with which they must work. And by materials, of course, what I mean is their understanding of the character of individuals or groups, adults or youngsters, whom they encounter for brief moments or over the long term. The overriding thought is that, much as in the case of the potter, the nature of the materials to be worked with is strongly related to how the material must be handled and what can be made from it.

In some very important ways, though, the case of the administrator's thinking about the materials she or he must work with is infinitely more complicated than is that of the potter. First, as mentioned in an earlier chapter, whereas the potter has the luxury of making choices about what is to be made and what type of clay would best fit that project, that luxury is denied the school administrator. What the next phone call will bring a superintendent or which teacher, student, or parent bearing which problem will next be sitting outside the principal's office is simply unpredictable. A related point of interest here, and another complicating element, is this: In the case of the potter, while there is an interaction between what is to be made and the choice of materials, it seems to be the case that the latter is almost exclusively dependent on the former. The potter decides what to make and chooses the clay, and avoids trying to make things that require the use of a type of clay with which he or she feels uncomfortable.

Things don't work that way for the administrator. Although it is probably true that an administrator can avoid engaging in some situations in which he or she may feel uncomfortable in the short run, it is hardly possible to escape them altogether. Sooner or later, in one fashion or another, they will have to be confronted. It is the nature of the materials with which an administrator must deal that frequently influences the image of the end product rather than the other way around, as in the case of the potter. That is, just about any administrator (or teacher) can give ample testimony to the idea that similar problems will yield to different solutions depending on who is involved and how the administrator understands the nature of that "who." Here is an example of just that kind of situation. Two young high school girls had received a little roughing-up through no fault of their own while they were spectators at a school basketball game. The mothers of the two, quite upset, made an appointment to see the principal about it. The principal stated:

> I knew one of them, but I didn't know the other. The one I knew was a real reasonable person. I knew that she wanted to be heard out and I wanted her to leave the meeting with the feeling that we really cared about her kid and we were doing the best job we could even if, at times, we simply couldn't prevent certain things from happening. So for her I knew I had to use my best listening skills and let her talk. I didn't know the other mother so I checked with the guidance counselor and he told me she was a little flaky and, on occasion, became a screamer. I didn't like that. But I had to meet her and I also thought I knew what to do, which was to take control of the situation, not let her talk very much at all, explain the situation as clearly as I could, and let it go at that. It worked. They both walked out pretty much cooled down.

As clear as can be, this brief anecdote illustrates the point quite well: Different strokes for different folks. That's too easy though because before one can put that adage into practice, one has to be aware of the difference in the "folks" and what those differences might mean for one's practice.

There is a further complicating factor involved as we think about the understanding and use of "materials" in the practice of administrative craft. Different than the potter whose thinking about the materials to be used to produce something is confined to the clay to be handled, the administrator needs to think about himself or herself as entering into the "material" scheme of things. That is, much as there is a need to be as clear as one can be about the nature of the people or groups involved in a particular predicament, so one must be clear about oneself: one's likes and dislikes; predispositions to act in certain ways; and conditions that evoke tension, anger, and so forth.

The oft-quoted comment from Pogo in the comic strip describes the implication of this idea quite well, "We have found the enemy and he is us." And this is by way of saying that for present purposes, in the practice of the craft of administration, the person of the administrator becomes an important part of the "materials" that are to be used and worked with as he or she tries to produce something in almost any problematic situation.

• The Self as Material

Understanding the idea of "the self as material" involves the way each administrator elaborates on Pogo's comment. If the enemy is us—better, if the enemy is oneself—what is it that needs to be understood about oneself that will help an administrator make use of that self better in the wide variety of situations that develop on the job? In other words, if you want to use yourself well it becomes important to know what it is that you are using and, more to the point, what part of yourself it is important to avoid using. That is the essence of Pogo's message: what it is about each person that must be borne in mind so that one does not become the enemy; does not, that is, through inattention to that something prevent from happening what one wants to happen.

The administrators with whom I talked had ready answers to the question as it was posed, not with the Pogo reference, but simply with the comment that "Most of us are aware of certain things about ourselves that sometimes get in the way of our doing our best work. How about you?" The responses to the question varied, of course. One person mentioned his tendency to be too slow about things when his school board wanted the tempo of problem solving to move quicker. Another talked of his tendency to be too trusting so that, at times, he got left "holding the bag." An elementary school principal spoke about his tendency to let himself be "tugged into a situation that I know I don't belong in." And a high school principal, formerly a very successful English teacher, spoke of her need not to come across as a know-it-all.

By far the largest portion of the responses were somehow related to the individual's tendency to want to be more directive, to be overly enthusiastic, or to be more forceful than was appropriate. By way of illustration, here are a number of comments which, in one fashion or another, make the point well:

 • One of the things that I have to watch out for is when I get on to something and I get enthusiastic about it, I really have to subdue my enthusiasm because it gets in the way of the feedback I want. That is, I don't want them to go with something because of me. So, what I have to do is consciously watch the way I interact with them. I've heard teachers sometimes make a comment like, "He really wants this," and I don't want that to be.

- It can probably all be characterized by the intensity that I have about education. It comes out in good and bad ways. People know I'm committed, that I work hard, and that they can depend on me. But the bad part of it comes out when I see people not working at the same pace I do or doing things the way I think they should be done. I tend to be sarcastic, then—but not as much as I used to be—and overly critical. I have to remind myself to adjust to the way others work. Sometimes I almost have to stop and say, "Hey, watch it. You're getting too intense."

- I have a tendency sometimes to be very opinionated, and I really have to make sure that I say to myself, "Be quiet. Bite your tongue. Hear everybody else. Don't say 'good,' 'bad,' don't be judgmental and just listen." You know when you're young and enthusiastic you want to cram it down everybody's throat.

- I really do like to control things, but I know that I have to keep that part of me under wraps. In the back of my mind, I frequently keep reminding myself, "Don't appear to be overly in control." Because if they feel everything is set before they even talk about it, then, in fact, it will backfire.

There are two reasons for including these particular interview excerpts. First, as noted earlier, a very substantial number of the responses to the question of what was it about themselves that these administrators thought it was important for them to be aware of focused on the way in which they used or possibly misused their authority. It is not, of course, the central purpose of this book to make generalities about school administrators as people. However, it may be worthwhile simply to propose the hypothesis that the need to be aware of and hold their own needs for control in check is a modal one, perhaps the most predominant one, relative to the things that administrators sense about themselves as they engage in their craft. The point is that the appropriate use of power and authority has implications for practice and for what I think may be termed practical morality, or the morality of practice. But that, I think, is another story and, possibly, another book.

Though it takes us ahead of our story by several chapters, one is forced to ask how these people, and many of their colleagues, became aware that they needed to attend to that part of themselves that was concerned with how they used their authority as they engaged in their practice. The answer seems to lie just beneath the surface of their comments. It seems apparent that at one time or another, each of these individuals made an error in their work that was somehow related to their use of authority. One doesn't learn about the misuse of authority in any way that has meaning for subsequent behavior unless one first misuses it. This is true despite the admonishments offered by textbooks or how-to-do it books such as *The One-Minute Manager* (Blanchard and Johnson,

1982). The misuse of authority as an abstraction has little meaning for a school principal or superintendent up to the point where he or she has misused it and, thus, both behaviorally and emotionally learned what it meant. Further, each administrator makes his or her own interpretations of that meaning. What is misuse for Administrator A in situation B maybe quite appropriate for Administrator C in situation D. And more, if Administrator A were to move to situation D, he or she might well find that what could be done in B cannot be done in D. It is the familiar "different strokes for different folks" theme—simple, perhaps, to the point of nausea, but unavoidable in its applicability.

A second point becomes important for our discussion of "the self as material" in the practice of the administrative craft. All of us have had the experience of talking to ourselves, of giving ourselves advice or warnings, of recalling previous experience to ourselves as we go about the daily business of living and working. Driving in snow, for example, may bring the continual advice to ourselves, "Don't accelerate too quickly" or "Don't brake too hard." Or we may remind ourselves on a sunny and warm day at the beach to be careful about too much exposure to the sun. Each of us has a repertoire of "tips" that we actively and consciously give ourselves to help us deal with the variety of situations we confront each day. Not every situation requires this tip-giving, of course. More of it is likely to happen in those circumstances where we see ourselves or the enterprise at some risk rather than those that are routine, matter-of-fact circumstances.

This brings us back to the interview excerpts we have just noted. They all involve situations in which the use of one's authority may become an issue, and implicitly this means that they are risky. Thus, the arousal of tip-giving behavior about oneself occurs. It is almost as though these administrators hold conversations with themselves. Note, for example, the use of phrases such as "I have to watch out," "I have to remind myself," and "I say to myself." Awareness of oneself as a material in administrative practice, then, particularly in situations that are risky, seems to be close to the surface.

• Others (or the Other) as Materials

That the practice of administration requires that a person have a keen sense of others conceived of as materials with whom he or she is working is patently obvious. It is so obvious, perhaps, that little systematic thought seems to have been given in the professional literature beyond prescriptive generalities such as, "Make sure you know the community power structure." Perhaps the reason for this neglect can be traced back to our discussion in Chapter Five of the need to attend to the commonplace. Recall, for example, the wheelbarrow story with its message that one must, indeed, look very closely at what is obvious in order to understand what the world is about.

In the present case, then, we need to look past the prescriptive generalities concerning the need to know the materials with which one is working. What becomes important is to provide some illustrations of the ways in which administrators think about the notion of "materials" as they work at their craft. We have several such illustrations and present them with the caveat that they are but a small sample of the universe of illustrations that might be provided. But, indeed, they convey the flavor of what we mean by the importance to the craft of administration of understanding that with which one is working. We start with some comments from a high school principal about her needs to know about her staff:

> You have to know people and you have to know their psychology and what makes them tick, what motivates them. I find that, as a rule, I spend 75 percent of my day interacting with people, either on a formal or informal basis. It's extremely important for me to go beyond the formal in order to learn about them. I stop and talk in the hall or cafeteria. I have an open door policy. I lose a lot of time. I know that, but I can't function without knowing them. I want to know whom I'm working with, what touches them, what motivates them, why they are in education. I want to know what's going on in their lives because so often things that are affecting their lives outside of school affect their performance in school. I spend a great deal of time trying to figure out my subjects as if they were models on a tapestry. Like each one is a great small part of that tapestry, but yet everyone of them has to fit together for the total tapestry to be complete.

Note how this principal moved from her general prescription to self ("You have to know people and know their psychology") to how she learns about people, to the things she wants to know about people, to how she then tries to use what she knows as she develops an image of the design of a tapestry she is weaving. And note as well that although she acknowledges that all this activity that focuses on understanding materials causes her to "lose a lot of time," she feels she "can't function without knowing them." Perhaps the time really isn't "lost," then, but used in a way that takes time from more routine administrative work and apportions it to that part of the practice that has a real payoff—building (or weaving) a school.

There is another part of this that I think is important to ponder over. It is this principal's ability to articulate what it is she is about as she talked about her needs to know her staff. Hers was not simply a stock answer. To the contrary, I got the feeling that our interview was not the first time she had given thought to the problem. You simply have to know how things fit together.

Another high school principal provided more detail concerning how people-materials fit together as she thought about her school in terms of a community:

> Well, in a sense it's like a community and within that community you have people who represent a lot of different skills. There are some you can count on to be real

hard workers but are not big idea people. They are the implementors. And you have people who may have good ideas but aren't very good implementors. You really have to know that. You may have people who may appear to be negative, but it's because they've had a bad experience and when you give them a little TLC or whatever, they respond. And then there are those people who don't want that. They want you to give them some responsibility so they can take it and run. So, I think, the real important thing is to learn where a person's at and learn how to use them all in tandem. Everybody doesn't do everything equally well and you have to find out what they can do.

Once more, then, there is this global concern about fitting the pieces together, about understanding that everyone doesn't do everything equally well, and that the only way to find out how things might conceivably fit is "to learn where a person's at." But note, as in the previous case, that the reason it's important to learn where that "at" is is so particular skills or services get utilized in community building. The linkage between the image of what is to be and what will be used to create that image is there, as well. And what this suggests is the possibility, at least, that as school administrators think of the image they have of what they want their district or school to be, they automatically start to think about the human (and sometimes physical, I suspect) materials they have with which to work. The parallel between this thought and the way we have noted that traditional craftspeople think when they contemplate making something is striking. It almost suggests a level of intuitiveness of thought that predates any ideas concerning those things that might make a difference between highly effective and less effective administrators.

The truth be known, though, much as a school administrator might prefer to spend most of his or her time thinking about grand designs and how things will fit together, the problems of their work life simply don't permit it. Theirs, as we have suggested several times, is a life of continually having to deal with the practical predicaments of others (and sometimes their own). These predicaments may be of a minuscule scale relative to the grand scheme of things or they may assume a size that is large. Regardless of the size, however, it is important to understand and deal with the materials that are there. Here, for example, is the thinking of a superintendent concerning the problem of declining enrollments with its consequent demand to close one of two high schools in his rather large, sprawling and thus fragmented, suburban district. A committee had been formed to make recommendations about what should be done.

The only thing that anybody knew was that we had to come up with two or three plans that would address a given problem. So maybe the best way to think about it craft-wise is that I've got a lump of clay and I've got to produce a pot. So I've got a feeling for where I want to go.

But really, there are different kinds of clay that make up the lump. For example, there were the band boosters from Hilltop High. They had always considered themselves as sort of a stepchild of the District. They were kind of fragile to deal with. And the Teachers Union. If there was any implication that closing a school would affect seniority, they would also be very fragile. It would all depend on how we put things. We knew all that going in. And things were up front right at the beginning. No games with seniority.

So if you go back to the clay idea, what you have to do is add a little water to it so you can work it. Like working with the Union so that we'd end up with their needs and the District's being served. The trick is to learn just how much water needs to be added so that you don't add too much and get mud, but enough to develop the kind of consistency you can deal with. Not too hard so that you can't work with it and not too soft so that it won't stand up.

We are down to cases, then, as different from thinking about materials in the context of an image of the future—an unmade tapestry or underdeveloped community—as was previously the circumstance. A problem had to be solved and the metaphor of administrator as potter seemed to fit. And, as we learned earlier, some types of clay are much more delicate in workability than others which are tough and can withstand being pounded. The fragileness of two groups was what he focused on. If he could get them to hold the form he wished, then other, more resilient parts of the design could be put into place, even if they had to be squeezed a bit.

Regardless of what solution to the problem was developed (the school was closed with minimal trauma to concerned parties), the important thing for us to understand is the character of thinking that occupied the superintendent. The precise nature of the plan ("we had to come up with two or three plans") apparently was not an issue with him as long as the system maintained its integrity. What *was* at issue was to make sure that all the different kinds of "clay" made a contribution to and were integrated into the final plan. There had to be a little patting here, adding some water there, supporting a handle on the pot until it became firmly attached to the side, and so on. The essence of it all was the superintendent's concern with how the materials would be used and transformed into the final product. Looked at this way, the image that gets conjured up of this superintendent is what has come to be known as the process-oriented leader—the type of person who is able to help the various members of a group or organization best mobilize and use their resources to solve the problems that confront them.

The thinking of this superintendent, as we have seen, was to make as sure as he could that whatever solution was arrived at by the group would be politically palatable to constituencies that were both internal and external to the system. His thinking about the materials to be used was conditioned by that prior consideration. In a way, what he had done was to create a microcosm in the committee of the potentially conflicting community groups so that when they reached agreement, he could be relatively sure that it would be agreeable to the community at large. Indeed, this is precisely what happened.

In the context of thinking about the school district, the school, or the subgroups within them as an interactive system, the need to think about "materials" is essentially a political imperative. We have some additional examples of the form this thinking might take. Here is a situation in which a central office curriculum director had been requested by the superintendent to take the leadership in a program of major curriculum overhaul. When I asked him to tell me what he was thinking about as he assumed leadership responsibility for the task, he said:

> Well, the first thing I think about when I receive this kind of responsibility, in general, is "Who are the key people out there that are going to be able to help me brainstorm this and pull this thing off?" The thing is to get people in key positions, not necessarily high-up positions, but people who are respected by their peers and who also know something. Further, in our District, you've got to have a balance between people who have respect, people that the Union will find appropriate, people who have knowledge of what you're talking about, and those people who are willing to volunteer their time to put things together. It's like I want to turn all that material into tools that will help me think this thing through.

What could be simpler? If you want a group of people to "help you think this thing through," convene a group of smart people and turn them loose. But, of course, there is much more to it than that. Somewhere and at some level, in situations such as this, an administrator has to have a sense of the appropriate. That is, which groups and which people within those groups most appropriately fit the requirements of the situation? On one level, the answer to that question is a political one if by that question one is also asking, "What constituencies must support be gotten from if the eventual problem solution is ever to be integrated into the system?" Rationality, sad to say, does not rule the day in matters such as this. And this is another way of raising the question of the power base that members of a group represent so that the right amount of leverage may be applied to sensitive points.

On another level, the answer to the appropriate mix of materials in the group is found on the level of knowledge of individuals, what they know, how interested they are in the project, and how willing they might be to be part of it. And on still another level, what is required is a sort of knowledge of the interpersonal histories of the people one is considering. Who will get along with whom? And who won't? These are critical questions for the administrator, as more than one problem has failed of solution because the people involved, almost literally, could not talk to each other.

Again, though, one might ask, "What could be simpler?" After all, the kinds of things that have been said in the previous two paragraphs are not exactly news to anyone. They describe thinking and events that probably transpire hundreds or thousands of times each day in American public life. Again, with reference to a point made earlier, it maybe that it is from the simple and commonplace that we have most to learn. It is in the course of making these very common decisions, doors become open for the administrator-craftsperson to learn about the nature of the materials he or she must use.

To open a door does not mean that one will enter a room. One must want to go in. And so it is that some administrators seem to be much more knowledgeable about the materials they work with than do others. They seem to have an almost uncanny sense of the proper mix, probably developed because they wanted to develop it. And this is not something we know before the fact. Rather, we come to understand it after we look at that person's history of leadership delegation.

The brief point of summary that has to be made here is this: At one level, the practice of the administrative craft is a highly political enterprise, the success of which depends in large measure on one's ability to sense the "material" requirements of a situation and to know what is available for use. This sounds highly manipulative and indeed it is. But if one can shed any negative values that one holds about the idea of manipulation—or at least hold them in abeyance—it can become less odious. We are simply referring to the pressing need for an administrator to arrange the human circumstances within his or her domain in such a way as to insure the highest probability of success for a particular venture. Nothing more and nothing less.

On this level of our concern, then, with the idea of the materials that are used in administrative craftwork, several things become important: knowing what is required in a situation by way of material, knowing what material is available, and arranging it in a way so that things become more predictable. It is not always the case, though, that the option to make the necessary choices is there for the administrator to exercise. Sometimes situations develop (the election of a school board, for instance) that are properly outside a superintendent's ability to control. There are some superintendents, though, who almost look forward to new members being elected to a school board. That circumstance, it seems, presents them with a challenge to their craft skills of molding and shaping the new board into the image of one with which they feel comfortable working, whatever that image may be. Or, to use the woodcarver metaphor, a superintendent, thinking of the Board as a log, looked forward to dealing with it as a new and perhaps exotic piece of wood whose properties were as yet unknown. The idea was to make that wood behave like others more familiar and workable. Not everyone enjoys this kind of work, though. Here is an example of one superintendent whose tone, as he talked with me, was a bit exasperated:

> You really have to be sensitive to the Board as a group, the individuals on the Board and what they're going to react to, and you also have to be aware of their impact on each other. For instance, this Board I have is a very young one. I've got five members on it with less than one year of experience. They've never gone through this budget process before. They want to go through every item, which is silly. You have to let them do it or let them think they're doing it. Sometimes I

deliberately set up things in the budget that they can pick at and do away with and I know it's not going to do any harm. It's almost as though I know what they're going to do so I set it up so that what they do won't hurt the whole picture.

The situation may not be as variant or, for some readers, as repelling as it may seem. Again, we deal with our idea of materials in the context of the political character of the superintendency. Or we can deal with it more directly in craft terms by suggesting that, for this superintendent, the tendency of his Board to attend to small budget details represents for him a "knot in the wood." When a woodcarver comes across a knot in the wood that was unexpected, there are three options available. The piece of wood may be thrown away as of no use; the knot may be excised, thereby radically changing the form of the product; or the knot may be incorporated into the design.

Analogically, the first two options are not available to the superintendent, much as he or she might wish they were. What can be done, though, is to exercise the third. That is, the superintendent somehow incorporates what he or she sees as a "knot" into the overall design for working on budget matters, at least. As any woodcarver will tell you, the problem is that working on knots takes time and usually results in one's tools getting dulled or broken. Sometimes, though, in the process, a lovely, eyecatching result occurs. And this, too, may happen with a school board, depending on the craft skill of the superintendent, particularly that part of the skill that involves understanding and predicting the behavior of the materials with which one works.

It is this ability to predict, stemming from an understanding of the materials one is working with, that brings things together. If one can predict with an acceptable degree of reliability how things will develop, then one can also monitor one's own behavior better as well as give oneself prior tips about what to do. Consider the following comments from a central office administrator as he thought of a school-community task force on the gifted that he chaired:

It's a mix of me and the group. The important thing for me to learn is where I fit into those materials and how I can push, or pull, or shape, or mold, or play with them.

We meet every two weeks and, of course, I think about it beforehand. I think about what will come up and who will talk about what. I think about Dan bringing up his usual characteristic points and how I will deal with them if I'm not comfortable with them. Then I think that maybe I better call on Bill because I know that Bill can deal with him better than I can. Then I think that at some point Jim is going to make his usual big political statement and again, as usual, it won't make any sense. So along will come Mary and blow Jim out of the water. And it's here that I will have to come in and support Mary. I'll have to clarify things and also blow Jim out of the water—but gently, absolutely gently.

So the scenario is created (perhaps a craft in itself) and its creation is wholly dependent, it seems, on this administrator's knowledge of the materials with which he has to work in this group. One may smile at his description of the sequence of action. But the smiles fade in what I think is a tip to himself that comes close to our potter's earlier talking about what a delicate task it was to work with porcelain. Note the last words he used after talking about having to "blow Jim out of the water." They were "but gently, absolutely gently."

There is another level on which one's ability to predict the behavior of another, based on knowledge of that other, comes into play an administrative life. It has to do with knowing enough about external educational organizations (the state education department if one works in a central office, for example) to be able to predict what it is they want when they issue requests for reports or other types of information. Certainly all of us who work in large, decentralized organizations know what is involved here. We make jokes about organizational functionaries who must justify their positions by collecting large amounts of information that we must supply. We "know" them even though we've never met them. And this knowing of that particular bit of material enables us to make judgments about what we have to do to satisfy their requests. In one particular case, for example, a superintendent was reviewing some requests for information regarding his district's compliance with several directives that were issued by the state education department. Said he, "All they want is a response. That's the game we play. They want a response." Knowing the "materials" enables him, very simply, to make some quick administrative decisions that would end up in the desired response, and no one would be terribly the worse off. Or, to think about administrative situations such as this in a slightly different way, knowing the "materials" enabled this superintendent to know how much staff time and energy should be put into providing the response. Not much, as the case turned out. And the time and energy that might have been expended in a situation where the superintendent didn't know the "materials" became available for use in other, more productive activities.

One thing that emerges from the discussion thus far is that there is a type of knowing of "materials" that is general and speaks to a class of actors (teachers or youngsters, for example), and there is a type of knowing that focuses on individuals within that class. The superintendent in the case immediately above knew, in general, about what it was that state education people were like and what they expected of him. And the anecdote related just previous to that spoke to the knowing of particular individuals and how they might react in particular circumstances.

These two themes of the need to know about one's materials in general and in specific seem to be consistent with the observations and discussions I held with administrators. Time and again it was possible to sense and talk about the way they both came into play, sometimes separate from each other and sometimes in interaction, in which case knowledge of the general case served as a ground for thought and action in the particular. But the general comes first, as it seems that administrators continually have in mind the question, "What is this class of people like?" as they move from situation to situation. Here are several examples of that question being answered, not in words, but in the behavior of an administrator.

In one case the choral group in a high school was invited to participate in a competition in another state. Participation would involve being away from school for several days, to say nothing of financing the trip, arranging for chaperones, and so forth. The principal arranged a meeting with the superintendent, the teachers involved, other pertinent central office personnel, as well as another teacher. The aim of the meeting was to raise formally for the first time the question of the feasibility of the choral group becoming involved and making the trip. No decisions were made at the meeting. It was all delicately exploratory. Later on, as we talked about the meeting, the principal said:

> I knew damn well that if I didn't start things this way it wouldn't be long before the rumors would start to fly and I'd have had a real problem on my hands, both with the superintendent and, more important, with the other teachers in the school. "What's going on?" they would have said. "All those kids out of school!" I know them and that's what would have happened. So I wanted to cut all that off by getting them involved with information right at the start.

In another situation, an elementary school principal had been asked by his superintendent to assume responsibility of a curriculum review project. The principal's preference ordinarily is to work with groups in a rather open-ended fashion and let specific tasks emerge as problems developed during the group's work. Things could not happen that way on this occasion because, as he stated:

> From my past experience I know that teachers are very task-oriented. They like to see results fairly quickly and I knew that this was going to be a working group process that would take some time. I worried about and tried to make sure that, even though things might get hazy at times, the teachers had specific things to do and could feel a sense of short term accomplishment.

And this is the way a principal of an urban middle school, not noted for the peacefulness of its days, reflected on problems of discipline in the school, particularly those that involved youngsters fighting with each other:

> You really need to understand the value system that kids hold when they get involved in a fight. It goes like this most of the time. First, "if people hit me, I hit them back." Second, "if I start something, I'll come up with an excuse why I started it, like I had no other choice, and I want you to make sure that you've caught everybody else who was involved." It really isn't so much that you're right all the time about these things, but if you have some sense of where the kids are in their thinking, it gives you a place to start.

The critical point in all this is found in the last sentence of the interview excerpt just quoted. Regardless of the problem, after some image is formed of what might be a possible solution, thought is given on some level of the general nature of the human materials with which one will have to deal. This is not to suggest that the character of that thought is slow and deliberate. I suspect that the case is quite likely the opposite—quick and intuitive for the most part. And what becomes important is not so much that one needs to be right all the time about the judgments that are made, but that one makes the decision and gives oneself a chance to test out whether or not that judgment will hold up or have to be changed.

Within these judgments that are made by practicing administrators about the nature of general categories of people with whom she or he comes in contact, there are, of course, judgments made about the "materials" represented by individual. No great insight is that, one might say, all of us do it all the time. True, without a doubt. It is our way to survive in a very uncertain world. But attend to the detail with which a high school principal described his thinking on the matter:

> First of all, everyone has a track record and I try to think of the track record of the person—kid or adult—with whom I'm working. Everybody has a certain consistency about them and I have to learn what that consistency is. There are some people whose judgment and credibility you respect and I, at least, tend to think that in a conflict situation their side is apt to have more merit to it. You know which people are out to get kids and which are not. The reputation of a person always comes into play. You have likes and dislikes. Some people, frankly, aren't so nice. Some people are out to screw you; they're out to screw everybody, even though they don't see themselves that way. Some of them are winners and some are losers. You simply have to know which is which and play things out accordingly.

Indeed, then, the practice of the craft of administration requires that the practitioner go very much beyond the general to the specific as he or she thinks about the materials to be worked with. And the specific may be thought of in terms that are elegant and delicate or common and crude—or anything in between. It is not so much that the school world is a sordid one. I think, for the most part, it is quite the opposite. However, it is true that every school or school district represents a sort of mini-community, bringing together a wide assortment of people with an equally wide assortment of problems, aspirations, and so forth. And, as our principal put it, some of these people are not so nice; and, some are winners and some are losers. The central issue in all this is not so much that one tries to make a winner out of a loser as much as it is that one needs to know if one is working with a winner or loser to start with.

How does an administrator learn about the materials with which he or she works? Are there special analytic skills involved? Or is it that the simple process of growing from child to adolescent to adult equips anyone to deal with the question we have raised?

As seems to be true with so many questions of leadership and organizational life, the answer to these questions is "it depends." It is probably true, for example, the experience of growing to adulthood has created for most of us a generalized healthy skepticism of the world that serves us in good stead in organizational life. It enables us to view things optimistically but with a tendency to test things before jumping in. We tend to understand and trust people, in general, until we learn, in specific, to be wary. It is also true that a small percentage of us seem to have traversed our rites of passage and emerged with a view that the world is a lovely place and no one is ill-motivated. (I had such a person as a student who did, indeed, manage to get a position as an administrator—but not for long. The discrepancy between what the world was like and what was his view of it was simply too great.) On the other hand, there also appears to be a small percentage of us for whom the world is a rather frightening place and who, thus, are led to view most ordinary events with suspicion. My sense of what happens to these people in the field of education is that if they remain in the field, they do so in rather low-level positions. Not trusting anybody, they themselves cannot be trusted.

Most people fall in that large area between the extremes. That is, the process of growing and maturing, particularly because our society is an organizational one, has equipped them both to understand and deal reasonably with the vagaries of organizational life and the ability to sense the general and specific characteristics of the "materials" with which they must work. Beyond that general sensing ability, though, it seems likely that each administrator gives thought to and develops personalized ways of making inferences about the nature of the specific "materials" with which they are working at particular moments in time.

This is not a startling statement in the sense that it is probably true that all of us at some time each day, for a brief moment or for a longer period, give some thought to the human "materials" we have encountered or anticipate encountering. We do this, administrator or not, because it is a very natural thing for us to do. People present themselves to us. We react to and make judgments about them and about what they are like. And it's probably true, though I know of no research to support the idea, that the way we describe people and the kinds of judgments we make from those descriptions reflect our own needs for compatibility. For example, I am sure that whatever are my own needs for power, wealth, commitment to task, and so forth are reflected in the way I describe and make judgments about others (colleagues, students, or administrators).

Thus, as each of us lives our daily lives, we quite naturally devote time and energy to trying to figure others out. And, as administrators practice their craft, they engage in this activity quite consciously, from time to time. What follows are a few illustrations of what they do and what they think about as they try and understand the "material" with which they are working. First, a superintendent thinking about his school board:

I always want to become quickly aware of possible trouble signs so I observe closely their body language while they're sitting around the table. You have to learn to read a board of nine people so you can tell if you're moving in the direction you want to move. Sometimes they're restless, shifting around in chairs, or heads going down on on the table. And when you get those signs, you know there's a problem. They really don't make very good poker players. They sort of wear their emotions on their sleeve and I've become very much aware of that.

A high school principal, new to the school, engaged in trying to revitalize its curriculum and its faculty's way of thinking about itself:

What I have to do is to put it together because they don't see the whole picture all the time as I do. That means I have to know my people and be able to play them at the right time. Like there are certain people I know I can count on to make remarks I can build on and there are others I feel I need to draw out. And yet there are others who might be very negative. Usually, these people have had experiences in which they've gotten burned. I try to bring them in for a personal talk to find out what's going on.

Another new high school principal talking about how she started to orient herself to the informal system that existed among the faculty:

What I did mostly was to watch and listen. I watched who talked to whom, who sits with whom in a faculty meeting, who had lunch together. In the faculty room, one person will say, "So and so said to me. . . ." I take it all in. I never wrote a thing down. Never really went out of my way to find out more than I was learning. I just watched and listened. You can hear a lot by being quiet.

An elementary school principal reflecting on his stance in any new and potentially troublesome situation that develops in his school:

The first thing you do is to observe and listen to the person who is presenting the information. That was tough for me to learn. The closer I listen, the more I learn. When someone comes in highly excitable, I immediately become skeptical of the information. I figure it's 75 percent fluff, but I have to find the 25 percent of what's really going on.

Another elementary school principal after having an early morning conference with a teacher new to her school:

I wanted to learn how she was starting to see her classroom. I wanted to know if her perceptions were somewhat the same as mine. I wanted to know in what areas she may need help. It was the first opportunity since she came on board to talk with her one-on-one.

These comments are simply illustrative of how a few school administrators think about learning about the "materials" with which they must work. There is nothing arcane or mysterious about it all, but what is important to realize is the large part that idiosyncratic preferences, needs, and so forth play in the way one's descriptions and diagnoses of the "materials" get made. We tend to be selective concerning what kind of information we attend to and the ways we go about getting that information. And though it is probably true that two potters will sense slightly different things in a lump of clay, it is also undoubtedly true that there will be more agreement about it between them than there will be between two administrators who may be describing the same "lump" of humanity or human organization.

The aim of this chapter has not been to prescribe, but to explain and illustrate the idea that both the general and specific nature of the "materials" with which administrators work seems absolutely focal to the practice of the administrative craft. This concern seems to be a result of a "learning through living" process—socialization, perhaps—to which all humans have exposure. This point, however, is not to suggest that all administrators are equally skilled in their ability to understand that with which they are working. It is to suggest, though, that the adequacy of their understanding probably fits their needs to know. And this may reflect the image they have of themselves and what they wish to do.

A final note: One may wonder about the relationship between our discussion in Chapter Five, "Getting a Nose for Things," and the concern of this one. What makes sense to me, to use a theatrical metaphor, is that the aim of "getting a nose" is to become aware of the backstage props and scenery, while the aim of understanding one's materials is to attend to the actors.

Chapter Eight

Knowing How to Do Things: Matters of Technique

Every craft or field of practice has techniques that are particular to it and, of course, every technique may be put to use with varying degrees of skill. The technique is the craft procedure deemed appropriate to a particular set of circumstances or functions, and the degree of skill refers to one's ability to use that technique more or less successfully so that its use achieves the intent of its user. These general ideas hold for practitioners as widely separated in the problems they face as surgeons, cabinetmakers, or school administrators. They all must know and be able to do something. Simply knowing how things work is not enough.

In this chapter we approach the idea of "knowing-how" through a discussion of what seem to be some central categories of administrative technique. In the next chapter, the discussion of "knowing-how" continues with a focus on skill. In both chapters it is important to understand that their goal is not to be prescriptive about the techniques or skills that make up the know-how of school administration, but to try and understand and illustrate its complexity.

One can get an argument concerning what I take to be the complexity of administrative know-how. After all, it sounds fairly simple. Learn a few techniques, practice some skills of application, and you, too, can be an administrator. This is a position held by large numbers of teachers and professors relative to the intellectual demands that are placed on an administrator. "It's a piece of cake," the thinking is, "as long as you're willing to put up with time demands and political hassles that seem to be part of every administrative job package."

Several years ago I had an experience that was almost a caricature of the "piece of cake" point of view. I was talking with a graduate student who was shortly to assume his first superintendency. We were discussing, somewhat abstractly, the superintendency as an organizational role. He had been doing a good bit of reading about it and he was raising questions with himself about the demands he would face and the skills he would have to use. "What do you think?" he asked.

My response was another question. I said, "Suppose you could have either of two jobs tomorrow morning, a school superintendent's or a fifth grade teacher's. Each was equally attractive to you. Which one would be more difficult?" We sat in silence for what seemed like a long time, but was probably about thirty seconds. Finally he said, "The fifth grade teacher because a teacher has to know something." And then we both laughed. Indeed, in some respects, I think being a teacher *is* more difficult than being an administrator.

My thinking about the matter, though, was beside the point. This man who was going to be a superintendent did not see the position demanding that he "know something" in the sense that a teacher has command of subject matter. It would not be that he wouldn't have to work hard and learn to become a highly political animal. It was just that there was no special subject matter involved in the job that he would have to produce on demand. A superintendent (or a principal) can easily, in ways that a teacher finds very difficult, tell a questioner to wait for half an hour while the answer to a question is sought.

In a way, I think my superintendent-to-be student was an unwitting heir to an accumulation of thought about administration that does, indeed, suggest that what know-how is required to be a principal or a superintendent is fairly simple-minded stuff, at best. Put another way, the lore of the craft is that the intellectual demands having such a position puts on a person are not exactly those that will send that person running off to the nearest reference library. For example, I know of a school superintendent who was quoted as telling teachers in his district who wanted to be administrators to go into an administrative preparation program at X College because "they will teach you the nuts and bolts" and not Y where "you will learn theory and philosophy." Further, there is a book (Stallings and Nelson, 1978) entitled *Nuts and Bolts of School Administration* which, it would not be expected, would likely excite the intellectual cockles of a physicist's or mathematician's heart. The book itself is a collection of bits of advice to a school administrator about what he or she should do to keep a school or school system running smoothly. Its authors state that the book's title starts with "Nuts and Bolts" because "they are the devices that will hold administrative behavior together" (p. iv). Well and good—and very necessary to think about, as a matter of fact. Unfortunately, though, it seems to me that the very use of "Nuts and Bolts" in that fashion suggests that the craft we are talking about requires little in the way of refined knowledge or skill and less in the way of thinking.

As another example of the character of thought that was part of the school administration tradition—one that thankfully is no longer in vogue—one can turn to *School Building Management* (Reeves and Ganders, 1928). This book was part of the School Administration series produced by the Bureau of Publications at Teachers College, Columbia University. Both its authors were professors of education, the first at Elmira College and the second at the University of Cincinnati. Including its bibliography of about seventy-five references, it is almost 400 pages long. What it is about is the care and nurturing of the physical plant of a school building. It has chapters devoted to using vacuum cleaners; sweeping; the proper way to scrub and mop; cleaning blackboards, erasers, and toilets; and so forth.

I make note of this book here, and it is not an isolated example, not to poke fun at it or its authors who saw themselves performing a much needed task for professors, students, and practitioners of school administration. Rather, I refer to it as an example of the type of thinking about school administration that once held some credence and, I think, in more subtle form is still with us today to some extent influencing both the thinking about and practice of administration.

It should be clear that my own thinking about engaging in the craft of administration, on the whole, is anything but a nuts and bolts affair. I say this knowing that there are some administrators for whom the "nuts and bolts" are the beginning and end of the job. I say this also knowing that there are some things an administrator does or rules of thumb to which he or she pays attention that are relatively mindless and, despite this, that are possibly quite important. For example, one of Stallings and Nelson's nuts and bolts is (p. 112) "K.I.S.S.—Keep It Short and Simple," and not a bad tip, at that. But the problem is, if that genre of thought about school administration is symbolic of what the field is all about, why bother to try to study and understand the work of administrators?

As much as anything, then, I suspect the field—both its study and its practice—has an image problem. And that problem is connected to the perception held by other "professionals" that what administrators do, for the most part, is turn nuts on bolts all day. That is, they start each day by applying Technique A to Situation 1. They then move on to Situation 2 where Technique B is appropriate. And then, perhaps, it's on to Situation 3 where, of all things, Technique A applies once more. According to this way of thinking, administrative craftwork is most aptly described as the routine and automatic application of one technique or another to any and every situation that occurs. This seems hardly a subject for inquiry unless the inquirer sees himself or herself in direct lineage of scientific management's Frederick Taylor or his apostle in the schools, Frank Spaulding (Callahan, 1962). There is, as I've suggested, much more to it than that, and the balance of this chapter will be concerned with trying to clarify that "much more."

We start by attending more closely to the concept of know-how itself. Implicit in the first paragraph of this chapter was the idea that know-how, or the quality of one's know-how, is a function of the skill with which a particular technique might be used in a particular situation. Thus, we might say about a principal who is able to deal very well with youngsters who are in conflict with each other, "He or she really has 'know-how' when it comes to helping kids resolve their problems with each other." Conversely, if the person in question is not very good at working with that kind of problem, we might say that he or she lacks "know-how" when it comes to helping young people work out conflicts that they may have with each other. Or we might deal with the idea much more generally and say, "If you want to see a real good running school system, go to X. The superintendent there really has 'know-how.'" Here we are not referring to a specific technique or even a specific set of techniques and their skillful use, but a sort of generalized ability, whatever that might mean, to keep a system running in a relatively unruffled manner.

Obviously, if our interest lies in trying to understand what it means to have "know-how," the first example is more helpful than the second. We could observe a principal in action in specific types of situations and learn what he or she did and how. On the other hand, the "know-how" of the superintendent of the good running school system is a many splendored thing. What does one look for in order to get an idea, a concrete idea, of the "know-how" that it takes to do that? The answer you will get to that question clearly depends on whom you ask.

So we must pursue things further with the thought at hand that, at the least, if we are to understand the concept of "know-how" as it applies to school administration, we must focus on specific things that administrators do and not on the very general. Unless we do this, we simply will find ourselves in the position of saying that efforts to understand administrative practice are doomed to failure; and that the only reasonable position to take is that that practice, the craft, is ultimately a mysterious enterprise that admits to no ordinary understanding. (This is no argument for the so-called administrative science which, as I noted earlier, I do not believe exists. Certainly, for example, most of us make daily sense of our world without resorting to scientific methodology.)

The idea of specificity of focus when thinking about "know-how" is reinforced by Howard (1982). In his discussion (curiously, for our purposes) of how people are taught to sing (an example of a craft), he refers to "know-how" as an "intelligent, trained ability" (p. 50) to produce certain kinds of sounds. In a chapter on "language of craft," he suggests "that we have a concept of 'know-how' that presupposes practice to be applicable to demonstrated abilities" (p. 66). In order to achieve "know-how" at some craft, then, one must focus on a set of particular skills and techniques, practice them until one becomes proficient in their use, and then be able to demonstrate them in a particular setting so that others will be able to say, "You have 'know-how.'"

Obviously, this scenario doesn't fit too well with what our intuition tells us about school administration, school administrators, and how they learn to do what they do (see Chapter Twelve). Who tells a superintendent what are the appropriate skills and techniques to learn? A professor? Another superintendent? His or her spouse? And where are the skills and techniques to be practiced? A superintendent's office, a school board meeting, or a meeting with a couple of hundred irate parents is not exactly the place to practice new ways of dealing with people or problems. (By practice, I mean the opportunity to learn, through repetition and critique, how to become proficient at the skill of using some technique in a safe environment, where not only is it permissible to make a mistake, but mistakes are encouraged as ways to learn.) There are no systematic practice studios for superintendents or principals in which they can "run something up the flagpole and see if it will fly," though a lot of that form of behavior does go on but for purposes other than practice.

As we continue our attempts to understand and illustrate the administrative craft, we cannot afford to be purists. School life is simply too imprecise and messy for that, and there are many places where it becomes apparent that half a conceptual loaf is better than none. Perhaps what is required, is to develop a different idea about the opportunity to practice techniques and skills whatever that idea might be.

At another point in his discussion, under the heading of "Types of Know-How," Howard (p. 66) suggests that the "know-how" concept is not a unidimensional thing. He states there are four types. We have already mentioned Type A—the ability to do something through practice at having done it, though the learning and practice may not be deliberate. A so-called "natural," a person who does something very well, perhaps effortlessly, and who simply seems to have a knack for his or her craft, falls into this category. Type B "know-how" is "knowing how, without practice, to make factual assertions and answer correctly questions presupposed by knowledge that, for instance, the earth is round" (pp. 67–68). It is the knowing-how to make logical reasoning inferences based on some previous information, and apparently develops without practice. Type C "know-how" is concerned primarily with knowing how things work, but not necessarily being able to do something. Old hands in organizations, for example, are important for newcomers to get to know precisely because they know how things work and can given the newcomer tips about the rocks and shoals of organizational life.

The fourth type of "know-how," Type D, is the main focus of our concern. Howard refers to it as "accountable 'know-how'" (p. 68). It is a combination of A and C and suggests that not only does an individual know how to do something, but he or she knows why doing it one way will work while doing it another way will not. For example, Howard says that "there are circumstances where we should be prepared to deny 'complete' or full-fledged 'know-how' of anyone who acquires even the most refined capacities . . . and yet who is unable to give any coherent account of his or her success" (p. 68).

In effect, being a professional involves Type D "know-how"—knowing what to do, when that "what" should be done, and being able to do it. Two additional points are important to think about within the framework of Type D. First, because it implies a "why" as well as a "how to," it suggests that the only legitimate teachers of a craft are those who possess Type D "know-how." That is, learning a craft from someone who knows how, but not why, is limiting. You cannot go beyond the technique. It is only when a person knows why one or another alternative should be considered for action—and the "why" of the practitioner does not have to be and most frequently is not the "why" of the researcher—that he or she can make intelligent and prudential use of self. This is what the craft of school administration ultimately is all about—the use of self in ways that, in one fashion or another, further the aims of the particular school or school system in question.

I think that this last sentence, which, for me, encapsulates the core idea of the work of school administrators, runs counter to prevailing and generally accepted wisdom. Such thinking places the focus of an administrator's decision making outside himself or herself. That is, classical organizational theory from which derives classical management or administrative theory tells us that the role of managers or administrators mainly involves decisions about planning, organizing, commanding, coordinating, and controlling—of others. As I have observed administrators at work and talked with them about their work, it became rather clear that the major decisions that they make involve self and not others. Although predicaments involving others or the larger system form the content and context of their work—and it is about these predicaments that decisions do have to be made—prior decisions about self and how one uses oneself with others are always involved.

This should not be taken to mean that the decisions that administrators make about how they use themselves as they confront the variety of conditions that develop daily at their work are conscious and deliberate ones. To the contrary, I suspect that what happens is that decisions about what kinds of things generally work in particular situations and about one's feelings of competence and skill in their use get made over a long period of time. They are already in place, as it were, freeing the administrator to concentrate on the situation he or she is facing.

So much for this rather lengthy introduction to the concept of "knowing-how" in the practice of the craft of administration. We turn now to matters of technique. A consideration of these things is a much more complicated proposition than one might think at the outset. Matters of technique initially seem not to be things that require much thought. However, as with the idea of "know-how," it will become more complex as we get into it.

• Matters of Technique

As I attended to matters of technique in this study of the administrative craft, I was not interested in developing a long list of procedural prescriptions or suggestions for action. Rather, what was on my mind was to try and understand what things occupied administrators' time during a day's work and what, in general, they did to help themselves cope with that day. As it turned out, the number of techniques that can be observed by watching an administrator during a day is relatively small, although there is undoubtedly an infinite number of variations in usage of any particular technique that would seem to be a matter of individual stylistic preference.

It is also important to note that I used the phrase "techniques that can be observed" in the previous paragraph. There are techniques (and skills) used in administration that cannot be observed. For example, all administrators I have ever talked with or watched reflect on how they "anticipate" consequences of one action or another. Anticipation is a technique, in one form or another, but it's about impossible to observe someone "anticipating." What would one look for? And how would one know they had found it if they ever did?

The balance of this section on techniques, then, is principally built around things I observed and then talked about as I accompanied a number of school administrators through a day's work. Additionally, as before, information is presented from interviews I had with people in their or my office, but with whom I did not spend a workday.

As I noted at the beginning of this chapter, a technique is a procedure used for performing a function or dealing with a particular set of circumstances connected with that function. And it rather makes sense to suggest that the major functions that are performed by school administrators, taken together, describe their work. We return, then, to Chapter Four at the point at which we discussed the several work themes or functions that seem to occupy administrators during the course of a day. Although the emphasis given these themes will undoubtedly vary from individual to individual or job to job, I think they are generic to what being an administrator is all about. In a sense, then, these themes constitute the imperatives of school administration. If they are not attended to in some manner, the system will be found lacking in some part of its being. I list them here somewhat differently than I did in Chapter Four, in the form of imperatives, not to be "how-to" prescriptive about the matter, but to say that it seems that these functions simply must be performed somehow and some way in the work life of administrators if a school or school system is to maintain its viability. With that in mind and also with the thought that many subfunctions flow from them, the imperatives of school administration can be thought of in the following way:

- School administrators must continually get, refresh, and refine their "nose for things."
- They must continually develop and maintain contact with people in the domain (school district or school) for which they have administrative responsibility.
- They must continually "keep tabs on things" by engaging in information-seeking behavior about a wide spectrum of events, problems, or opportunities with which they are confronted daily.
- They must spend a great deal of time in situations that call for conflict resolution techniques.
- They must continually be aware that their system is a very dynamic thing and that its development depends on their moving it along in one fashion or another.

One thing that becomes immediately clear from this list of imperatives is that it does not imply a discrete thing being done at any moment in time. There is much overlap. Numbers of different problems, for example, are apt to develop while a superintendent or principal is working on his or her "nose." Or, while maintaining contact with people, the chances are good that a superintendent or principal will find herself or himself engaged in conflict resolution. What all this suggests is that much as the imperatives are not discrete in the sense of being sharply separated from each other, so there is overlap in the way techniques are used. That is, no technique is reserved for conflict resolution that would not be used for some other purpose. To put it quite squarely, we are engaged in trying to understand a very messy business, even though it might not appear that way to a casual observer.

What seems to occur in the work life of administrators is that they engage principally in the following:

- They reach out to people.
- They "seed" their staffs with new ideas.
- They unravel problem situations.
- They negotiate.

If you observe a principal or a superintendent for either a short or long period of time, you will see them, for the most part, reaching out, seeding, unraveling, and negotiating. As a matter of fact, on the technique level, I think a case can be made that those are the things that are the stuff of administrative life. Here are some examples.

• Reaching Out

If the schools (or most other organizations) really behaved like the classic bureaucracies their organizational charts say they are, there would be no need to "reach out." The very act of doing that communicates that the people who work in the schools (or most other organizations) simply don't respond in the impersonal, objective, task-oriented manner that the chart suggests that they do. Somehow and in some ways, it seems, school administrators need to step outside of an "organization-as-machine" idea, if they ever conceived of things that way, and think of the people who work in their systems as individuals for whom the very act of being "reached out" to by their principal or superintendent is of value to them. I really think that an administrator cannot succeed unless he or she is able to enact behaviors that lets teachers, for example, know that their principal cares enough about them, both personally and professionally, to "reach out." Time and again, I have heard teachers speak with respect, admiration, and affection about their principal who not only "knows what's going on all over the school" but knows each teacher and makes a point continually to enhance his or her knowledge. And this is not done, of course, with the idea of prying into personal or professional matters, but with the idea of developing what might best be called a caring culture in the school.

Besides making a point to see and talk with each teacher in his school each day, usually in the morning, an elementary school principal talked about reaching out like this:

> When you reach out, you let people know you're thinking about them and their problems and you're also telling them that you are a person who is concerned. But it has to be real, nothing phony. Like one of the things I do is ask people for favors—again nothing phony, it's just part of me—and when you do that, I think that's reaching out and saying to people, "You're valuable. You're helpful."

And, another principal:

> Well, there's the usual stuff, you know. Talking with teachers, visiting classrooms, let them know that what they're doing is important. They have to know that you value what they have to say or do about something. And here's something I do. I'm real concerned about my teachers letting me have access to them and the primary way I get this is by reaching out and letting them have access to me. When I do that they feel valued. I let them know, by being around, in their rooms, in the halls that I want to experience their world and I want them to feel free to come into mine. I ask them for their ideas about problems I have to deal with and they get to know that I think their ideas are worthwhile.

There are probably as many ways of "reaching out" as there are people who want to do the reaching. Each person puts his or her own twist on the generalized idea. So, in a way, what we have is a fairly simple concept. But one must notice the thinking behind the concept, which is not simple at all. At least it is not simple if one wants to inquire beyond the obvious. For one thing—a point that emerges repeatedly in this discussion—there is an element of authenticity involved: No phoniness allowed. If an administrator has learned somewhere that a good technique is to reach out because it will make teachers (or others) feel valued, but he or she places no particular premium on this idea, it is simply better not to try and do it. Teachers will spot the phoniness in an instant and more harm than good will be done to the relationship. This point holds across the board. That is, I have no doubt that teachers with their principal—much as principals with their superintendent, and students with their teacher—are very adept at knowing when he or she is behaving honestly with them. (People, I think, learn the skills of recognizing phony behavior very early in their lives. It's a case of survival.)

There is a second point here that is quite important. It has to do with the school's reward system, which is a sometime thing relative to a principal's or superintendent's ability to provide extra financial compensation for a job well done, for example. There are other forms of rewards, though, that are important to school people even though, as one teacher told me, "They don't buy groceries." One of them is being told by the behavior, more importantly than by words, that one is considered to be of worth by one's organizational supraordinate. Though neither of the principals quoted talked in terms of the reward system and "reaching out," they both took note of the importance of having their teachers feel valued and how they felt they accomplished this end by their "reaching." On some level, then, they seemed quite well to understand what it was they were doing and why they were doing it.

So, once more, we have the mixture of simplicity and complexity, as is the case of so much that goes on in an administrator's life. And, as an aside, it may be the ability to understand the implications of this mixture that separates administrators who are masters of their craft from those who are apprentices. If a technique is understood only as a technique, without regard to the way its use may relate to other parts of school organization life, then we limit our understanding of administration to the simple use of technique and our concept of administrators as little more than technocrats who are good at doing some things but cannot step beyond the techniques themselves.

• Seeding

One thing that becomes very obvious if one spends time with school administrators on the job is that a great deal of "seeding" takes place and in a variety of ways. In a very real way, I think, this suggests a subtle recognition on the part of the administrator that even though he or she may occupy the top rung on the organization chart, there is no necessary relationship between this fact and being the boss (the boss in the sense of being able to get people to do what one wants them to do and when). There are parts of school or school system life, of course, over which an administrator has direct control, but I think they are limited in the way they may make an impact on the school as an educational organization. Curiously, administrators tend to have more direct control over those parts of the system that are oriented to organizational maintenance matters rather than matters of what the school is all about—curriculum and instruction.

What is at issue is the matter of territorial prerogative. In schools, curriculum and instruction is a class of territory that tends to be owned by teachers, even if the administrator in question is a central office person formally charged with the responsibility for that territory. What this means for the administrator, in particular, the principal, who would exert an influence in matters of curriculum and instruction is that she or he must have the teachers' "permission" to intrude into that territory. I use the term *intrude* advisedly in the sense that not only is it the case that teachers tend to see themselves as exercising ownership of the curriculum and instruction function, but that it is only in relatively few situations that they see their principals as having expertise in the area. And certainly, the cases are far fewer where a central office person is seen as having much to offer. They simply live in another world, as it were.

The rational bureaucratic mind may interpret this discussion of territory and the need for the administrator to gain the teacher's permission to enter it as bordering on the ridiculous. Doesn't the leader of any organization have the right to engage its members in talk about the goals of the organization and the methods by which those goals may be best met? The answer is in the affirmative in the sense that organizational leaders have a discussion-convening authority that tends to be recognized as legitimate. For example, a principal or a central office curriculum director may legitimately call a meeting of a group of teachers with the aim of examining curriculum issues, or perhaps considering the efficacy of a particular teaching methodology. But the legtitimacy of things stops at the point of convening—at least in the eyes of teachers so far as the demand may be that, once convened, they must be motivated to devote time and energy to the problem. What we are discussing, then, is a set of conditions in school organizational life that bears a close parallel to the old saw that starts, "You can lead a horse to water. . . ."

The school administrators whom I observed and to whom I talked seemed to recognize the situation that I have just described, though I doubt they saw it in quite the same terms (territory, permission) as I have written. Regardless, what they did convey was that they understood how these things worked—they planted seeds and seemed prepared for a long growing season, although, as we shall see, the length of the growing season is a relative thing. Further, seeds are planted in a wide variety of ways and in an equally wide variety of situations. Some principals do most of their "planting" on their "nose-getting" walks around the building—a question here and an opinion sought there seems to suffice, although there must be follow-up activity, as well. Somewhat differently, a high school principal, a subscriber to and a voracious reader of numbers of educational publications, said,

> Here's the incoming mail pile here. I'll look through that tonight and there will be a zillion notes to people tomorrow, like "Will you stop in and see me about this or that?" Sometimes it's just that I want them to be aware of new things for the kids that they may want to check out. And I want them to know that I'm aware of what is going on and I want them to stop in and talk about it. I don't like to write them memos that say, "Stop in and see me when you can." I want them to know what I'm interested in.

And here is a superintendent in a rather large suburban district just after having talked with a nonprofessional-level administrative employee about the development of a rather mundane, but nevertheless important, transportation policy:

> You have to plant seeds. And, of course, if a seed of an idea is planted and someone picks it up, it becomes their own program. And once they have ownership, it becomes important and it's done very well. We probably could have written that policy in ten or fifteen minutes. This way it'll take two days, but it'll work well because it'll be his and he'll make it work well. You have to have patience.

Somewhat differently, an assistant superintendent for curriculum said, mixing our metaphor,

> When I want to get teachers motivated I think of it like I'm fishing. What I do is to throw out the line, but there are four or five different pieces of bait on four or five different hooks. I want to attract them to bite on one of them.

But a principal, reacting to this anecdote, said,

> Sure, I throw out bait and let them chomp on it, but before I do, I make sure that I can live with the alternative. If I have two pieces of bait and I don't care which one is taken then I'll just throw both of them out. But if I have four and know that I'd have trouble living with two of them, I won't throw out all four of them—only the two I can live with.

And on the matter of the relative length of the "growing season," a high school principal noted,

> Early in September, I knew we had to give consideration to the State's Master Plan. So I went to see the foreign language teachers and asked them to think about getting Spanish into the curriculum as we had only French and German. I didn't bring it up again for two months and that gave them plenty of time to mull it over. And they became very receptive to the idea, but primarily, I think, because they had the time to think about what it would mean for the whole program.

There is an infinite number of variations on the theme of seeding, much as there is with any other technique of the administrative craft. What is done specifically and how it is done is a function of the individual administrator, his or her objectives, personal style, and assessment of the demands of the confronting problem—at the least. As one superintendent put it, "You've got to match the seed with the soil." And, one might add, one has to feel comfortable with the way one goes about planting. For example, some administrators adapt an informal style—"What do you think about X?" during a chance encounter in the hall. For others, more formal means appear to fit—"I'd like you to think about X and test things out with your people" during a meeting of a superintendent's cabinet. Or "I do a lot of verbal sparring and people get my messages that way—at least most of them do."

Just how one goes about seeding, then, is less important than recognizing the fact that if an administrator wishes to get teachers, in particular, to start thinking about and then doing things somewhat differently, seeding must take place. School administrators, at least the ones to whom I talked, seemed to understand this quite well. Along with this understanding is the tacit, sometimes explicit, knowledge of the concepts of territorial prerogatives and ownership of ideas and plans. Further, there is the knowledge that once seeds are planted, whatever emerges from the ground needs to be cultivated—we call it *follow-up* in administrative jargon.

• Unraveling

The role that administrators take on when they engage in unraveling is frequently called being a "detective" or "putting on my Sherlock Holmes hat." It is a role familiar to most adults, administrators or not, at least those who are parents. The times are without number when our children have come to us with a complaint about a sibling or a friend. We learn to unravel things in a hurry because if we don't, we find ourselves acting on only one side of the story. It becomes a matter of parental survival.

I don't think I'm stretching the case too much by suggesting that the technique of unraveling is a survival tool in the craft of administration. Administrators of every stripe are confronted with a great variety of problems each day, many of which involve a conflict of one type or another—a teacher has treated a student unfairly, or so says the student; a student is blamed for starting a fight which was started by another, or so says the one who was first blamed; a teacher meted out unjust punishment to a child, or so says the parent. The starting point in all these situations seems to have two things in common: (1) there is one person who is the initial information-giver and complainant, and (2) based on the initial complaint, the administrator is asked to make a just and equitable decision about the outcome. To do so on the basis of the initial information, of course, with the exception of possible emergency situations, is a rather unwise thing to do. The administrator must engage in unraveling the situation so that he or she can come as close to the truth as possible before making a decision.

There is more to it, though, than trying to make a just decision, important as that may be. There is also an issue of administrative reputation at stake, particularly with regard to principals as they deal with problems of discipline. They are under the scrutiny of teachers, parents, and youngsters, each group of which has its own particular stake in the principal's behavior and decisions. It starts out with varying ideas about what is fair and just, and members of each group will certainly have different thoughts about that. Beyond that, though, teachers want consistency, parents want leniency, and students want consistency and leniency. But even beyond that, particularly in the case of principals, the reputational questions get raised as to whether or not he or she is a person who is inclined to try and listen to and understand all sides of a problem. Or, put in the context of this discussion, is he or she inclined to act on an initial impression or to unravel the problem to get at its roots?

It is not hard to observe principals trying to unravel a situation. They tend first to talk with the parties involved by themselves, searching for congruities and incongruities in the way each tells the story. Then, as they begin to understand things, they frequently bring the parties together and confront them with the things they agree on and disagree on. "Whom am I supposed to believe?" is the question that gets asked and the unraveling continues until eventually the principal—detective, judge, and jury—feels secure in his or her knowledge of what really happened.

Unraveling, like other administrative techniques, is not a particularly difficult behavior in which to engage. But as we have noted before, behaviors that are simple to enact may well have a highly complex side to them. For example, in one school where I was spending some time, I noted the principal stepping outside of his usual rather gentle approach to problems and taking on what seemed to be a tough and unyielding stance with one particular youngster who, it appeared, was trying to avoid responding to him. When I noted this change in our later conversation, the principal was also quite aware he had shifted styles. He said:

> Oh yeah. Well, I just had a sense that it would work to get him to tell the truth. And it did. It usually does.

Then he went on to say,

> There's really a danger in this when you sense yourself on automatic pilot, like you've seen it all before. When this happens, you may get too mechanical. You may forget to listen carefully to the kids, hearing their side of it, helping them sort out what went wrong, what their feelings are, and what the consequences of their actions are.

So it is not a simple matter of getting at the truth in situations, because getting at the truth may well involve helping to build and maintain the dignity of those involved. Once more, then, although the technique and its usage are not difficult to master, how it is used may be a much more complex affair.

There are times, of course, when things go beyond unraveling petty conflicts and the principal almost assumes a bona fide investigator role. The principal of a high school got a call from the central office informing her that information had been received that a student had drugs in his locker. A search of the locker was made and no drugs turned up.

> We called the student down and asked him questions. "No, no, no, no." "Do you have them?" "Do you use them now?" "Empty your pockets," and boom, there they were. And then he told us about two other kids.
>
> It's like being a detective. You have to take one little clue and go a little further and a little further. And with this student, if we had stopped questioning him at one point in time, we probably would not have gotten the other two. The procedure is very important and the fact that you get the kid is important. You try to treat people with respect and yet, at the same time, get what you want.

It goes without saying that most principals find this type of activity distasteful, taking away, as it does, from what the schools are supposed to be all about. Yet it is a function that has to be performed for the most basic of reasons—to keep the school on an even keel. I also suspect that there are some principals for whom their expertise at unraveling is considered a matter of pride and who look forward to opportunities to use it. They have their eyes on the hole and not on the doughnut.

Finally, lest I be misunderstood, the technique of unraveling finds application in many other areas of school life besides the discipline of students. Adults misunderstand each other, quarrel with each other, complain about each other, and fault each other. Unraveling needs to take place and gently so, at that, so that the integrity of those involved is maintained.

• Negotiating

How one describes an organization or a role within that organization is very much related to the theoretical perch from which one views it, of course. And one may choose to see the dynamics of school and administrative life as being centrally concerned with narrowing the differences between the basically incompatible needs and demands of individuals and groups through the process and technique of negotiating. Or another theoretical perch that might lead one to view schools as essentially settings for negotiation is one that suggests what they are all about is competition for scare resources, thus leading to a dominant negotiating mode.

Whichever is the case is less important than the fact that administrators are continually involved in negotiating. Principally, they negotiate with others over time, money, and personnel. They also negotiate over the gray areas of school policy that may be related to practically anything else. In fact, there is little that develops in a school day or week that is not somehow subject to negotiation if someone wishes to move in that direction. A central office administrator put it this way:

> Sometimes I feel as though I'm negotiating all the time and the thing I have to be careful of is that old saying of not getting in a position where you give away the store. You know, there is always this question of power that comes into play. You have to be careful about how widely you use your power. So I find myself negotiating a lot. Everyday I'm negotiating.

And from the very general to the more specific, an elementary school principal said,

> Whenever a teacher walks in, I can feel myself starting to negotiate. I simply assume, and I always seem to be right, that they're here because they need something I don't have a lot of. If there was a lot of whatever it is they want, they wouldn't have to come and see me. Some teachers are more aggressive than others and are not afraid to come in and say, "I need this for my program." So I negotiate. But what that means is that you've got to keep your eyes open for those who don't come in and make sure they get their share of things.

And more specifically, still, a high school principal recalled,

> We had a parent call who did not want her youngster to come to Saturday detention, didn't want to get up and drive the kid into school at 8 o'clock. Our negotiation was to present the alternative. "Well, if your child doesn't come to Saturday detention, then there will be an in-school suspension and your son will miss all his classes which we presume you don't want to happen." Maybe that's not real negotiation cause we don't give in. I guess we try to get them to negotiate with themselves over consequences.

What we have here, then, is the notion of the pervasive presence of the need to negotiate in the practice of administrative craft. And, indeed, it *is* pervasive. All that needs to be done to confirm this is to watch and listen to what administrators do during the course of a day, in addition to the other things that have been discussed. Further, like the other techniques that have been discussed, the technique of negotiation is quite simple yet quite complex. How and with what skill it is employed can play a major role in the success of an administrator on the job. For example, we use the phrase "tough, but fair" with admiration and respect. And we laugh at a "pushover" who "gives away the store" at every opportunity, or so it seems. "A nice person," we say, "but not much of an administrator."

I suspect that any school administrator, upon finishing this chapter, is entitled to a "Yes, but . . ." reaction. This translates into an agreement, by and large, with what has been written "but you've left a lot out." I think that's undoubtedly true in the sense that situations arise during the course of a superintendent's or principal's day that do not fall under the categories of technique that have been discussed. What are techniques for dealing with a hostile newspaper reporter, for example? Or for gathering information about an alleged incompetent teacher in anticipation of building a solid case for dismissal? Or for leading a productive meeting?

Recall that the focus of this chapter (and the next) is on starting to develop an understanding of the concept of administrative "know-how," of which matters of technique are a part, and not simply a discussion of technique. The point is, I think, that as we start to understand what appears to be some major categories of technique in both their simplicity and complexity, we can also subject the concept of "know-how" to a more rigorous analysis.

Chapter Nine

Knowing How to Do Things: Matters of a Basic Skill

We all know how essential it is to ask the right question at the right time. How does one write about that except to say that it is important for an administrator to do that? The answer is, I think, you don't. And the same holds for any of what must be an infinite number of skills that are important to administrative work. Such prescriptions do little to help us understand the notion of skill, and this is the focal purpose of this chapter. Our primary aim is to understand and possibly provide a model for thinking about what it means to be skillful as a school administrator. I believe, incidentally, that this is a very complicated business and that the best we will be able to do is, as professors are fond of saying, "I'll provide the theory; you see after the details." We start out with some thoughts about skill that come from outside the field of administration—baseball and medicine.[1]

I have always marveled at the ability and skill of those professional baseball players who can hit a ball that is traveling at a speed of ninety miles an hour after having left the pitcher's hand a mere sixty feet away. What I observe, of course, is the swing, and if I hear something I know it's the ball being hit. (Or I might hear evidence of a miss—the ball hitting the catcher's glove.) But I think that the ball being hit is only the end product of the totality of skills that need to be employed by the batter in a split second. Here is what I, clearly an amateur, think is involved in the ability of a batter to hit the ball. First, there is the ability to see the ball in ways most of us undoubtedly cannot; to follow its path from the moment it is thrown until the point of what it is hoped will be contact between it and the bat. For example, legend has it that Ted Williams was so good at this that he could see the seams on the ball as it traveled toward him. I can't imagine that actually being so, but it does make for a colorful story.

Within a split second the batter must make a judgment, another skill, concerning whether or not the ball will arrive at home plate inside or outside the strike zone. If he thinks it will be outside, presumably he will not swing and if the umpire agrees with his judgment the pitch will be called a ball. If not, of course, it will be called a strike. If the batter judges that the ball will be in the strike zone, he then has to make a decision whether or not to swing at it. Even if he knows it will be called a strike he may not swing because it is not "his pitch," which translates into his knowing what kind of pitch he is best able to hit. Another skill is involved, then—the skill of sensing what is right for him at a particular moment in time.

A decision is made to swing, which involves a sense of timing, the ability to bring the bat to meet the ball on the right plane of flight at precisely the right moment. There also may be involved an ever-so-slight change in the way the batter is standing. When everything I've described, and more, of which I'm surely unaware, occurs, we onlookers hear the contact between ball and bat and we see the ball going in one direction or another. And we cheer or groan.

It's important to understand here that my aim is not to try and make a case for something that might be called the craft of hitting a baseball. It is also important to understand that although every craft has skills attached to it, a set of skills can exist without being attached to a craft. The baseball scenario is useful for our purposes because of the generic nature of the skills it involves, not because of whether or not the batting sequence can be described as a craft.

Let us try to understand these skills. First, skills may be categorized as those we can see and those we cannot. Perhaps it might be better to say skills we *think* we can see, because the only thing we know for sure is that we see the bat being swung and meeting the ball. It may even be better to say we can see the results of it having met the ball, the naked eye being unable to pick up the point and moment of contact. The swing and the hit, though, are the end product of the employment of several other skills that we cannot observe. These include the ability to see the ball in certain ways; to make judgments about where the ball will be when it passes over the plate; to decide if the pitch is in the strike zone; to determine if it is "his" pitch; to have a sense of timing, so that the batter swings neither too early nor too late; and so on.

Besides categorizing these skills into what can be seen and what cannot, we can think of them in terms of their content and the contribution that content makes to the end product, hitting the ball. There is obviously a skill of observation and description involved, seeing the ball and its path toward home plate. There is a skill of diagnosis apparent as the batter, seeing the ball approaching, makes a judgment from his observation about whether the pitch will be a ball or a strike. There is a skill, indeed, that we might call a sense of timing. And certainly there is a skill related to knowing "his" pitch, which relates to the actual decision to swing. And, once more, the only thing we can see is the swing and its result, and we must assume a great deal of motor skill goes into making just the right swing.

Whether these decisions and actions take place in a deliberate fashion or are intuitively reflexive is not the point. Rather, what needs to be understood is that all these actions actually do occur in the process of trying to hit a ball with a bat. Like every schoolchild baseball player, I can attest to that. I can recall seeing (and striking out on) the first curve ball that was ever thrown to me and knowing that I had to develop higher skills of observation and timing to deal with similar pitches in the future. And I can recall seeing a ball coming at me and knowing it was "my" pitch. Observing, making judgments, and deciding to act—none of it can be seen but all of it constitutes skills learned mostly by practice and coaching. And these skills and their sequence are a necessary prelude to the final act of swinging and hitting.

In this example, something has been left out that we must consider in our thinking about the components of skill. It is simply, but perhaps quite mysteriously, the fact that some people are "naturals" when it comes to hitting a baseball. They can't tell you why or how they are able to bat well. They just do. And coming back to the craft of administration for a moment, this is another way of saying that there is something we might call the idiosyncratic use of self that enters the picture in what may be a confusing, unaccountable, and delightful way, providing as it does the opportunity to spice things up.

Another example of skills, this time from the practice of medicine, fits my concept of craft quite neatly (however, I'm sure my physician friends prefer to think of it as an art). The first thing a physician does when you go to his or her office is to say things like, "Tell me about the problem," "Where does it hurt?" and "What are the conditions under which it hurts?" Naturally, the physician wants to know as much as possible about what it is that brought you to the office. Questions are asked so that he or she can understand things better. We may become aware that the questions have become narrower, but we can't see or hear what the physician can see and hear. Training, practice, and experience have enabled our medical friend to be alert to certain kinds of cues that our answers provide. Being alert to certain cues in the materials one is working with is a craft skill. After asking all the questions he or she deems germane (another skill) and after collecting other information through one test of another, the doctor says to you, "Let me tell you what I think the problem is." The diagnosis is made on the basis of the information provided, plus what has been learned through training, practice, and experience. As in the case of the baseball player, it is probably an idiosyncratic intuition that confirms the hypothetical rightness of the diagnosis.

After the diagnosis, we are told what the remediation for our complaint might be. This is the physician's (batter's) "swing," even though I suspect there are many MDs who would reject that analogy. Nevertheless, I think it holds as, from our own experience, we have known of cases where medical people have "hit homeruns" with their diagnosis and action, and we have also known cases where they "struck out."

It is important for us to go back over this example of the physician at work and treat it as we did that of the batter. First, there are things we can observe and things we cannot. We can observe (hear) the questions asked and we can observe (feel) a hand poking at our kidney. But we can't observe what led him or her to ask a particular question, or to poke us in a particular way, or in a particular place. Our answers to the questions and our body's reaction to finger-poking provide our physician with ways of understanding that we cannot see. It is not a magical skill; most of us could probably acquire it. Yet, as I have suggested, some physicians are simply better at seeing these cues than others, and it's hard to say why. And it seems to be without question that some of them are better diagnosticians than others—again, a skill that we cannot observe.

Though the totality of the medical model of remediation tends not to be accepted by those of us who work in the "softer" crafts, I do think that the analogue it presents for our concern with administrative craft skills is a workable one. Stemming from that analogue and the one about the baseball player we can develop a prototypical way of thinking about these skills. Some of them can be observed; some of them cannot. The content of the skills generally has to do with (1) understanding what's happening (and some people are simply better at this than others); (2) understanding why it's happening (and some people are simply better at *this* than others); and (3), based on (1) and (2), taking some sort of action than one judges to be appropriate (and some people are simply better at *this* than others).

Two other points in this general approach to understanding the notion of craft skills are important to consider before we become more specific about the administrative craft. First, the skills that we observe in action, the actual doing of something, represent only the tip of the skill iceberg. That is, ways of seeing, thinking, and interpreting constitute the critical mass of the skill of any craft. Second, my own inferences from the statements in the previous paragraph that some people are simply better at a skill than are others is to suggest that there is an element of not knowing about it all, which I would just as soon see remain unknowable. In fact, because I think this element is a function of some type of idiosyncratic intuition, I suspect we have no option but to settle for not knowing all there is to know about things. A "natural" is simply a "natural."

Using the backdrop already provided, we will now attend to the notion of skill in the life of administrators at work. Two caveats are important to consider at the outset. First, different from the batter at the plate or the physician examining the patient, there is no prototypical administrative situation that we can use as a learning model, as there is a baseball player at bat or a physician in his or her office or operating room. That is, we cannot say that if you want to learn about administrative skills, turn your attention here or there. There is no special place in which skills get played out nor is there a hallmark set of circumstances that somehow define "Administrator at Work." So the situations to be used are simply a matter of my personal choice because they provide good opportunities to understand the notion of skill in administration, and not because they are modal to the life of a principal or superintendent.

The second caveat is that I do not intend to provide the reader with a litany of administrative competencies. Given the highly individuated way that administrators play out their roles, I think to do so would border on both the boring and the ridiculous. Rather, I will propose a way of thinking about administrative craft skills that parallels the analytic method of the baseball player and the physician. Certainly, though, it won't be as distinct as either of those situations for at least two reasons. First, as has been noted several times and in several ways, the work environment of school administrators is messy and cluttered. Lots of things are jumbled together, making it difficult to be precise about what is happening, why it is happening, and what should be done about it. Second, unlike in baseball where the measure of the result of one's successful use of skills is obvious—you either get on base or you don't—there are few unqualified successes and few absolute failures in school administrative life. Furthermore, if a superintendent or principal feels a need to improve a particular skill, it is hard to find a place to practice. There is no administrative "batting cage," nor is there a place like a hospital clinic or "grand rounds" where a physician gets practice in diagnostic skills, for example.

All this notwithstanding, I think it is possible to create a scenario that will enable us to put the issue of administrative skills into a usable perspective. We start with an excerpt[2] from an interview with an elementary school principal who was describing how she went about providing computer instruction in her school. Because I wanted to understand how this principal thought about success on the job, I had prepared her for our discussion some days prior to it by telling her I would be interested in her telling me about a time when she felt she had done something that she had considered a "smashing success." Here is the way she thought about that:

I think things are more subtle than smashing. I'll share with you something that I can see as a success, but how smashing it is is someone else's judgment, the eye-of-the-beholder kind of thing.

I felt a need to provide some kind of computer instruction and awareness for both staff and students, but I didn't want to get swamped. The district had no budget for it, so if it was to happen, I would have to make it happen. I knew I would have to work slowly. I started with the idea that I would have to become computer literate first. I purchased $5000 worth of equipment in my home by convincing my husband I was buying it for his business, but really knowing I was buying it because I wanted to become somewhat computer literate before I could even begin to suggest that other people in my district become so. I was able to persuade a local business to donate a computer and some good software. I also tapped a lot of resources of other schools that had computer programs and I attended a conference at my own expense. I wrote a grant for equipment and we were funded. Teachers were very skeptical about it all and I recognized those attitudes. I started with the kids before I started with the teachers. I was thinking about all the arguments that people would have about why we don't need computers in the school and why we shouldn't be bothered by them. I listen closely for cues all the time. I'm a good listener. So I was anticipating all these arguments, but I was also becoming more conscious of the need to do something. So I was thinking about how I was going to resolve that. I was thinking about strategies that would get people to buy into it or, at the least, not oppose it. And I think that's what led me to think about starting with the kids first. They would be the entree into the faculty. I ran a mini-course for fifth and sixth graders. They went back to their rooms all excited and the teachers became curious. I knew the kids would be easier to capture. I've had that experience before—that is, working through the kids to get teachers excited. I've used this strategy before—working with one group to get something from another. That really seems to work for me, but I don't know where I learned to do that. I think it was probably trial and error at some point. But there was never any conscious intention to learn something. Anyhow, I did a lot of careful planning about the computer lab. In my own mind, I knew what I wanted, but I really didn't share it with the Board because if I had told them we needed 20 computers, it would have seemed exorbitant and the idea would have simply been rejected as being foolish and unreasonable. But little by little we did it, including a volunteer staff development program for teachers which was so-so. I took part in the program, too. I was a learner along with them because I knew that would be important to their accepting the idea. They had to see me struggling along with them. We now have a computer lab with 20 machines and a full-time staff member, too.

Although innumerable conversations continued to occur during this process, which lasted over a year, I think we have enough data to enable us to think in general terms about the skills that were employed. What we don't have, nor can we have, is a sense of the individuated flavor with which the skills were used—in this or any other situation. In more or less the sequence in which they were described and in not too great detail, this is the way this principal's description of what happened can be analyzed for its administrative skill components:

- A skill related to one's ability to *be aware of how much is too much:* "But I didn't want to get swamped," said the principal. All of us have known people who lack the ability to recognize that they are overloading themselves, with the typical result that nothing gets done well or on time and the individual involved becomes anxious and possibly debilitated.
- A skill related to the *sense of the possible,* of knowing where the responsibility for work would end up: ". . . So if it was to happen, I would have to make it happen," said the principal. Very much related to "how much is too much" is the ability to sense who will have to do what, at least at the start of thing.
- A skill related to having a *sense of work tempo:* In this case, the skill is shown by the principal's ability to realize that things would have to move slowly.
- A skill related to being aware of *how to use oneself* so that other people will be tempted to try something new: This principal had the ability to

be aware that she could not get others simply to "do as I say." They had to see that she, too, was involved. Said she, ". . . because I wanted to become somewhat computer literate before I could even begin to suggest that other people in my district become so."

- The skill to *persuade others* to offer support for one's ideas: In this case it was the ability to get a local business to understand the importance of the program and to donate a computer and software so that things could start.

- The skill of *knowing when outside help is required* and where that help might be: The "resources of other schools" was the answer to "where." But I think the ability to know "where" may be more important. Perhaps the skill is also concerned with knowing "when" so that the project doesn't break down if help comes too late.

- The skill of *persuasion through writing:*   "I wrote a grant for equipment and we were funded," stated the principal. Writing successful grant proposals, after all, is the ability to persuade someone whom you may never have met that the case you present for assistance is a worthy one.

- The skill of *recognizing teachers' skeptical attitudes* about innovations: Perhaps there is another skill implied here—that of remembering what it was like to be a teacher.

- The skill of *listening* and, based on this, the skill of *anticipating* arguments: Being able to understand what others are saying and then to predict accurately what positions they will take are critical skills in change situations.

- The skill of knowing which of a variety of avenues would lead to a *potential breakdown* in teacher skepticism and possible resistance: In this case, the principal said, "I started with the kids before I started with the teachers."

- Directly related to this last point, the skills of *timing:*   As the principal realized, noting that she was anticipating teacher arguments, "I was also becoming more conscious of the need to do something." As we have implied on a number of occasions, although talk is the administrator's stock in trade, what administration ultimately is about is doing something. And frequently it is the sense of timing that plays the critical role in whether or not what one does has the consequences originally intended.

- A skill of *political awareness:*   She stated, "I knew what I wanted, but I really didn't share it with the Board because if I had told them we needed 20 computers, it would have seemed exorbitant and the idea would have simply been rejected as being foolish and unreasonable." Knowing how a board will react seems like a fairly simply skill, but a number of school administrators have had a project fail precisely because they didn't know.

- Once more, the skill of knowing more than one way to *gain acceptance* of an idea by others: "I was a learner along with them because I knew that would be important to their acceptance of the idea," said the principal.

Having said all this, what then can be said about the skill side of administrative "knowing how to do things"? Do we find some direction here or do we find simply a continued muddle? I suspect the answer is a bit of both—direction and continued muddle.

First, the muddle. According to the inferences I made, there were thirteen different skills (some with overlap) that this principal talked of having used, although, for the most part, she didn't talk of them in the context of skills. She was simply "seeing" things in the situation. But there appeared to be little in the way of a systematic plan in it all from which we might deduce the skills that would be necessary, yet neither did it all appear to be a random effort. To further the muddle, I have absolutely no doubt that a different principal, faced with the same desire to develop a computer-literacy program in her or his school in a similar district environment, would have decided on a different strategy that would require different techniques and the use of different skills—though most certainly there would be some commonalities. Certainly, if we look for a list of skills that would apply universally to situations such as this one we are doomed to disappointment, and just as well. The old saw, "Different strokes for different folks" stands up well here. What is at issue, of course, is the comment that has been made numbers of times concerning the practice of the administrative craft as being a highly idiosyncratic endeavor. People simply sense different things, make different inferences from what they sense, and decide on and act out different scenarios to accomplish similar ends.

It may well be that this last thought is as crucial as any to our thinking about skills. That is, when we say that different people will decide on and act out different scenarios to accomplish similar ends, we are invoking the principal of equifinality, an important part of thinking about open systems (Katz and Kahn, 1978). Put rather simply, the equifinality idea means that there is more than one way to skin a cat. Put in the context of the prior discussion, *As long as the dignity of individuals and the integrity of the system are maintained, do what you think you should in ways that work for you.* Indeed, one does enact administrative craft skills idiosyncratically, and so the muddle about what to do continues.

There is some direction to it all, however. If we look back over the list of skills that my inferences said this principal used, we find ourselves returning to the model that developed from the discussion about was involved in the skill of hitting a baseball. For example, it is apparent that much of the skill that was exercised by the principal was unobservable. These unobservables and the way they were used were absolutely critical to the success of the project. They laid the ground upon which other things could happen. The ability to make a realistic assessment of what one can do, the ability to sense the possible, the ability to sense the way the tempo of activities would have to develop, the ability to anticipate the reactions and sentiments of others—these and other similar abilities, all unobservable, are the necessary starting points for intelligent administrative craftwork. And, of course, listening, about which we will have much more to say later in this chapter, is also unobservable.

One does have to *do* something, though, and there are several points of skill, kin to the ballplayer swinging the bat, that are observable. Curiously, though, they well might not strike the outsider as a skill. For example, simply seeing the principal teaching youngsters how to use a computer might not be seen as an administrative skill important to the whole enterprise. And, in a way, it is not. It is one of the observable "swings" that took place that was dependent on some unobservable things having happened. The same might be said for the principal's having tapped resources of other schools or becoming a learner along with her teachers. That is, these activities took place because some other unseen skills had been exercised.

There were some other observable skills involved that we might be inclined to describe as behavioral and apparently well exercised. In particular, I have reference to the face-to-face persuasiveness of the principal and her ability to write a grant proposal that was funded.

Using the ideas and images developed earlier from the baseball and medical analogies, we can break things down a bit farther. That is, some of what this principal described had the quality of "seeing the ball" or being aware of the school's emotional pulse in the sense of having knowledge of a variety of circumstances, including the state of oneself, that would or might come into play as the program developed. And depending on how things were seen, judgments had to be made about the why's of the reactions of people so that appropriate remedial action could be taken. We don't have any direct evidence about these judgments—the diagnosis—but we know by inference that they were made. The several comments concerning faculty skepticism, gaining faculty acceptance, and not approaching the school board with the whole package at one time tell us. Decisions to do or not to do one thing or another were not merely made on a whim. This is obvious, of course, but for our concern with skills it needs to be noted. As with physicians, some administrators are better diagnosticians than others. How they achieve that high degree of skill is a matter of conjecture. That it exists is not.

The purpose of this chapter thus far has been to develop a loose framework for understanding the meaning of the idea of the skills of administrative craftwork. To summarize, the framework suggests two major categories of skills—those that involve some type of action and are observable, and those that involve the use of the senses (primarily seeing and hearing) and cannot be observed by an onlooker. The specific substance with which the totality of these skills deals has to do with (1) skills related to understanding the "what" of the environment or those parts of it that are pertinent to the problem at hand; (2) skills related to understanding why what is happening is, indeed, happening; and

(3) predicated on the adequacy of one's ability to understand the what and the why of things, skills of enacting particular behaviors that are judged to be helpful to the solution of whatever problem in which an administrator is engaged. The framework suggests that we make judgments of relative skillfulness on the basis of what we can see or hear—how a question is asked, or how a discussion is summarized, or how much understanding is conveyed in an empathic response. Curiously, though, the ability to understand the what and the why adequately or the development of a sense of timing, for example, are probably more difficult skills to learn simply because one cannot observe and comment on the thought processes of another as he or she tries to understand what, know why, and then make a decision about when and how to do something.

What is at issue here is not only the question of learning, however. More important, I think, is that what we are talking about is a sort of basic skills notion of the craft of administration. Just as we speak of reading, writing, and arithmetic as providing a basic skill foundation for a successful adult life, so it seems that the skills of understanding what is happening, understanding why it's happening, and having a sense of timing are basic to engaging successfully in the craft of administration. But I want to reduce the matter more than that, at least for the purposes of this book.

Every time I asked an administrator what was most important for him or her to be able to do well, the response was, "Listening." When I asked why this was so, the response, expressed in different ways, was, "So I can understand what's happening." In other words, I reduce the idea of basic *skills* to that of a basic *skill*—that of listening in order to understand. It is not my intent, by this reduction, to negate the importance of being a good social diagnostician or of having a sense of timing in the work life of an administrator. It is only to say that if you don't understand what is happening—and you do this mostly by listening—the chances of your doing anything else well are minimal. It is really a corollary of the phrase we used earlier in the baseball analogy: "You can't hit what you can't see." It is also true, of course, that one "listens" with one's eyes in the sense of gathering information through observing the environment. But because most of administration involves working with people (verbal interaction with individuals or groups) and not with the physical environment, one's visual observations simply do not loom as large as one's listening observations in the total scheme of things. In fact, it is not difficult for me to conceive of a school principal or superintendent who is blind. Indeed, there may be some. I can't, however, picture an administrator who is deaf, and for obvious reasons.

There is another reason why I chose to reduce things to a single basic skill. It is that by doing so I eliminate a great deal of the idiosyncratic component attached to diagnosing or to a sense of timing. This is not to say that people do not listen idiosyncratically, however. For example a colleague and I might attend to different parts of a group discussion. Different topics might affect us differently and we become more or less attentive. (It is to say, though, that I think matters of individual judgment may come into play while one is listening to a much lesser extent than when one is drawing an inference about why something is happening.) On the other hand, one's individual judgment plays a major role in one's sense of timing about when to intervene, to make a comment, to ask a question, and so on.

What, then, can be said about this basic administrative craft skill of listening beyond speaking of it as being fundamental? A good bit, I think, that combines some definitional thoughts, some theoretical ideas about the listening and communications process, and some comments of school administrators about both the need for and theoretical ideas about the listening and communications process, and some comments of school administrators about both the need for and aim of listening in a skillful way.

We start with the idea that sometimes, perhaps most times, that which is simple in its initial presentation is most complex in its elaboration. Thus, we have Webster's giving us a rather simple definition of the verb form of the word *listen*. It is "to hear with thoughtful attention." Not only must you be attentive to what others are saying but you must be thoughtful about it, according to Webster. A nice idea, for sure, but it is not very helpful if we want to think about what is the nature of the skill involved. Further, the modifying phrase "with thoughtful attention" is open to a theatrical factor. In discussion with students of mine in a supervision class, for example, I frequently take note of the fact that any teacher worth his or her salt practices looking interested so that "thoughtful attention" will be communicated to a supervisor's comments during a conference. The fact that when I make this observation it is always greeted with laughter tells me that Webster's definition has problems even though, as I noted, it has a nice ring to it.

A more adequate way to think about this basic skill of listening, and one that has clear behavioral implications, is to place it within the context of the broader process of interpersonal communication. Ruesch and Bateson (1951) explain the process in the following way, and though their focus was on the cycle of the communication process, the role of the listener will become quite clear.

1. Person A wishes to communicate some idea to Person B. He or she does this mostly through words but sometimes with gestures. For example, we see a friend walking on the other side of the street. Not wishing to shout, we try to catch our friend's eye and wave a greeting.

2. Person B hears the words or sees the gesture. We cannot observe this happening or, in fact, that it has happened at all until

3. Person B, in one way or another, lets Person A know what it is that has been *received* and *understood*. We don't know whether our friend has seen our wave, for example, unless he or she waves back or acknowledges it in some other way with a nod of the head or, perhaps, with the shout we didn't want to give in the first place.

In the context of the communications cycle, interpersonal or group, the role of the listener then is crucial. Up to the point that he or she lets the communicator know what has been received and understood, the latter doesn't know (1) what has been communicated, or (2) if, indeed, anything has been communicated. All of us have had the experience, for example, of being in situations (mostly classrooms and faculty meetings, I suspect) of absolutely not attending to what is being said by our professor, principal, superintendent, or dean. For whatever reasons—boredom, anxiety, or simply lack of interest—we "tune out."

The point in the cycle where the listener lets the communicator know what he or she has received and understood is the test point in it all. We even sometimes use the word *test* as we enact that behavior, that is, we use or hear the sentence, "Let me test out what I hear." Or the testing takes other forms: "What I hear you saying is. . . ." "What I understand your intention to be is. . . ." Sometimes remarks such as these have the character of being rote responses and they may be reacted to with ridicule. Regardless, though, without testing of this nature there simply is no way to know whether or not someone has heard "with thoughtful attention."

Here is the way one principal expressed his critical role as a listener:

> Everyone has something to say and they know that I am listening to them, really paying attention. I have to listen to all the testimony. That's my data. I keep on checking it. That's how I know what's happening. And I need to let them know what I think I know so that they can let me know if I've listened to them correctly.

Broadly speaking, the administrator's skill at listening is analogous to the baseball player's skill of seeing the ball. In both cases, there is an absolute need for information, which the batter tries to get with his eyes, and the administrator with her or his ears. Everything else that a superintendent or a principal may do depends on the adequacy of the information, mostly received orally, that that person has at hand. A high school principal made a similar case for this most basic of all administrative skills with words that are more familiar: "Above everything else you've got to be a good listener because this is what opens the door for you to do the right thing at the right time."

Notice the link to action. It is a sort of administrative parallel to the "you can't hit what you can't see" bit of wisdom about hitting a baseball. And, once more, notice the implicit chain of familiar thought involved: "As I listen, I find out what's going on and from a variety of sources. I process this information. I put it together and make inferences from it about the why's and where-for's of a situation. Then I make a decision about what to do and when to do it."

In what is not so neat and tidy a form because action in a school or school district is simply not as neat and tidy a thing as is writing about it, this is the way I believe things get played out with the information-gathering function of listening. And though it sounds simple, as with examples we have used previously, matters do become exceedingly complex. Note that the further one moves from the basic act of listening along the way to some type of action, the more the process becomes open to individual and not necessarily widely shared predispositions and skills of making judgments and decisions. For example, the same information may get interpreted differently by different people; decisions about what to do based upon the same information and interpretation may well vary among people; and the same holds for when to do it. And so what we have is another argument for the fundamentality to the practice of the craft of administration of the ability to be a good listener. That is, first, everything else appears to depend on it, and second, the further one moves from it in the direction of action, the more individual (not generalized) judgment comes into play.

Having made the case for the very fundamentality of the skill of listening in the context of "Knowing How to Do Things," it becomes necessary to inquire a bit further into the thinking of administrators about this skill and its meaning to them. Several illustrations follow of what a principal or superintendent talked about, unprompted, immediately after having told me that being a skilled listener was their indispensable stock in trade. Here is a superintendent being more explicit about his own listening behavior:

> I have to listen to their ideas, to what's on their mind and I also have to listen for any emotion that's there. And, for example, if there's anger there I have to listen at whom it is directed. Sometimes it seems like it's all directed at me but it really isn't. I have to think about that and test it out.

Not only the words but the musical accompaniment become important to the listener. And along with picking up the existence of the music is a need to sense the underlying refrain and its meaning. What is being implied is that a bit of fine-tuning is necessary. These points are valid in that along with the content of what it is we talk about, we unavoidably convey our feelings about it. This is true even though we may very deliberately try to hide our feelings. Something typically creeps through (sometimes through body language in which case our skills of observation support those of listening) that lets the listener know about the refrain: the joy, anger, enthusiasm or lack of it, and so on.

In other words, this superintendent's elaboration on his need to listen suggests that if he really wants to understand the what of things, he has to make himself open to listening to and trying to understand the emotionality of the other. And, indeed, this is not so terribly easy to do. It is less taxing on a person not to attend to that deeper level of meaning that accompanies our idea. And, of course, the potential of hearing something that may produce anxiety is much less when we don't attend to that deeper level. But as we engage in this avoidance, the obverse implication of this superintendent's comment is, we find ourselves at some point making decisions on the wrong information.

At times I have observed people engaging in this avoidance almost eagerly, as if not to avoid would be frightening. In fact, that potential is clearly there. The point is that if one doesn't listen for the emotional side of school life, one doesn't have to deal with it. And, indeed, it is possible to live a long administrative life in precisely that way.

A high school principal, after noting that by concentrating on listening she allows herself to pick up on thoughts and emotions that might otherwise have slipped by, said:

> And when I get an angry person, perhaps a parent, in my office and I sit there and listen to them, let them talk, let them know I am listening to them, you can almost see their anger coming out of them, almost like a hot air balloon coming down. All of a sudden, you've got them back in their seat and they're not off the wall as they were when they first came in. You can talk with them.

These thoughts were echoed any number of times by the principals and superintendents with whom I talked. There is an interesting intuitive psychology to it all which seems to make abundant sense. For example, as important as it may be that a parent is able to take a complaint to a school administrator, it is perhaps more important that the parent receives the sense of having been listened to, particularly when the anger is very overt. As we listen and convey our nonvalued understanding of the anger, we also convey a couple of other things—that anger is a permissible emotion to have, and that the other is a person of value (because I wouldn't listen to him or her otherwise). In other words, the notion is that that as a person receives the sense of having been listened to, particularly by a person of some prestige, one gets the feeling of having been confirmed as a person of worth. And that, in this day and age, is no small matter. In the context of this principal's remarks, I suspect that what happens is that once the angry parent feels listened to, thus confirmed, it is no longer necessary to be angry. Adult discussion can take place.

In another setting, I studied a situation in which a highly respected and admired school administrator had moved to another position. I wanted to know the basis for the respect and admiration. Over and over again, teachers to whom I talked told me that whenever they went to see the principal, for whatever reason, they left his office with two central reactions: they felt that his very focused listening had made them the center of his attention and that, thus, they were important. I repeat, this is no small matter—especially in the schools.

Of course, this discussion does not apply to only adults; youngsters also come into the action. And they are quite aware of those adults who listen to them and those who don't. They gravitate to the former and shy away from the latter. My suspicion is that the dynamics of these situations are similar to those obtained with adults. The principal who listens, and who youngsters know listens, confers a certain type of dignity on them. Although administrators may not be able to intuit the theory behind it all, they are quite aware of the power that resides in the skill of listening. As one person said, "When I listen to people, my behavior tells them I respect them."

We must peek around another corner in our concern with the basic administrative craft skill of listening. It has to do with the unintended action commitments that get implied as an administrator listens to people with problems. Curiously, there is a certain amount at risk as an administrator listens to his or her constituents, school, or community. For example, as a principal or superintendent solicits information from people about the schools and listens to them in the process, it frequently happens that an expectation gets created that he or she will act on the information or opinion that has been solicited. The activity and skill of listening, originally intended for understanding and/or diagnosing a set of circumstances may, at times, end up in the development of what I call an "expectations box," out of which the administrator may have trouble escaping. The expectations have their roots in this thinking, for example: "If the principal (or superintendent) thinks that it is important to listen to me and learn what's on my mind, then I expect he or she will use the ideas I gave him." Thus the risk that in the process of listening, expectations are created that the administrator has no intention of fulfilling.

As we have noted several times previously, it is a messy business, a messy craft, we are trying to understand. It is not the same as the woodcarver who makes a perfect cut in a piece of white pine and knows that nothing will alter the way the cut has changed the wood, unless it is the woodcarver. What is at issue, I think, is the problem of control over one's work. The woodcarver has almost total control over that with which he or she is working. No such circumstance exists for the school administrator, and indeed, we must be thankful for that, lest we lose our own humanity.

This chapter has presented an approach to understanding the problem of "Knowing How to Do Things." It involves accepting the idea that there is one skill that is basic to all others—listening. To be able to be a skilled listener, although a necessary requirement for administrative practice, is not a sufficient requirement. One cannot *only* listen and be an effective school administrator. But if one is not a good listener, becoming an effective administrator is something that is hardly likely to happen—"you can't hit what you can't see."

• Endnotes

1. Using illustrations such as these may seem like an odd way to start a chapter on skills of administration. I chose to do so, though, because (1) they appealed to me in a playful sort of way, and (2) they provided scenarios that would be familiar to and have meaning to just about every reader of this book.

2. This excerpt is reprinted from A. Blumberg, "The Work of Principals: A Touch of Craft," in William Greenfield (ed.), *Instructional Leadership* (Boston: Allyn and Bacon, 1987).

Chapter Ten

Knowing the Right Thing to Do

Thinking about the idea of administration as craft ends up being a fairly sloppy conceptual business. Though it is possible to separate the elements of craftwork in fairly discrete ways, as the chapter titles of Part Two of this book indicate, the realities of practice are that there is a great deal of overlap in the way these elements enter the thinking of an administrator as he or she engages with daily work. For example, it is certainly the case that a superintendent cannot form a useful image of the solution to a problem without an informed awareness of the nature of the human materials involved. Nor can one understand the nature of these materials without having developed the basic skill of being able to "listen to the music as well as the words."

The list of examples of how the conceptual elements of the craft overlap with and influence each other could be extended endlessly, but that is not the point of these introductory comments to "Knowing the Right Thing to Do." Rather, what I suggest is that the closer we get to thinking about an administrator's actual doing of something, the more the tidy neatness of categorical thinking tends to be nonfunctional if one really wants to understand how and why school administrators do what they do. Things simply become somewhat confusing conceptually the closer one gets to action. This point holds most truly for school principals because of the extremely quick tempo of their work. But it also holds for superintendents and members of their staff even if the pace of their work and the urgency of demands placed on them for "doing something" may be somewhat toned down compared with their collegial building administrators.

Any framework for understanding the practice of administrative craft must, at its base, include the idea that it is not a neat business. As we approach trying to understand the actions of any particular administrator we must (1) acknowledge and deal with this messiness, and (2) acknowledge that some things are simply unknowable. And so it is that I think our discussion of "Knowing the Right Thing to Do" will end up with more questions than answers, and even perhaps a bit of mystery.

In the concluding section of his book *Artistry,* Howard (1982, p. 189), as he reinforces the craft-art linkage and as he wonders how artists or craftspeople know what to do next in their work, quotes Picasso:[1] "A painting remains there like a question. And it alone has the answer." Howard then goes on to say, "In the end, for the artist, artisan, or athlete, it is a matter of finding the right response, the 'better way' of doing things." He then suggests that finding this "better way" or the right response is a goal in its own right and rarely a matter of the individual craftsperson developing a better theory of craft.

There are a couple of thoughts here that, for our purpose, are worthy of further comments. First, stemming from the Picasso quotation, is the idea that the substance of the solution to a problem is a way of understanding the problem itself. "A painting remains there like a question," and if you study the painting with the kind of understanding required, at some point you will know the question to which the painting purports to be the answer. That is, the painting is the artist's efforts to "know the right thing to do" in order to symbolize the question that it attempts to answer. I don't think it's stretching things too far to say that this concept may be transferred to our thinking about the practice of school administration. If the solutions to problems that are arrived at by an administrator represent her or his ideas about "the right thing to do," then we might say that imbedded in that solution were the questions that got asked in the search for the right response. The significance of this point for our understanding the work of school administration as a craft is this proposition: If we are interested in knowing how an administrator conceives of his or her work, a good way to do this is to learn what solutions to predicaments he or she arrives at. Inherent in the solutions are the questions that were asked, and inherent in the questions are clues to one's views of the nature of one's work. And moving more to what I think are both the practical and conceptual focus of this book, as we come to understand the way one views one's work, we become enabled to learn and use the language of that work as it is used by the other. And so, perhaps in somewhat of a circular way, if we want to learn the work language of a particular administrator, it might be worthy to focus on the substance of the images that he or she develops as the most appropriate way to resolve particular problems.

The second point that we should attend to from Howard's discussion is concerned with finding the right response as an end in itself and not simply as a means of developing a better theory of a craft. This thought is a rather forthright acknowledgment that what is and probably should be most important for practitioners of any craft is the quest for better ways to do things, for refining one's know-how, and not the quest of a better theory of that craft. What becomes crucially important to understand about this idea is that it contains no intent to relegate practice to a less worthy form of intellectual activity. But for certain, it is to say that "knowing the right thing to do" or "finding a better way" places intellectual as well as emotional demands on a practicing administrator that are different than those placed on people (professors) who theorize about administration.

• Knowing the Right Thing to Do

The question of how one knows what is the right thing to do can be dealt with somewhat abstractly by appealing to theory in the form of "rules of thumb," by ignoring theory and relying on experience, or by rejecting the question altogether as inappropriate in the sense that there are no "right" ways to do things but there may be somethings that are wrong.

We start with this last idea, which we might call idiosyncratic intentionality. To put it quite simply, each of us brings with us to our work our own particular life history, set of skills and attitudes, views of the world, and so forth, that rather directly affect the way we see things, the images we form, and the notions that we develop about what is "the right thing to do." We noted this inferentially in Chapter Four, in our discussion of a school principal dealing with a discipline problem, and in Chapter Nine, with the problem of developing a computer literacy program in an elementary school. To repeat, the point quite simply is that different administrators would have had different intentions about their work and would have found different "right" responses.

If, according to this way of looking at things, there are no right responses to which we might find general agreement, are there wrong responses? I think the answer is in the affirmative. For example, though different principals would have different "right" responses to a particularly frustrating discipline problem or a particularly frustrating circumstance with a barely competent tenured teacher, there would undoubtedly be agreement that, in the first instance, you should not hit the youngster and, in the second, you should not hold the teacher up as a bad example of teaching for the rest of the faculty. Or, superintendents would tend not to agree with each other on what to do with a troublesome school board member, but they would undoubtedly agree that the person shouldn't be held up to the public ridicule as an example of unparalleled stupidity.

I exaggerate, of course, to make a point. Knowing the right thing to do in the practice of the administrative craft is an idiosyncratic matter. Knowing what not to do or what things to avoid are matters about which more general agreement may be found. And the former thought, dealing with idiosyncratic predispositions in what we might think of as problem sensing and defining, takes us back to the previous chapter in which we discussed the principle of equifinality—there is more than one way to skin a cat. Or, to bring the thought closer to home, in schools or school districts there is simply more than one right way to deal with the daily problems of work.

If there are no generalized right ways to deal with problems of school life in the specific, I think there are abstract ways. This refers to the rules of thumb that have come to be associated, certainly in no systematic fashion, with the craft of administration. A rule of thumb is defined as "a method of procedure based on experience or common sense" and is further elaborated, definitionally, as "a general principle regarded as being roughly correct but not intended to be scientifically accurate." I am not talking about a series of rigid and universally correct do's and don't's, of course. But I do think there exists (Hines, 1987), quite uncatalogued because its existence rests in the experience and minds of untold numbers of school administrators, a storehouse filled with rules of thumb, ways of doing things that have worked and are predicted to work, about how to deal with problems that occur in an administrator's daily life. Additionally, it needs to be understood that there are general statements about what is the right (or wrong) thing to do that are not specific to a particular situation. In a very real and important sense, they constitute the lore—the traditional knowledge base—of the craft of school administration.

Here are some examples of administrative rules of thumb. I must admit to feeling somewhat hesitant about putting them in print for they will appear as rather simple-minded statements of truth about the very complicated everyday life in school organizations. But that, of course, is precisely the reason that they receive general support. They represent the reality of school administration that every superintendent or principal lives and understands. So, as examples, some rules of thumb might be:

- "If you want to make some changes in a school, make sure the teachers share ownership in the change."
- "Boards of education do not like to receive surprises. Keep them informed."
- "If you have to confront an angry parent, make sure you keep your cool."
- "If you give teachers a sense that you are really listening to their problems, they will get the feeling that you respect them."

All of this, of course, does not answer the problem of the right thing to do or say in any particular situation. But I think it's probably true that, even if unarticulated by an individual, most important rules of thumb are part of the very general craft knowledge held by practically all school administrators. Importantly, though, we must take note of the fact that though rules of thumb speak to the generalized "what" of action, they don't speak to the skill of action. And this, as we noted in Chapter Nine, is a very complicated business.

Still, with the acknowledgment that the question, "What is the right thing to do?" can receive no universal answer, we are faced with the question of how individual school administrators know—for them—what action is right in any particular situation. In my talks with administrators, this question was confronted over and over again. That is, as superintendents or principals would tell me about a particular situation and how they dealt with it, my almost invariable question was, "How did you know that was the right thing to do?" And their invariable response was, "Through experience." That response should come as no surprise to any reader of this book but, at the same time, it's not very helpful if one is trying to understand why particular action decisions are taken as different from other alternatives. And so, the questions become: What is meant by reference to experience as the source of learning what is right? And, in companion fashion, what is meant by the phrase "Experience is the best teacher" as it may be applied, once more, to knowing the right thing to do?

A start on my own understanding of the problem with which I was dealing—the meaning of experience in the context of knowing the right thing to do—came during a discussion I was holding with a high school principal after having spent the day with her observing her at work. We were talking about how one learns to deal with the action and quick decision demands that are placed on a principal. Her first response, of course, was "experience." Then, she went on to say:

> In my first year as principal, I remember saying, "Please, Lord, let me get through the first year so that, after that, there won't be any surprises." I know there would be surprises personally, but there won't be any organizational surprises. I'll have gone through my first graduation, my first January Regents. I will have lived through my first yearly cycle and I will know what that cycle is apt to bring. I'm going into my fifth year in February and, though things used to be new, I haven't found a new thing in quite a while. There are, of course, some bizarre things that happen, but they all seem to fall into familiar categories now. I don't have the anxiety I used to.

There are several thoughts imbedded in this interview that are most pertinent for our discussion. First, what the idea of experience means becomes much more clear. It means, as I understand it, the development of one's memory of events, of categories of events, of a repertoire of feasible solutions to categories of events, and of those decisions and actions that worked. Note, for example, how after her first year as principal that with which she had to deal all seemed "to fall into familiar categories" although it was and is still true that within these categories bizarre things could and did happen. But one can deal with the bizarre fairly readily, it appears, if it can be organized within some categorical framework.

Note, as well, what appears to be the criticalness of the first year one works as an administrator for the development of one's work-event memory, so to speak. There is, indeed, something to the seasons as they become reflected in the life and times of the schools. You must live through the opening of school in September to have a sense of what that means to administrative work—its excitement and its anxiety (for adults, youngsters, and parents). You must live through, in your role as principal, the February "blues" in order to develop a memory for and, thus, know how to deal with the emotionality of that time. As a superintendent, you must experience the development of a budget that may get turned down in order to have a memory for doing it differently (or the same) the next time around. You have to experience, as a superintendent, the often agonizingly political machinations of collective bargaining meetings in order for your memory to guide you to finding the right response in the future.

So we have, at least initially, a way to think about "knowing the right thing to do." It is lodged within the notion of experience which, in turn, translates into the idea of developing a memory for categories of events. This thought, incidentally, probably accounts for the thoughts our principal expressed about the anxiety that was associated with her first year on the job. She had no memory for events—they simply had not yet occurred so that things that happened were indeed new to her experience. Perhaps most important, in a vein we have referred to more than once, she had not, in that first year, developed a conceptual language to deal with that experience. To be somewhat anxious as a result of all this is certainly not surprising. What would be surprising is not to be anxious, but my suspicions are that most first-year administrators, regardless of their position, tend to deny their anxiety. To admit it may seem to be a sign of emotional incompetence (which it is not).

The general idea, then, of "knowing the right thing to do" suggests that one comes to know this through the experience of engaging in practice from which one develops a memory for categories of events and categories of responses. In the process of building that memory bank before one has had the experience necessary in order to make "deposits" in it, a fair amount of trial and error takes place (as we shall discuss in Chapter Twelve). Without the experience-based memory, an administrator in his or her early years on the job is continually involved in testing operations. "What works?" is the question that continually gets asked, though not in a consciously articulated fashion. And though "What works?" is clearly a survival question for neophyte administrators, the answers provided are what builds one's craft memory. And this is not to say, of course, that after the first year of practice the memory bank is filled. At least for those administrators who see their work as never quite done, it seems reasonable to suspect that they are continually expanding, perhaps consciously, their experience so that they develop a memory for a wider range of events. Conversely, my suspicion is that those administrators to whom we attribute a "Stone Age" mentality are those who stopped making new deposits shortly after they started.

Taking things a bit further, another principal echoes the idea of the strangeness of the first year on the job, the development of a memory, and then elaborates on the notion of events cueing his memory. In a fairly lengthy comment, he said:

> You see situations that come up that are like other things you've done and, consequently, you know what kinds of responses are appropriate. It's rare, it really is rare after five years as principal, that I would see somebody who presented a

completely unique situation. The first year everything was unique. But after these years, I learned that people come across in certain ways and I develop ways of responding. One thing I learned not to do was, I won't scream back at a screamer.

So how do you make the judgment about what to do? The only thing I can say is I think you begin to feel safe in what you do because you had good, safe experiences with something and you work out of that mold. You make a judgment as to whether you've seen this problem in other places, other settings. You make a judgment based on how they approach you, the kinds of things they say, the adjectives, the tones, the kinds of judgments you think they will make. Then you go back to the things that worked. And some people might not like the idea, but the truth is you reach into your little bag and find some ways that worked to get a dialogue going. The point is that over the years you develop a repertoire of behaviors that work.

So we have reinforcement of the idea of building one's memory in order to know the "right thing to do." It appears that what happens is that one develops coding and cueing systems to enable oneself to make judgments about both when to "reach into your little bag" and what to reach for. The "when," of course, refers to timing and is probably as important as the "what" in the whole process. As implied in the baseball analogy used in the last chapter, the swing of the bat may be perfect but without timing it results in just another strike.

There appears to be more to the whole memory process, though, and that has to do with what this principal referred to as working out of the mold of "good, safe experiences." What I suspect happens goes something like this: As you accumulate experience, as you respond to events, your memory for the events and your responses to them builds up. But there is a hierarchy of "what works," if we are to accept this principal's ideas, that is based on "safety" of experience. In other words, what may be the case, and it is certainly worth thinking about, is that what is first reached for in the bag is the low-risk response. If it works, fine. If not, you reach for something that is a bit more risky, and so on. It is important to understand that as an administrator increases the riskiness of responses, he or she also probably increases the amount of emotional energy that is being used. No wonder that the days that are filled with risks of one kind or another leave a person exhausted.

Sometimes, of course, no right response can be found. In that case, particularly if the other party is an outsider to the school (a parent or other community member), it may be that

> . . . all you can do is shut them off, be tough, take a stand and say, "This is how it is." And then you say, "And this is my boss's name" and give them his card and say, "If you have any problems, you call him." You simply have to shut the situation down and, sometimes, rather crudely.

High risk, indeed.

Knowing the right thing to do involves not only developing a memory for coding the large number of short and fragmented events that occur in a school administrator's work, but for those tasks that may be anticipated and involve long periods of time. A classic example of this is the preparation of the school district budget, surely a task that is anticipated and is likely to take a long time. Here is a superintendent talking about budget work with his new business manager:

> You learn to do a budget by doing a budget. The courses in budgeting you take at the University? They help you, but until you have gone through the process, you really don't know. And every district does it differently and you have to learn that, too. So, I said to my new business manager, "I'll help you with it this first time around and then you'll have to go ahead and do it on your own. I'll help you with it once and we'll mold things within the budget." It's like your memory comes into play and you say to yourself, "Well, I've been here before and I know how to do it. I know what the red lights are and what the caution lights are because I've been there before and I can help you."

What makes this anecdote interesting to me is that it takes the process of budget building, clearly one in which knowing the right things to do is critically important, but also one in which I find myself personally disinterested if not bored, and makes it a very lively thing. The very first sentence is as Deweyan as one can get: "You learn . . . by doing" (and, of course, this is how your memory develops). And this point is buttressed by the next reference about the nature of what you learn at the University. Technical-rational stuff [2] it is, and though it helps, that's all it does, until you do it *in vivo* and develop your memory for the red lights and the caution lights. And notice, as well, the budget-making process involved "molding." So we have a potter at work, teaching another potter about how to make something in a new studio, as it were. The red lights and caution lights, to continue the analogy, become bubbles in the clay or circumstances that might become bubbles.

Perhaps I make too much of this, but I think not. Those few brief sentences speak volumes. Most important, in a fashion about which I am not clear, they speak to the relationship between memory development as it occurs in the process of finding the right response to a circumstance and the parallel learning of a common language. "Red lights" and "caution lights," one would presume, would soon come to have a similar meaning to both the superintendent and his assistant. And in the process, of course, the superintendent helps build his staff member's memory so that, at a later time, he will be able to find the right response on his own.

The whole idea of the interplay between experience and memory as a means of understanding how administrators know what is the right thing to do and developing a common interpersonal language about it also relates to what I think is the development of a workable intrapersonal language of craft. That is, this is the type of language that we speak to ourselves and is concerned mostly, it seems, with the cues that we attend to as we go about, once more, deciding on the right response. A high school principal talked about the cues the language he attends to in these terms:

> So a stranger, a parent, comes into your office. There are lots of things I pay attention to, 'cause I have to make a judgment about what to do. First, I try to remember if I've seen them in other places, in other settings. I watch how they approach me. I listen to the kinds of things they say, the adjectives they use, their tone of voice. I try to get kind of a sense of whether or not they seem inclined to be even-handed or whether they seem to be exaggerating. And all those things put together helps me understand the kinds of things I may be able to do in the situation. Whether, for example, we can hold a dialogue with each other or I just have to use my authority and shut them off.

In less detail, but dealing beneath the surface with the same kinds of issues—cues about the nature of problems and a language to communicate to oneself about that problem—a superintendent spoke to the way he categorized problems that he sensed as he worked on "his nose":

> Along with everything that has to be done each day, you have to be picking up cues about the nature of the problems out there. You look ahead and say things to yourself like, "Is this a problem that just needs a bandaid solution? Or is it a problem with the system or a problem with the program?" And you try to analyze very quickly. You know, "Should I put a cap on this to take care of it or is it symptomatic of something else?" It's really important that you think this way 'cause how you think determines what you do.

It all gets to be a very complicated business—more complicated, I suspect, than anyone might imagine. Perhaps at its root, its complexity derives from the idea that there is no common way of thinking about the cues that one attends to nor the language one uses when talking to oneself about what the cues mean and what judgments should be made from them. What occurs is a highly individuated exercise in sensing and deciding. What one attends to, the inferences and decisions one makes, are clearly a product of one's experience and resulting memory. One plus one adds up to two for Superintendent A, but the same one and one adds up to two and a half for Superintendent B. The point is that the development of a language of the craft of administration is likely to be highly refined relative to a person's intrapersonal level of communication. But its refinement at the interpersonal level is likely to be relatively elementary. What is at issue is the thought that common languages develop from common work and the amount of common work that occurs among school administrators is typically rather minimal.

An illustration may make the idea more clear. The language that the members of the symphony orchestra must learn and through which they come to know what to do is the language of the gestures of the conductor. To play softly, slowly, or with vigor gets communicated through gestures of the hands and arms, posturing of the body, or perhaps even wrinkles of the nose or forehead. Members of the orchestra, I suspect, can tell you very quickly the meaning of different words in that gestural language with a great deal of precision and agreement. Were they not able to do so, the orchestra's performance would disintegrate. I think it's clear that the only kind of agreement about the meaning of cues and, thus, the development of a common language in administrative life, is that which describes broad categories of events, not the smaller circumstances within those events from which ultimate meaning is drawn and upon which decisions are made about the right thing to do.

To return to the examples that were used to start this discussion, in the case of the principal it is fair to say that what he attends to, or feels should be attended to, would probably find pretty wide agreement among his colleagues. The particular cues he attends to and the interpretative language he uses to discuss those cues with *himself* would find less agreement. And, of course, his decision about what to do would find even less. This line of reasoning is based on the idea that the further one moves away from description of events in the direction of interpreting them and acting on one's interpretation, the more one's idiosyncratic memory comes into play and the more the language used becomes variant.

A similar situation would hold with the superintendent in his brief comment about the character of problems that are encountered. There would certainly be wide agreement that some problems need only bandaids and that another category is somehow reflective of something going awry in the system, thus requiring a different type of resolution. Beyond that, though, things become hazy as, once more, one's personalized memory comes into play, affecting the cues that are taken to be important, the language used to describe and interpret those cues, and so forth.

It all sounds very rational. The very use of the word *memory* implies rationality, suggesting the process by which our senses communicate information to our brain which, in turn, stores that information in particular types of memory categories. And perhaps it is true that things work that way most of the time in the sense that information is processed, memory is activated, and decisions are made in relatively orderly fashion even though a person may not be conscious of the process that is taking place.

There are times, though, when the circumstances of life combine (or conspire) to upset what otherwise may be this neat and orderly process. These are times when one's *emotional memory* intrudes into and, anthropomorphically speaking, does battle with our rationality—and, I suspect, usually wins.

In a conversation I was having with a central office administrator, just such a circumstance was discussed as we talked about a situation (a student discipline problem) that had arisen that he had quite deliberately passed off as aberrant and more to be ignored than anything else. The memory process had been activated and the "right thing to do" was to let it pass. But there are times when to act out of one's memory does not serve us well. And by this I mean that there are conflictual problems that occasionally arise in which "the right thing to do" involves the person of the administrator as well as the objective nature of the problem itself. This administrator said:

> Sometimes, of course, even though the problem seems like one I've dealt with previously and have let it pass, I don't let it pass. I think that happens mostly if I sense that if I ignore it will be a major reflection on my integrity. And I'm the only one who knows that. It's almost as though my brain says one thing and my gut says another. And I go with my gut. I can tuck away a little of not feeling good about myself, but if it goes beyond a little then I can't do it.

A high school principal spoke of using her "gut" in a situation where it was necessary to provide feedback to a potentially excellent teacher who seemed not to be able to get the type of student reactions to him that were desired. The principal talked with colleagues and studied some articles she had about how to work with the situation. And then,

> I did what I thought I was going to do in the first place. I ended up doing what my gut reaction said to do.

What her "gut" told her to do was a high-risk enterprise. She arranged for a feedback session in her office in which a group of students described to the teacher what he was doing that stood in the way of their reacting to him the way he wanted. As the principal said:

> The teacher agreed and before he came down I told the kids that I wanted them to be honest but not to attack the teacher in any way, shape, or form. Just tell him what behavior he keeps doing that bothers them. And I told him not to get defensive and just to explain why he does certain things. It worked out very, very well. I had no idea if it would or would not, and I was scared to death it might blow up in our faces. But it worked out super, but you know, you don't open up the magic principal's journal and find out what you're supposed to do. A lot of it is just plain "feel."

It may well be, then, that all of us have an "emotional memory" that tells us what we will feel relatively comfortable doing as well as a rational memory that, in a sense, presents us with alternative ways of doing things or focuses on what worked previously. I have no doubt that the specific conditions under which one's emotional memory comes strongly into play vary with each individual. But

I also think that a common denominator has to do with the amount of risk, to self and/or to the most desired problem resolution, that is perceived by the administrator to be inherent in one action or the other. A reasonable hypothesis, in this connection, would suggest that the higher the perceived riskiness of a situation, the more one's emotional memory comes into play as a source of "finding the right response."

Quite related to the questions of deciding on high-risk ways of working on problems is a part of the process that I think is largely ignored in the study of administrative behavior. It has to do with the conditions under which administrators give themselves tips about what they should do—a type of "silent rehearsal" (Howard, 1982, p. 194). For example, in the situation just described it will be recalled that the principal noted that she had told the students "to be honest" and "not to attack the teacher in any way or shape." She also told me that she had prepared herself to deal with the students. That is, she had given herself tips about what to do and how to do it; she had coached herself. This, of course, is not an unusual set of circumstances. All of us give ourselves tips about how to behave in situations that we know we will have to confront, particularly if we see those situations as containing a relatively high element of risk. For example, one superintendent talked with me about an appointment he had with a teacher a week from the day on which he and I were talking with each other:

> The last time we met, it was a disaster. I did everything wrong. When my secretary told me that he had scheduled another meeting with me, my first inclination was to want to run away which, of course, I couldn't do. So I've been prepping myself. Almost writing a script for myself. I know now what things to stay away from, because I don't want any more disasters.

The craft metaphor becomes clearly relevant here. One can almost visualize a woodcarver, for example, having botched a figure he or she was carving, and contemplating working on another one from a piece of wood similar to the first. The woodcarver recalls what it was the previous time that led to disaster and engages, so to speak, in a self-coaching clinic. "Do this. Don't do this. Be careful here." This is, indeed, the type of scenario in which school administrators engage, and in a manner similar to the hypothesis we suggested earlier about the relationship between the degree of perceived risk in a situation and the invoking of one's emotional memory. One can quite suppose that the amount and intensity of tip-giving behavior to self is related to the degree of risk that one predicts to be present in any set of future circumstances.

Finally, in this chapter, we deal with the other side of the memory coin as it alludes to "knowing the right thing to do." The central thrust of our discussion, thus far, has been to suggest that the development of a memory for categories of events and for a category coding system that is activated by cues in each situation that arises is what enables school administrators to meet and deal with the wide array of predicaments they encounter each day. During the first year when one is in a new role[3] no memory for "knowing" exists. Indeed, it is possible to think of the first year that a person is playing out a role new to him or her as memory-building time. This is not to suggest that this is a deliberate process, although (as we shall note in a later chapter) under certain conditions it does become deliberate. For the most part, though, what occurs seems to be a rather natural, unsensed, and probably unconscious kind of thing. Something happens in the course of a day. The new principal or superintendent deals with it in one fashion or another and observes the results. If the manner in which things were dealt with seems to have led to satisfactory problem resolution, a "deposit" is made in the administrator's memory bank of categories of events about which he or she "knows the right thing to do." To continue the bank metaphor, when things don't work out (a matter that will be treated in a later chapter), it seems likely that a deposit is made in the "things not to do" account, never to be withdrawn but to exist in one's memory as a warning.

It should be obvious that this very natural process of developing a memory and using it in the manner that has been described may lead to practical problems as well as problems with understanding the complexity and advocating the use of the craft concept of administration. With reference to the latter point, recall that in Chapter Three I noted that objections have been made to the appropriateness of thinking of teaching in craft terms because of the routineness and unthinkingness of response it implied to Broudy (1956). And it was Shulman who used the adjective *mere* to modify "craft" as he tried to differentiate teaching-as-craft from teaching-as-profession. What seems to be at the root of both Broudy and Shulman's aversions to thinking about the work of teachers (and administrators) is, in the terms that have been used here, that the development of a memory for the "right thing to do" implies a routineness of reaction to events, or, perhaps a better way to express it, an automaticity of response. In Pavolvian terms, almost, the thinking seems to be that the concept of administrator as craftsperson means that when one's memory suggests that an event falls into Category A, Response B is in order; Category C yields to Response D, and so forth.

There is a certain amount of reasonableness derived from experience for thinking in these terms. That is, it is probably true that all of us have known or observed school administrators or teachers whose responses to a whole variety of circumstances in their work seemed to be automatic, unthinking, uncreative, or whatever. A demands B and that is that. On to the next case.

If conditions such as this were the rule or even obtained in more than a very small minority of cases, I suspect there would be reason to be concerned. Further, it is undoubtedly true that there is a certain amount of necessary automaticity of response in all administrators' daily reactions to predicaments they encounter. Some problems are or become routine and thus deserve routine responses if for no other reason than to conserve one's time and energy. And some types of problems, though not routine, have occurred in sufficient numbers so that the administrator can make quick judgments about what ought to happen even though the circumstances are serious. However, all the administrators who were subjects of this study, either through observation and interview or just interview, were aware of the pitfalls that might attach to the condition of "having been there before."

We have some examples. First is an automatic response of the "right thing" in a case that was far from routine. A boy in a suburban high school had been a source of trouble for some time. In addition to repeated truancy, he had violated enough rules "to fill a book." The problem was whether or not to recommend that he be suspended from school or to retain him and continue to try and influence him to be a more appropriate member of the school community. The vice principal was in favor of the latter; the principal favored the former. He said:

> When I was newer in the job, I think I was more willing to carry these things further along. But with the experiences I've had, I guess I just feel I know where this is going to end up. I'd predict this kid is not going to be in school much longer so I'd get on with it. It sounds bad for an educator to talk that way, but I believe that not all kids belong in school and I get angry at the amount of time and energy that one kid can cost us to the detriment of the kids out there who really need our help and are not getting it.
>
> My VP said he's going to talk to the boy more, but he has no control over the boy. So that's not going to help. I've got a feeling he's not going to make a suspension yet. I would have gone ahead with it 'cause I know it's going to happen.

Notice that the principal's response was not reflexive nor unthinking. But it was more or less automatic in the sense that having experienced similar situations in the past, he felt he was in a good position to deduce the scenario of the future in this particular case. In fact, it turned out the way he thought it would. But the principal also said, with reference to his vice principal, "He'll learn something from this, maybe." Or, in the language that has been used in this chapter, another deposit will have been made in the memory bank.

It's important to note, as well, that this principal was not reacting automatically to a single development at a brief moment in time. He was responding to an ongoing series of events and he recognized the pattern. His memory told him, given this pattern, how things would almost inevitably end up, and his automatic response to being cued by his memory was to shortcut the whole process. I think it may be true that the only viable argument to that response can be made by people with different memories or those with no memories for events such as this.

Being on "automatic pilot," though, as several people referred to their reactions in situations where they'd "seen it all before," clearly has its problems. Here is the way several people reflected about that:

> • I guess that sometimes I have the fear that I've seen it all before and so I don't get as emotionally involved as I ought to. I become hardened to it and

and forget that each kid has to feel listened to, regardless of how automatic the situation is. The point is that the kids are not automatic.

- You know what the scary part is? It's when I become overconfident and it becomes too mechanical. And then I start to wrestle with myself, like "Have you done it so often that it's too mechanical?"
- Sometimes, because situations repeat themselves in a school, you feel like you're on automatic pilot. But you've got to be aware of that possibility—it's happened to me—because then you start to treat things by the numbers. You've always got to listen to kids. It lets them respect themselves. But when things get mechanical, you're apt to forget that.
- When I come into a situation and sense that I've been there before and that I know what to do, that's when I'm least reflective. I don't say to myself, "Uh-huh, I know what to do this time." I just do it, reflexively, I think. A great deal of my job involves types of situations I've handled before and those are the least challenging parts of it.

Thus, although the automaticity of response in a very real way enables school administrators to deal with a large range of events in school life, it also contains the potential for creating other kinds of problems. One of these is the problem of just being bored, even though it may be hard to believe that the job of superintendent or a principal can be boring. It can be, though, particularly in schools where one can observe a half dozen youngsters at most any time of day, sitting in the school office and waiting for the principal to deal with them about one or another type of disciplinary problem. Indeed, the principal has seen it all before. The office resembles an assembly line—and *that* is boring.

What does appear to be the antidote to problems of automatic response is simply being aware of when that is happening. It's as simple and as complicated as having enough of a sense of self to know that you are reacting in a reflexive, automatic way to a particular situation. And once this knowledge is produced for oneself it becomes possible to make a decision about whether to continue automatically or to bring into use the basic administrative craft skill—listening. Regardless of the situation, the rule of thumb on which everything else is grounded holds sway: You can't hit what you can't see.

• Endnotes

1. In his reference to Picasso, Howard is unable to provide a precise citation. He states, "I am not sure of the origin of this quote except that I heard it on a television program on Picasso, who reportedly said it" (p. 199).
2. See Donald Schon (1983, 1987) for discussion of the problems the professions face in their search for technical-rational-based practice.
3. By the use of "new role" in this context, I mean the first experience a person has had as a principal, for example. This is different from a "new position" where one may have moved from one principalship to another.

Chapter Eleven

Knots in the Wood; Bubbles in the Clay

Some months ago I was talking with a doctoral student of mine about his progress on his dissertation. It had been going quite slowly. Toward the end of our discussion I asked him what he had in mind to do with himself when he finished his work. My intent was to be helpful in his search for a job. He replied that he wanted to engage in full-time research and was going to look for a position as a researcher in a private sector research organization. When I opined that I thought he probably didn't have the necessary skills and might have difficulty finding a job—again, trying to be helpful in the sense of leading toward alternatives—the result, hardly what I had expected, was an emotional explosion. In language that potters understand very well, I had not kneaded the clay sufficiently to get all the bubbles out. As a consequence, the clay I was working on exploded when it was put in the kiln. In language a school administrator will understand, I had not explored with the student sufficiently his thoughts about his future to be well enough aware of what might be an issue too sensitive to be talked about, at least the way I talked about it. Indeed, something had gotten in the way of what I wanted to accomplish.

In this chapter, my concern is to illustrate several of the "somethings" that get in the way and, at times, alter both the image and results of what an administrator is trying to produce over the short or long term. They take the form of responses that I received from central office people or school principals when I asked them how they think and what they do when they encounter "knots in the wood" or "bubbles in the clay" as they are working on a project. The use of these metaphors communicated very well what was on my mind in the sense that people were well able to identify with and talk about conditions in the "material" with which they were working, or for which they had responsibility that got in the way of what they wanted to do. (As an aside, it almost seemed as though the use of such metaphorical language constituted a more focused and cordial invitation to conversation than had I framed my questions in what I think is some pseudo-scientificese of the behavioral sciences. That is, people tend to respond to questions within the framework of the language in which they are asked.)

There is another interesting thought attached to the use of these two metaphors, in particular. It is that though both of them deal with something about the material being worked on that is interfering with the production of the original design (though sometimes a woodcarver deliberately looks for wood with a knot), the implications of finding an unexpected knot or bubble are very different. In the latter case, there is no question that a bubble has to be popped or kneaded away. If not, as was the case with my graduate student, there will be an explosion in the kiln. Encountering knots, as we shall see, presents a different problem. The woodcarver has options about what to do when this happens. He or she may indeed find that the knot is so ill-placed, so big, or so hard to manage that the piece of wood must be thrown away. Or there may be alternate ways of dealing with it. We shall see these differences emerge in the discussion that follows. As a starter, though, many more people chose to talk about knots than bubbles. The reason, I think, has to do with this point about the variety of options available to a woodcarver when she or he discovers an unanticipated knot as opposed to what has to happen when a potter finds a bubble in the clay.

Bubbles, then, come first in the discussion, and our first illustration involves a central office curriculum director who had responsibility for convening and chairing a school-community task force on program development for gifted and talented youngsters. It was a sensitive topic to deal with in this particular community because an earlier experience with this type of program had, indeed, "exploded in the kiln." The administrator was very much aware of this history and, without doubt, did not want it repeated for reasons having to do with the youngsters, his career reputation, and his image of self as a skillful person. He talked about his work with the group:

> . . . I talk with the teacher members weekly, with the administrative members weekly, touch base with them about the project, talk with the assistant superintendent and the superintendent probably every other week, talk with a parent of a child in the program who is not on the Task Force and was totally turned off by the parents of other children in the program. I see him weekly. So, from all this, I could see concerns developing that might become problems, but we could deal with them before that happened.

And then, in response to my reflection that, "If you catch the bubbles before you put your clay in the oven . . . ," he said:

Yeah, if you keep on massaging what you're working on, you get the bubbles up. And I guess that's a real analogy for what I do, because my almost constant communication with people is very much like massaging a piece of clay, trying to find bubbles, which are their concerns. And then I try to bring out the concerns so that they are expressed and so they don't lay inside to explode when the finished product is done.

The imagery is both delightful and instructive. It is almost as if this administrator uses as a guide for his thinking a sort of Murphy's Law that says, "If anything can go wrong, it most certainly will." And this is not to be tentative, doubtful, or "paranoid" about administrative work in the schools. Rather, it seems a quite reasonable anticipatory stance to take in situations where one does not exercise direct control over events, a point that was made earlier in this book. The message is a pretty simply one, but also one that has continual and, perhaps, overriding meaning for how school administrators think about and engage with their work. It is that it is just naive to assume that because a group of well-intended people have been brought together to work on a project everything will fall into place over time. For a variety of reasons familiar to any administrator, it is probably a safer bet to assume the opposite—that without care being given to the circumstances, to the group, and its development, the project will disintegrate through inattention to "bubbles" or potential ones.

Thus, we see the administrator "massaging" his materials in order to get the bubbles up and popped before there is an explosion. Notice, too, that it seems not to be a heavy handed kind of thing he does. Rather, one almost gets a feeling of gentleness about the way he described what he does and thinks about. In effect, as he talks with and listens to the various parties that make up the group with which he is working, his behavior allows the bubbles to become visible. The point is well-taken in the sense that it appears that the way he thinks about working at his craft is that it involves a dictum, "The more you force, the less you get." Unless you are looking to force an explosion, that is. And there are times, of course, when an explosion *is* desired but one would have to say that this would be an infrequent set of circumstances.

There is another point that I think needs to be raised about the idea of gentle "massaging" in order to bring out the bubbles. Simply put, it is an adult way of working. By talking, listening, and seeking out concerns so that they can be dealt what gets communicated by this administrator is that he has confidence that the group will be able to deal with them. Put another way, what to my way of thinking occurs as this administrator seeks out bubbles in the clay is that he performs an educative function with the group by helping them learn how to confront and deal with the problems that emerge during their work together.

To elaborate a bit, school administrators are always teaching, and the content of the lessons they teach is concerned with their own preferred way of working at their craft. It is not likely that they think of themselves deliberately doing this, but deliberateness is not the issue. The people, particularly other administrators or teachers with administrative aspirations, with whom administrators work, I believe, are continual observers of his or her behavior with the idea of learning from it—learning what to do or what not to do; how to think or how not to think.

Everyone, of course, develops their own cueing systems that helps them become aware of potential or actual "bubbles" in the material with which they are working. For example, a superintendent I know pays particular attention to the nonverbal behavior of members of his school board during a meeting. The way they sit, whether or not they shift around a lot in their chairs, the amount of "gazing at the ceiling" that occurs all have meaning for this man. For one school principal, "It's almost as though caution lights go on in my head whenever I hear anybody say, 'I want this done' or 'This has to be done.' I start to delay things a bit to give myself time to poke around." What is important is not the content of any one individual's cueing system but that it works satisfactorily for her or him. Recall, for example, the quotation from our potter early in the book when she said,

> You have to watch out for air bubbles. Sometimes you sense that something's wrong and sometimes you see it. Sometimes you feel it in the clay. You can feel how things are going and you simply learn to make judgments about what's going on through experience.

Substitute a word here and there, and instead of a potter and clay you have a school administrator sensing how things are going with the human material being worked with.

As I indicated earlier, there was more talk in the interviews I held about the analogy of "knots in the wood" than about "bubbles in the clay." And the reason for this, I suggested, is that the concept of "knots" as obstructions to work permits alternative ways of working in a manner that "bubbles" does not. You must get rid of the bubbles but not necessarily the knot. And certainly another difference between the two ideas is that bubbles have to be actively looked for and "popped," whereas knots are simply in the wood. You don't have to look for them. They become known to the administrator-craftsperson in the ordinary course of working through one situation or another.

What seems generally to be the case is that when administrators reflect on the notion of "knots in the wood," their thinking goes in the direction of people's behavior or attitudes or organizational conditions that somehow are perceived as standing in the way of something the administrator wants to do. And this point, too, suggests a difference between the bubble and knot ideas. There is a certain type of transiency associated with the former. Bubbles may be elusive, but they don't resist being found or popped. Knots, on the other hand, as we noted, are not hard to find. They can be seen with no effort. But, of course, they cannot be simply done away with by popping them. In fact, you cannot pop them at all and, as any woodcarver will tell you, because the wood in a knot tends to be very hard, you may break a knife blade trying to work with or around one.

Under this very general category of "standing in the way" of something the administrator wanted to do, four themes seemed to emerge from my observations and interviews. Certainly, these themes do not represent the universe of resistance-oriented themes, and they are not used here in that sense but, once more, as illustrative of a concept. These themes had to do with "knots in the wood" being symbolized in the form of vested interests in particular ways of doing something, territorial concerns, teachers who resist changing their ideas about teaching, and occasions in which it appears that an individual is placing his or her personalized interest in a matter ahead of the district's or school's. We have examples of these themes. First, is a case of a person or group having a vested interest in a previous way of doing things, starting with the thoughts of a new high school principal:

> People have been very receptive to me. I think there was a real need to make some forward motion in this school and people are really happy to see that happening. So there hasn't been a really awful barrier. There is one thing, though. A few years ago, they started a program here called the Pre-Competency Program. Some of those involved are still here and were part of it and they cling to it still as being a panacea for ninth graders. And they don't want to really look at other options.
>
> So if I think about that as a knot, I think my decision is almost always to include it. And I think that most of the time, unless it's something that would be really destructive to the group, it's better for them to work it through than for me to do it. And sometimes it's a good knot to have as part of it all, because it is viable. It's a choice that should be presented along with the others. But if I thought I couldn't live with something, I would probably tell the people involved so that they wouldn't bother to pursue it.

Take note of the character of the thinking used by this principal. The first paragraph in the excerpt sets the stage. The knot is observed and it takes the form of some teachers wanting to retain a program that had, for most intents and purposes, been discarded. What to do? is the question with which the principal is confronted.

With practically no hesitation, the decision is "almost always to include it," make it part of the design, as it were, except if by such inclusion it would be destructive of the grand design or, possibly, of some of its aesthetics. What we are dealing with is a critical rule of thumb by which this principal—a very successful and prestigious one, I might add—guides her administrative life. The rule of thumb "almost always to include it" (the knot) provides the key. That is, we have an image of an administrator-craftsperson playing the role of instructional leader but with an eye on maintaining the wholeness of the organization.

A side point is, then, that as we attend to the way administrators think about the decisions they have to make, we also start to develop an image of the way they see themselves in their position.

If maintaining the wholeness of the organization sounds like a complicated task, then the reader is correct. It is the polar opposite, for example, of the attitude of a principal I once knew who, bent on creating radical change in a school, took as his guiding rule of thumb: "If you aren't with us, you're against us." A heavy hand was at work in that case, with a quick decision "to get rid of the knot" and, as a matter of fact, the principal in question was quite successful in doing just that. In our present case, though, it seems to me that the principal was gentler and perhaps more skillful at her craft. It was important—and this, as I implied, lay beneath the decision to include—to maintain the wholeness of things, to avoid "splitting the wood."

But note, as well, that this desire to maintain the school's wholeness did not extend to every circumstance. Where it stopped was "if I thought I couldn't live with something." To go back to the woodcarver metaphor, the point is this: If the inclusion of a knot would have the effect of unacceptably violating the woodcarver's image of what he or she was trying to produce, then somehow the knot has to be excised. Or, if this doesn't work well, the piece of wood can be thrown away. Woodcarvers, of course, can do just that. School administrators most certainly don't have that luxury. In effect, what this means is that they may, at times, have to tolerate "knots" they'd rather not have and try to work in ways that diminish the knot's impact on the total scheme of things.

In school systems, as in any other type of work organization, problems associated with territorial prerogatives need continually to be recognized and attended to. In one school district, for example, a predicament had arisen concerning the high school honor society and the basis on which youngsters were selected for membership. For years, in fact from the inception of the honor society, a committee of teachers had the responsibility for establishing criteria for membership and then making the selections. But problems had developed and there was a good bit of dissension about things. The school board was unhappy with this state of affairs and inserted itself into the situation. As the superintendent said:

> They kept trying and pushing and pushing and shoving. My solution was to leave it alone. I told them that if they got into it, they'd make it worse. I felt like a woodcarver. I knew what I wanted to do, but the Board's desires—it was like a knot in the wood. So, in a sense, I had to build the knot in the wood into the design of what I was trying to do. And I had to protect them, the Board, from themselves in the sense that if we ever want the honor society in this district to survive, we've got to keep the Board out of it. Teachers volunteer their time for this kind of thing and if they sensed the Board wanted to move into it, that would be the end of that. And that would be detrimental to the kids.
>
> So what I had to do with the Board was to create an illusion that got them to think that they were going to be part of the picture. And yet I knew they were

not goint to be part of the picture. They had a little piece, but it was a cosmetic thing. I had to keep sidestepping and I took a few potshots for it, but I think the thing is alive and well because I managed to keep the Board out of the teachers' territory.

As in the case of the earlier anecdote about the principal who included vested interests into the overall design, so too it appears is this case of territorial encroachment. There are differences, of course, as one gets the feeling that the including efforts of the principal were nonmanipulative whereas the focus of the superintendent's work was clearly manipulative—to create an illusion when little actually existed. This, incidentally, is not to suggest any negative value should be attached to the notion of manipulation, which I take to be a value-neutral term. What is interesting from the point of view of administration-as-craft is the thought that the ability to create an illusion that something is so when it really isn't is probably as important a craft skill as one can think of, particularly from the vantage point of the superintendency. For example, Burlingame (1981) suggests that two primary ways that superintendents have of maintaining power are by using the tactics of mystification and cover-up.

As a political institution the focal point of school is the superintendent's office, and the superintendent is chief political craftsperson on the levels of both strategy and tactics. And part of his or her craft work, whether we find it appealing or not, is at times to create illusionary designs that communicate a picture that is believable but really does not exist.

Creating the illusion of including a territorial knot into an overall design takes on somewhat of a different flavor in the following comments of a superintendent, which are hypothetical in the sense that he visualizes a situation that might happen.

Well, we have a District Planning Committee and suppose they started to get involved in an area of a negotiated item on the union contract. That does not have a place in the discussions of the Planning Committee. It's not their territory and I would probably tell them that. However, I might not and that would depend on whether or not, if I let it develop a bit, I could get some advantage by dividing and conquering. That might be viewed as devious, but because of some particular district need, I might want to think twice about stepping in and reminding them that they overstepped the boundary line. I might want to use their interest in the item as leverage to change the contract the next time we negotiate.

So we have two ways of dealing with territorial knots in the wood; the use of either seems to depend on the superintendent's sense of what can be gained by going in one direction or the other. Clearly, this is the type of thinking that attaches to any craft, as in the question "How can I use my skills and understandings to make the best product with these materials?" And, in this case, it is answered in two ways. First, it was to observe the emergence of a knot and, to continue the metaphor, to excise it in short order—"That does not have a place in the discussions of the Planning Committee." Further, one suspects, if this is the tactic taken, then it best be done quickly before it becomes too big to deal with in this manner. The larger a knot becomes, the more difficult it is to get rid of by cutting it out of the wood.

Second, the administrator might decide that more is to be gained by letting the knot become bigger because she or he might use it in other things that need to be done. Thus, I sense, the administrator includes it in the current project that is being worked on but with the foreknowledge that, as in the previous territorial case discussed, he or she is engaged in creating illusions.[1] Further, if the administrator is skillful (and a little lucky), the illusion becomes part of the reality of a different project somewhere down the line a bit. Being able to do this well involves not only an administrator's keen sense of the present and what is happening of the moment, it also involves a sense of how this present may relate to a number of possible futures. Highly skilled administrative craftspeople, I suspect, do indeed have to live in two temporal worlds, now and the future. And certainly they need to have a sense of the past, what it means for now, and what it may mean for the future. One of the implications of this is that to be skilled in the craft of administration is a much more intellectually complex enterprise than it is if one is a prize-winning potter or woodcarver.

If you ask a school principal who is interested (as are most of them) in the quality of teaching that goes on in his or her school to describe the expertise of the faculty to you, the chances are the principal will respond in the normal curve fashion, without the jargon. That is, within the faculty there will be a few "stars," a bunch of "okay teachers," and a few duds—tenured faculty who never were good teachers, were good at one time but have "lost it," or are barely adequate and show no inclination to want to change. They are the instructional knots in the wood, so to speak, and probably account for more frustration in the lives of committed principals than any other single or combination of factors in their work world. It is about such a teacher that one principal from a small rural district said to me, "I'm ashamed that this person has the right to call himself a teacher." But what to do about it? The teacher has tenure and is not grossly incompetent. But he is poor enough to cause this principal frustration and not a little anguish—a knot in the wood in the image of a school she would like to create. In the following interview excerpt, this principal talked about herself and her problem of dealing with the knot. We had used the craft and woodcarver metaphor fairly frequently in our discussion, and she said:

It's sure like a knot in the wood, but it's also me. If I had a block of wood from which I wanted to make a cup, and yet the form of the wood, the grain, the lines would really be conducive to make a duck, I would more than likely still try and make it a cup. And I would probably feel frustrated through the process because part of me would know the wood was intended to be a duck and I think it would

> bother me. And I think that's what it is with this guy. He's my knot in the wood of the school and it seems like I can't turn him into anything else. I have not made him a good teacher. I try to work with his strengths, use him in some way, put him in charge of the bus routing kind of thing and yet I'm frustrated because I still want him to turn into a good teacher and I don't think he ever will. So the wood and its knots talk back to me and let me know that it doesn't matter what I want to make. It'll be what it'll be, but that's not good enough.

It's almost a classic case of "You're damned if you do and you're damned if you don't." Nothing seems to work in trying to get the teacher to change or to include the teacher's skills, which are apparently minimal, into the instructional image the principal has for the school. On the other hand, to do nothing is not satisfactory either, at least for the principal's peace of mind. She cannot excise the knot, nor can she throw the piece of wood away, and its continued existence spoils the way the school looks, at least through the eyes of the principal. The point is that situations do exist, particularly in smaller systems as this one is, where people can be moved only with difficulty, that the options about what to do with a knot such as we've described are extremely limited. The principal in this case, for example, has to live with the knowledge that there is little that she can do to alter what she sees. And curiously, she seems to acknowledge that part of the problem is her own in the sense that she hasn't learned, and, thankfully, probably won't, to settle for less than what she really wants. Perhaps this is one mark of a person who is master of her or his craft. But it is also a sure recipe for frustration, particularly when the essence of that craft involves working with and through other people.

A sentiment similar to the principal's was expressed by a superintendent who, by the very nature of his position, had more options available to him. His position was that everybody had a niche and part of his job was helping to find it. He said:

> I really try to match up the principal and the teachers. I'm not always successful, but I do a lot of it. So, in your terms, I try to incorporate the knot into the design. Unless the knot is filled with worms and there's no hope for it. . . .

Thus in situations such as these, where bothersome conditions exist and there seems to be little hope of changing things, I suspect that school administrators, like the rest of us, try to bury their frustrations in the deep recesses of their psyche in the hopes of making peace with themselves. It is all part of the yin and yang of school life.

So far we have been talking about knots in the wood as potentially obstructive situations that exist without regard to anything an administrator may have done. They are simply part of the conditions of school life, to be encountered and handled hopefully with satisfactory outcomes. The implication of this thought is, of course, that administrators do not err and that problems they encounter are always associated with the materials they work with, not with anything they may have said or done. Nothing could be further from the truth. Superintendents and principals do and say things that have the effect of creating knots where none had existed. I recall, for example, some years ago a colleague of mine at another university telling me that he was going to devote the rest of his career to bringing about the downfall of a recently arrived dean who had taken positions that had resulted in the creation of several knots, and in politically wrong places, I might add. And my colleague did precisely that.

Admittedly, that was a rather extreme case, but the point is well taken. Sometimes, administrators, with all the very best intentions, do or don't do things that have the effect of creating problems (knots) for them whether they recognize them or not. The knots are induced into the wood (a physical impossibility unless one thinks metaphorically) by an administrative error. There is a further complicating factor about all this. It is that the knots that have been discussed previously as already existing in the wood tend to be easily discernible. However, those that are induced by the administrator tend to remain beneath the surface and not exposed to view.

As noted earlier, the knots in the faculty's "wood," for example, are not difficult to observe once a principal starts to work with that faculty, particularly as she or he tries to induce change in a school. This is another way of making the point of a statement that has been attributed to psychologist Kurt Lewin who reputedly coined the term *group dynamics*: "If you want to learn about an organization, try and change it." It is a neat thought with the implication that as a person tries to alter established patterns of thinking and action in an organization's life, the very effort of doing so almost automatically uncovers resistance—the knots we have been talking about. This resistance, of course, can take a variety of forms, running from behavior that is overt and above board to that which is covert and possibly subversive. In any event, one doesn't have to be an extraordinarily aware person to understand (1) that knots exist, and (2) where they are and what they look like. The reason for this is that through the very process of living into adulthood and, possibly, with additional conceptual help of some academic experience, most administrators are simply aware of the fact that when they embark on a program of change, they will encounter resistance. They may even have foreknowledge of where to look for it. In fact, I suspect if they are highly skilled, this will indeed be the case.

These circumstances, though, are different from those that occur when an administrator, perhaps mostly through an unintended error of one sort or another, creates knots in the wood where none had previously existed. And the critical point is this: Unless the feedback channels are open, which is typically not the case, the administrator is (1) aware neither of having erred nor of having created a knot, and (2) surprised to find out at some point further down the road that he or she did.

These conditions are common to the experience of all of us. For example, who among us has not had occasion after having attended a staff meeting to stop in a co-worker's office in order to hold a confidential postmeeting critique in which the administrator's insensitivity or lack of skill has not been the topic? When we observe knots being created, albeit unintentionally, there is a tendency for us not to engage in authentic feedback about it. It is easier to withdraw or, if our own ox is being gored, simply to fight.

The following is an example of the opposite having occurred. It involves a superintendent and his assistant, a close colleague and confidant, who erred in an important way and created a knot in the wood which they would not have been able to work with had the character of their relationship not been what it was.

Every once in a while, I guess you forget the things that work. You make some assumptions you shouldn't and try to become cutesy. Here's an example. My superintendent and I, every once in a while, spend some time thinking and reflecting about what we've been trying to do in the district over the last ten years.

Last year, after one of these sessions together, we said, "Hey, you know what, we have a total system model here." We talked about it, we wrote it up, and we looked at the interrelatedness of it all, and we said, "Boy, you know, it really makes an awful lot of sense." And we decided that we'd just get the message across to our staff and our staff would know and feel that they are part of a much larger goal than just being a good teacher in a classroom.

The way we decided to do this was to bring twenty people together and tell them about our great insight. But we miscalculated. We didn't do the preparation. We didn't prepare ourselves and we didn't prepare the materials, that is, the people. We were thinking as administrators—theoretical.

Anyhow, we got them together and we had our legs knocked out from under us. Their rejection was completely unanticipated. It was a total shock to us. Our problem—he and I decided as we talked it over on the way home—was that we were talking in two different languages. The superintendent and I were talking in one and the teachers in another. We were talking about the grand plan and the teachers were saying, "What do you mean?" They were polite, but that's all it was. They were being polite.

It really took us a full year to make the connection between what we thought was important and the practices we used. They were saying, "When you talk that way to us, that's not where we live." What we had to do is to get down to where they were so we could bring them up. One of us alone couldn't have done it. There would have been no one to talk with.

On the one hand, this anecdote is a rather simple example of skilled administrative craftspeople at work. They knew what they wanted to produce, found out that they had made a mistake in the way they were working, and started over again. A relatively uncomplicated business, one might think. On the other hand, as is so often the case, there was much more going on than met the eye at first glance. For example, the cue that their approach had created a knot was the response of the teachers, which was, as the assistant superintendent said, "polite." There is nothing wrong with "polite" responses, of course, unless they are somehow out of context. And this is not to say that rudeness should have been the order of the day. Rather, the politeness is taken to mean a sort of distancing noninvolvement. But the critical point is that both of these people had to understand what the politeness meant and, in terms of our present discussion, it meant that they had created a knot in the wood. The teachers' response, though, was not to tell the two of them that they had created a problem. Rather, they were simply polite—a response that was apparently atypical, its very atypicality providing the cue that something was wrong.

And so we have the remainder of the story. The two were able to understand what they had inadvertently done. "We were humbled a little bit, but we said, 'Hey, is it still good?' And we said to ourselves, 'Yeah, it's still good.'" Back to the drawing boards, then. Out went the piece of wood with the knot in it that they had created. And a year later, after relearning the fact that they had to talk the teachers' language, they produced what they originally had in mind.

I close this chapter with a thought that I think has been implicit in everything that has preceded it. Although there are rules of thumb to guide the practice of administrative craftwork, what rule to attend to and how to attend to it inevitably becomes a matter of an individual making a judgment about the state of affairs with which he or she is confronted. It is simply not true that what is good for the goose is good for the gander, at least in the type of concerns that are the focus of this book. And this is simply a way of saying that you, the reader, and I, the writer, will arrive at different decisions about whether or not a knot in the wood should be incorporated into what we're trying to do and how to do it, or to excise the knot and, hopefully, not break our carving knife in the process.

• Endnote

1. Lest the reader become upset with these two descriptions of superintendents thinking about their work, let me say that I know both of these individuals quite well. One would be hard put to find people more interested in and committed to the quality education of youngsters than they. However, their work world is a political one and they must behave politically in order to survive and get things done.

Chapter Twelve

Learning the Craft

This chapter is a companion to Chapter Nine, the focus of which was "Knowing the Right Thing to Do." The idea that undergirded that theme was the development of a memory bank out of experience. In fact, it was posited that when administrators talk about how they know what to do because of their experience, they are really talking about their memory. In this chapter, we will explore in more detail those elements of their experience from which they seem somehow able to learn and both open their memory bank account and continue to make deposits in it.

The following two anecdotes are very striking. A veteran superintendent told me this story:

The superintendent of a neighboring district, a guy in his first superintendency, called me one day. There was going to be an open school board meeting in his district that evening about moving kindergarten classes to different buildings because of declining enrollments. He wanted to know if I had any advice for him. After he described the situation, I told him that though I didn't know exactly who the actors in the play would be and how things would come down, I thought he ought to expect several things. First, when the public participated, there would be people who started with the kindergarten issue, but that pretty soon other issues would be introduced that were totally unrelated. This would happen because a good number of people really don't know what they're doing at the meeting. The next thing I told him was that if he needed support from key administrators, like his principals, and he wanted to make sure they would be there to respond to questions, they should be seated with him. Otherwise, when the pressure got intense, they would most likely go out for a walk in the halls or underneath the bleachers.

The next morning, bright and early, I got a phone call from him. What I told him to expect had happened. The kindergarten issue didn't last beyond the first person. They they were all over the lot on unrelated issues. He had not asked his principals to sit with him. And three out of four had disappeared when he looked.

The second anecdote explores a situation that occurred while a student of mine shadowed a principal around during a school day as part of a study of the principalship in which she was engaged. She said:

As we were walking down the hall there were these common, ordinary noises that would probably exist in any building, not necessarily a school. They're the kind that you sort of sift out of your own mind and continue on. Then *she* heard—I didn't—a noise which to her was distinctly different than other kinds of subtle noises that were going on, and she said, "Wait a minute. I hear something upstairs." I was puzzled. I said, "What do you mean?" And she said, "There's somebody up there who I don't think belongs in the school." I didn't have a clue to what she was talking about, so we ran up the stairs and, sure enough, we found three young men up there from the high school. She ushered them out.

I have no doubt that circumstances such as these occur innumerable times each day in the school year as principals, superintendents, and their administrative colleagues sense something, observe and interpret something, or perhaps simply intuit something in ways that others of us are not able to do. I, at least, would not have been able to give the same response as the superintendent did to his colleagues, nor would I have heard the same kind of noises as the principal. Somewhere and somehow, it seems, a special kind of learning took place.

When asked about how he knew to give the response he did, the superintendent said:

Over the years, particularly in situations where the public became openly involved in an issue, I began to realize that patterns of behavior that develop were similar regardless of what the problem was. I suddenly discovered that in a public meeting only a few people really know what it's about. The others come, or so it seems, because they are opposed to the established order and what you are trying to do. So the meeting provides an opportunity for them to bring up issues that have been festering a while. And I think what happens with the principals, because they live closer to the parents than the superintendent, is that they figure when the going gets hot, it's better not to be visible so that they don't risk the possibility of being identified with an unpopular decision.

With regard to the principal's ability to hear and interpret particular kinds of noises in a school, my student said:

> Afterwards, I asked her how she knew; how she heard the noise I didn't hear; and how she was able to decipher that the noises were not the ordinary ones of the school. And she said, "If I have to tell you explicitly, I couldn't. I just felt it. It's in my sensors. I just knew that these were not the noises of my school."

Both responses, situation-specific as they were, shed a bit of light, but by no means the whole story, on how one learns to know things about practicing the craft of administration. In the case of the superintendent, what seemed to be operating was his ability, in an inductive fashion, to develop a rule of thumb, a nonscientifically arrived at principle, from a large number of experiences in which similar patterns of individual and group behavior had been observed. Having tested out that rule over a period of time and more or less confirming it, he was able to say with some sense of reliability, "Under Condition X, the chances are pretty good that you can expect Behavior Y."

The situation with the principal, though, is different. The parallel with which all of us are familiar is the manner in which parents (mothers more reliably so than fathers, I suspect) seem able or say they are able to tell what's troubling an infant by the nature of its cry. Based on their experience with the particular infant, they are simply attuned to it in ways that nonparents of *that* infant are not. It is important to note the particularity noted here. By that I mean that it is undoubtedly true that the principal could not walk into a strange school and make the same judgments about, in this case, noises that she heard. Indeed, in order to do that, one must live with, be part of, and want to understand a school in ways that others cannot. Further, I think it's true that experience is only a good teacher when a person understands that experience can be a good teacher. It is the old story of whether or not a person has thirty years of teaching experience or one year of teaching experience thirty times.

We are led, then, in this chapter to the task of trying to understand the various answers that may be given to the question of how administrators learn their craft. Three major learning conditions seem to be involved. First is the formal graduate school course of study that all administrators must engage in in order to take a step on the road to receiving state certification as an administrator. Second is the administrative internship experience which is typically, but not universally, part of a prospective administrator's graduate program. And third is the continuing experience of holding an administrative position.

• Learning in Graduate School

What becomes critically important to understand about graduate programs in school administration is that in them one does not learn how to be an administrator, though indeed one may learn about administration. This difference will become clear by a brief comparison between these programs and, for example, dental school. In the latter, over a period of three full-time years, a student studies such things as the basic physiology and anatomy of the jaw the treatment of tooth decay and gum disease. One learns and practices a variety of dental skills on models of the jaw and teeth. And, while in dental school, a student has "hands on" practical experience in the school's clinic. The result of all this is that when a person graduates from dental school, he or she has learned the basic skills necessary to start the practice of dentistry. Most dentists will tell you, of course, that the start of their practice was when they really started to learn dentistry.

There are structural similarities between a graduate program in administration and dental school, as well as some very marked differences. Depending on the college or university they attend, administrative students may study some "basic" sciences in the psychological or sociological tradition, mostly with a concern for application, however. They also may take course work in such fields as staff development, supervision, curriculum, organizational change, and so forth. These courses are likely to have both a theory component and a skill component in which they may learn and practice, in a sort of make-believe laboratory setting, such things as how to listen better, how to summarize group discussion, or how to analyze and diagnose school organizational problems. The practical clinical experience is the internship. Finally, most people enrolled in administrative programs are part-time and the total time they spend in study and practice certainly comes nowhere near the dental student's three years. Perhaps this is a way of suggesting that society considers our mouths more important than our schools, or that mouths are much more difficult to learn about than are schools.

But perhaps the most important thing to attend to is the matter of skill development. In dental school, the learning of skills is not left to chance experience. There is learning and practice and more learning and practice. And there is close clinical supervision of the results. No such parallel exists or possibly can exist in administrative programs. There may be some focus on skills, but it is far removed from the real "tooth."

If graduate school programs in administration really don't train people in the practice of that field, as it may, in fact, be logically impossible to do, what do they do? What is it that prospective administrators learn about their craft from going to graduate school? I asked this question of the people whom I observed and with whom I talked. A few, a distinct few, of the responses had to do with the learning of techniques or, as one man put it, referring to his Masters Degree program, ". . . that was the nuts and bolts sort of thing." Predominantly, though, as the superintendents and principals I talked with reflected on their graduate school experience, their thoughts had little to do with skills or techniques they had learned. Rather, what they talked about centered on ways of thinking about administration, on concepts. Here is a fair sampling of their remarks:

- My professors . . . what I really got from them was a philosophical base for administration. There was not too much from the practical side of things, but they helped me think about decisions I would have to make. The practical part comes with doing the job. But the experience of putting things into a philosophical frame of reference—that was really important, and it's stuck with me for a lot of years.

- What really happened in graduate school was that I started to develop a perspective on what it was like to be a school administrator. And then I took that perspective to the job and exercised my own skills through it. And another thing. My graduate program helped me understand that it was important to continue to learn.

- It helped me tie things together. And I guess I can say that it tied in very nicely because I enjoyed it so much. It helped me describe social behavior in a way, in a vocabulary, that I hadn't had. I got handles for things and I was able to describe things for myself and, more importantly, I was able to describe events to others in that language and that helps me understand it better for myself.

What is being said, then, as these people were able to reflect on it, was that the major contribution their graduate programs made to their practice is that they started to develop a way of thinking about being an administrator and "doing" administration. They learned about administration, what administration is about, but they didn't learn administration.

And notice this. While both the prospective school administrators and the prospective dentist leave graduate school supposedly prepared to practice, it is the dentist whose practice skills, it appears, were learned in school. For the most part this is not so for the administrator, who may indeed learn *what* to do but almost for sure, not *how* to do it.

One may ask, then, if what happens in graduate school is that a person may (1) learn some techniques or nuts and bolts of administration, and (2) develop a perspective of administrative work and a language with which to communicate about it, is that enough? Given my concept of administrative practice as being highly idiosyncratic, I'd have to say, "I think so." In fact, to perform those two functions well may be precisely what is needed and, indeed, all that can be expected.

• Learning in an Administrative Internship

As I noted previously, the administrative internship is the structural parallel of the clinical part of dental training. The parallelism, though, doesn't take us too far as there are distinct differences in the dynamics of the two situations. Some of these have already been mentioned, the most important being the opportunity of budding dentists to learn and practice skills under close clinical supervision.

The circumstances of close clinical supervision simply do not exist in administrative internships. There is another potentially very important difference in the two training experiences. It is that every clinical instructor in dental school is a dentist whereas it is not necessarily the case that every intern supervisor is or has been an administrator. The import of this is that if I am supervising an administrative intern, as I once briefly did, though I may help him or her understand a situation in ways not previously thought about, and though I may offer opinions about what to do and how to do it, I cannot do that based on things I learned as a school administrator. I simply have never been one. Regardless of what may be its problems as a learning vehicle, the internship does enable prospective administrators to learn what they, at least, think are some pretty important things.

I talked with numbers of interns, both in one-to-one meetings and in a group situation. Some important things were said, as these people reflected on what they were learning as administrative interns. What follows provides a flavor of what that learning is all about.

Perhaps what is learned most centrally as an intern is what it means relative to one's perspective on education to move out of the classroom into a position where one has some responsibility for broader organizational functioning. It is, indeed, an interesting thing to understand that a teacher may teach for years without finding out what it means to run a school. Engaging in an internship quickly changes that situation. The change of territory and territorial responsibilities may come as a rather rude shock. Again, though I may use only one or two examples of a particular idea, they are representatives of the whole. A woman stated the following about her seeing things and herself differently:

> I've learned a lot about myself, so much about myself. And there are days when I'm having a bad time and I'll say, "Why did I ever leave the classroom? In the classroom I was queen for a day. I had the kids and a whole lot of autonomy and it was terrific." But then I've said to myself, "You know what? There's a part of me that's become so stretched by this experience. It's so much more validating about who I am and what I'm about."

At least part of the experience and what people learn in it cuts both ways. They leave the classroom with its relatively certainty of structure, process, and control for an environment that is characterized by uncertainty of these factors. So, in a way, they learn more about the classroom. Another intern put it this way:

> You know, I was a teacher. I had my room and my kids. It was safe. It was my territory. They were my rules. The kids knew me and I knew them. All this is not true now. So one thing this job has done for me is it has taken away my tunnel vision of one room—my territory. I'm getting a picture of the whole school. Things I took for granted as a teacher I now see as part of the whole process of running

the school. I told my wife. I said, "You have to be alive. You have to be on your toes, alert. You have to make some decisions on the spot. You have to not only be an administrator, but a counselor, teacher, disciplinarian, supervisor. And you play in the whole ballpark and there's no single mode of operating."

Change of perspective, indeed, and not only relative to the environment for which one has responsibility but for the role one plays—a person in charge of things. One intern put it this way as he thought about his experience of hiring teachers aides:

All of a sudden in these interviews it dawned on me, "Whoa, I'm sitting here and I'm being perceived as the boss." I've not been perceived that way before. You know, there are different sets of rules people use in each situation and when you're perceived as the boss, people act differently than when you're seen as a peer.

I think this is a critical learning juncture for prospective school administrators. They have all been teachers and are accustomed to being in control of and "boss" of their classroom (made clear by comments about "my room," "my rules," "my kids," "my territory"). But classrooms are populated with youngsters and we expect them not only to defer to teachers as teachers but also to teachers as adults. Once into administration, though, the scenery and the *dramatis personnae* change. The classroom as a place of work changes to the office, hallway, or conference room. In addition, most of the people with whom one deals are adults and so the question becomes, How does one learn about authority and its appropriate use when all one's prior experience has been with youngsters who, by their own training, were taught to acknowledge your authority, even, at times, your absolute right to do certain things?

Each intern must find the answer to this question for himself or herself. And its answer, as well as the answer to many other questions about oneself as an administrator, seems tor revolve around the ability, as several people put it, to become a "sponge." Further, I suspect, the extent to which one can become a learning sponge is related to the extent one perceives the internship as a potentially powerful learning experience. As an example, one person said that she realized:

This was my time to learn the ropes. So I've often had talks with myself about being a sponge and saying, "Okay, soak it in. Watch them. Watch how they handle certain situations." I was very deliberate about it and I made sure I asked a whole lot of questions.

This idea of being a deliberate and conscious learner during an internship was echoed many times and in many ways. It was almost as though the people involved understood the need, if they were to become school administrators, for starting to develop a usable memory of techniques, skills, or understandings for their future work. Observations of others as a way to start to learn was apparently the primary initial learning mode. And, indeed, this is a safe way to start; that is, it is hard to make a mistake while observing. Of course, it went beyond that. Individuals sought or were given unsolicited tips about how to do certain things, for example. And they seemed to be acutely aware of the kinds of learning experiences they needed to get quickly under their belt so that they could begin to function as a colleague. One person said, in this respect, "I sat in with her on discipline cases. I asked to sit in, especially in the beginning, because my background is elementary and this was a junior-senior high. Very different."

The list of things learned and how they were learned by these people could be extended at some length. To do that, though, would miss the point, which is that there is probably a psychology of learning a craft, any craft, that is different from those psychologies that may be useful for understanding the learning dynamics of a classroom. In particular, if the administrative internship is considered to be a first formal learning experience aimed at learning the craft of administration, consider these points:

- Participation is voluntary.
- Participants need to learn in order to survive.
- The learning that takes place, for the most part, has immediate application to the task of survival.
- The internship is seen as a first step to new career opportunities and advancement.
- Given the previous point, the internship provides a relatively safe environment in which to see how well the "shoe fits."

These and probably other factors combine to make for a rather unique learning situation. It may possibly be a more powerful one than student teaching is considered to be for undergraduates. And I think if this is the case, it is because undergraduates are just that—students in college. Administrative interns, on the other hand, are experienced adults who have made a decision to try out something new. They seem to be highly motivated to learn and the internship is, so to speak, their learning oyster.

Through it all, though, there is an underlying point that needs to be borne in mind, particularly when we address the problems of learning administrative craft skills. One intern expressed the point this way:

What I've come to understand and what I think is very important is that as far as the skills are concerned, it is probably more a matter of refining those that I already have than learning brand new things. What I mean is something like this: I've always thought I've been a good listener, but I've learned I've got to be better. Or, I've always been able to ask good questions, but I've got to learn to ask better ones.

To start to understand these thoughts about refining one's skills, about becoming better at doing things one already knows how to do, is to start to understand a lot about the essentials of the craft of administration. The point I want to emphasize, and I believe it to be critical to our understanding of the work of administrators, is that what is involved in learning to be a school principal or a superintendent is learning to transfer and elaborate on the skills and understandings one already has about living and dealing with individuals and groups into a new work environment. Having made such a general statement, I now need to pull back a bit and explain myself.

It was not my intent, for example, to suggest that administering a school or a school district is a simple or simpleminded matter. To the contrary, to be a school administrator, particularly if what is desired is beyond routine organizational maintenance, is a highly complex task that is intellectually taxing and physically and emotionally draining. But, by the same token, to be a school administrator, even the very best one, does not mean that one has a type of knowledge or a type of skill that is the property of only a few highly trained individuals. (This is not to say that there may not be something special about the ability of some administrators to lead, a matter to be taken up in Chapter Sixteen.) Quite the opposite; the kinds of skills necessary to administer a school or school district are very widely shared. We all learn them in other contexts through the experiences of growing up, going to school, and working for a living. And, though it is not a necessarily essential part of this living and learning package, I suspect it is helpful to marry and raise one's own family.

Clearly, though, there is more to it than that. I think the person we last quoted put her finger on it when she said that the problem was "more a matter of refining those [skills] I already have than learning brand new things." She went on to say, as an example, that she had to learn to be a *better* listener and to ask *better* questions. If we had pursued the conversation, I have little doubt that she would have agreed that she had to learn to refine other skills she already possessed—of problem solving, of disciplining, of public speaking, of negotiating, of working with groups, and on and on—all within the context of a school's social and work environment. I do not intend to imply that that is a simple matter. However, I do maintain that the knowledge and skills necessary to become a functioning school administrator are not of the same order as those needed to become a nuclear physicist. In a curious way, though, if we really considered what was involved in the crazy quilt pattern of administrative life, we might say that it was as complex a type of work as that of the physicist.

I close out this section of the administrative internship and learning the craft of administration with this summary thought: People start to learn the "know-how" of being school administrators in infancy and they add to that knowledge as they grow to adulthood. Implicitly, what happens more or less to interns is that their "know-how" is formalized a bit, perhaps codified, adapted, and refined.

• Learning the Craft On-the-Job

As with the learning of any other craft, learning to be better skilled at administrative practice is not a task that is completed at the close of what is taken to be the formal experiential training period, in our case, the administrative internship. However, there does appear to be an interesting difference in learning perspective between a person who is engaging in an internship and one who is engaged in full-time practice. With regard to the former, and quite properly so, we have a condition in which learning how to be an administrator is very much of a direct focus of the individual involved. He or she actively seems to seek out help in whatever form it may be available; actively appears to have her or his antennae out and tuned into the possibility of new learning experiences; and almost eagerly seems to engage in reflection on the what it means to view work in the school from an administrative perspective rather than that of the classroom. My sense is that most interns see that time as the one time they have in their prospective careers when they can be active learners and recognized as such. And this means that it is the one time they can make mistakes that can be treated as the errors made by anyone learning a new craft. What this suggests, in a way, is that mistakes made in the course of an internship may be made without the individual having to take responsibility for them as a full-fledged administrator. There is a certain freedom to err. This is not at all to suggest that interns don't feel a great deal of responsibility for what they do and the decisions they make. Indeed they do, for they still operate during this time in the very real world of the schools with real people and real problems.

It seems clear to me, though, that once a person becomes a full-time administrator of whatever stripe, his or her perspective on learning the craft changes and, again, quite properly so. Much as the focus of the internship is to learn how to be an administrator by being one, so the focus of being a school principal is, quite simply, to be a school principal—to decide, to act, to do. Another way of putting it might be to offer the thought that the intern is interested in *learning how to be* a principal whereas our full-time appointed person is concerned with *being* the principal. Learning about administration is not a focus for the latter; doing administration is. In other words, the conscious learning perspective of the intern becomes a thing of the past when one "plays for keeps."

This is not to say, of course, that once on the job, a person stops learning. It is to say, though, that learning how to be an administrator assumes a distinctly secondary focus in the life, for example, of a new school principal or superintendent. When hired, they are assumed to be competent, certainly not an unreasonable assumption, and for them to take the public position that they are still raw beginners would be highly impolitic and downright risky as far as their survival on the job is concerned. Obviously, a school board does not hire a person to be a superintendent so that the person can learn to be a superintendent.

Nevertheless, learning does occur in the sense of people adding to and refining their memory for their work. But it is also true that practicing administrators have much more difficulty talking about what is being learned than do interns. This is probably so because after having been on the job, minimally for a year so that they have the chance to live and work through a full cycle during which time they learn to be *the* administrator, they stop seeing new categories of events and primarily engage in refining skills and understandings they already have. So, once more, each day is not looked at as an opportunity to learn new things but perhaps as an opportunity to do new things.

If one is interested in what and how practicing administrators learn, one's approach to inquiry must be different than it is with interns. As the administrators I held conversations with reflected on their own learning of the craft of administration, they talked about four categories of events of experiences that had made an impression on them and that they could recall rather vividly; (1) situations in which they had made a glaring error, (2) learning to develop and trust their "sixth sense," (3) having had a positive role model, and (4) having had a negative role model.

• Learning from One's Errors

My initial approach to studying what it was in their work lives from which administrators learned, was to ask them about "peak" experiences they had experienced that had affected the way they practiced their craft. My approach was unproductive; the responses to my question were almost invariably fumbling ones. It was not that they could not recall a so-called "peak" experience but that the experience seemed not to have been used as a learning vehicle. It was not so much that the experience had occurred without regard for anything they might have done, any skill they might have exercised, but that it was unimportant. It was enough to get a feeling of having accomplished something very well without having attended to what one may have done to enable that accomplishment to take place. And this is not to say that these people did not learn anything from a very positive experience, but only to say, for the most part, that they could not recall with clarity what it was they had learned.

A much different response occurred, though, when the opposite question was asked. That is, when I asked if they could recall an experience in which they had learned something very important from having "screwed up," there was an abundance of laughs, rueful smiles, and clarity of memory. I am quite certain that the reader of this book will be able to smile his or her own rueful smile at this point with a rather clear memory of having "screwed up," which is simply a part of living and working, familiar to us all. It is common knowledge that we learn by mistakes, but it is still worthy of illustration as a way of understanding one way that school administrators learn their craft, and remember what they learned, while on the job. For example, here is how a superintendent replied:

> I remember my first year as assistant superintendent on my last job. Very early on, during the first month I was there I was given a pretty large staff assignment. I went off and did it by myself, alone, in isolation. When I brought the finished product back to our staff meeting, people were aghast that I hadn't even asked anyone's opinion, neither a peer nor a subordinate. And I guess I learned, really learned, that if you make decisions in a jar, even though they may be good ones, they just won't fly.

And here are the reflections of an elementary school principal:

> It was my first administrative job in a very small rural district. I had had a run-in with a teacher and my superintendent said, "What you should have done was jump right down this person's throat and let her know who's boss." Well, I tried that and the whole situation blew up. It took me six months to fix it.
>
> What I learned from that was not to be or try to be somebody I'm not. I'm not a stern confronter, by nature. Particularly with adults. I have to stick with who I am, soft spoken, and part of that means I never raised my voice at an adult since that time.

And, in rather direct fashion, a high school principal smiled and said:

> You bet. I once went to a superintendent's hearing with not all my ducks lined up. The parents took me on and that was that. I had not prepared properly. Since that time, I've never been unprepared.

As I implied earlier, the list of mistakes made and things learned from them is endless, and it is not our purpose to make some sort of category-oriented "mistake" statement about it. Rather, what is important is what appears to be the deliberateness of learning that attaches to having made an error. What is learned from making a mistake, especially where a person's competence is called into question more by himself or herself than by others, seems not to be treated casually, at all. If we can judge by these few examples, it is almost a case of each of these people giving themselves a little lecture on having discovered what for them was an important rule of thumb. The titles of the lectures might go something like this:

- The Superintendent: "If there's a chance that others should be involved, even a small chance, involve them."
- The Elementary Principal: "Don't let anyone push you into a role that doesn't fit what you think you are."
- The High School Principal: "Always make sure you prepare yourself well. Leave as little to chance as possible."

There is little that is complicated about all this. But the interesting thing about rules of thumb, it seems, is that the way to learn about them more vividly is to violate them. I have little doubt that each of the people we have discussed has heard the title of the "lecture" they gave themselves, undoubtedly if not the precise words, in some other context—in graduate school, in their family, at a professional development program, for example. Lectures, though, may not have much meaning without being accompanied by the experience to which they are supposed to apply. So, in a real sense, for example, one does not learn to make sure to involve others simply by involving them. One learns this by not involving them, finding out one has made a mistake and paying for it. At least, that is the theory of learning by error that seems to pertain to learning to practice a craft.

I don't think that this is a very startling insight; it is pretty common knowledge. What might be a bit surprising is that knowing it, we seem not to use our knowledge in any type of public forum. But this, too, is not startling given that we seem to be more prone to use our mistakes for personal and private learning while maintaining, if we can, an image of competence. It is simply more confortable and safe to do that, or so it seems. This personal and private comfort and safety may perhaps be best symbolized by the comment of an elementary school principal who was reflecting on a mistake she had made and what she had learned from it. The last thing she said about it was, "I guess I have my never-to-do-again file."

• Developing and Learning to Trust One's "Sixth Sense"

It should be abundantly clear by now that administering a school or a school system is not a logical, step-by-step process. The circumstances of work simply don't permit that, particularly during the daily rush of events. Further, what seems to be the case is that when we talk about learning to be an administrator and we use the word *experience* to describe that learning, we mean that one's work experience is the source of "deposits" in a "what-to-do-now" memory bank. This, of course, is not a mindless process; to the contrary, it may involve some judgments and decisions that are almost exquisite in their delicacy. And, of course, this is not to say that any particular superintendent, for example, may be aware at the time of the nature of what it is that has been learned and stored away for future use.

Ill-defined and sloppy as this "what-to-do" memory development may be, there is another that it is even more ill-defined and sloppier. It has to do with the learning, or as several people put it, of being able to trust their "sixth sense," their "gut." Certainly, this is not a new idea, but equally as certain, it is one that tends to be ignored by academics, perhaps because it is not possible to subject it to rational analysis.

I don't think that the "sixth sense" phenomenon is mystical, but I do think there may be a bit of mystery attached to it. Further, I do not have reference to an ESP type of idea, a premonition of something that is going to happen. Rather, what seems to be involved is the development of some sort of reliable intuition (1) for things that might occur, and (2) for making decisions that one senses are the right ones, popular wisdom to the contrary. It is most important to learn to trust that intuition. What follows is a sample of what people talked about as they thought about the notion of their "sixth sense." From a superintendent:

> It's a funny thing. It's almost as though my antennae go up without my even knowing it. I just sort of know when trouble is brewing. And it's not as though I remember having learning anything in specific, but there seem to be times that I react to cues that I can't be too clear about.

And from another superintendent:

> Sometimes we people who are university-trained are so used to the concept of expert that we tend to defer even when our sixth sense tells us not to. If you've got a sixth sense, go with it. Trust yourself. All of us have a voice inside. You've got to pay attention to it. It's a sense of feel that you get through experience. Like somehow to know that some answers are more right than others.

And a high school principal who had also raised the "sixth sense" idea in relation to his need to anticipate events said:

> I don't know how it happens. You build it up, I guess, over a period of years. You learn to have a sixth sense about certain things, like you have a feeling for what could happen. And like I know that even though there's a demand for quick action on most things, I can usually sense when there is something that doesn't have to be acted on quickly.

Perhaps it is enough simply to leave this discussion of one's administrative "sixth sense" at this point. In fact, there is not too much to do about it except to acknowledge its presence, for what is being talked about is the slow experiential accumulation of a particular kind of "know-how" that rather defies description. Everyone's "sixth sense" is as different as the individual involved, attuned somehow to differences in the subtle nuances in the environment and making varied inferences from them.

There is one additional thought that can be offered, however. It is not about the development of that intuitive sense but trusting it. "The proof is in the pudding," and by that I mean that people apparently learn to trust that intuition by experiencing confirmation of it. Or, as numbers of my interviewees told me, "You learn to trust your gut by taking a risk and trusting it." The rule of thumb might be: When you sense something is right, even though other things might add up differently, go with your sense of things. Otherwise, you simply never will know whether you know certain things or you don't.

• Learning by Modeling—
Or Not Modeling

Most of the administrators with whom I talked seemed to recall people who had served as a learning model for them with regard to specific skills and techniques or for learning a more generalized perspective on the work and craft of administration. Some of them, as well, recalled administrators who served as a "don't be like this" model of an administrator. Here are some examples of role modeling from which people said they learned important things:

> Frank is one of the few intellectuals in the superintendency, one of the very few. I observed him closely but, of course, he never knew it. He taught me the value of extensive reading, of being prepared, and of being able to stand up for your convictions in the light of ten people sitting around and not agreeing with you, and do it in a way that's classy. You know, not in the way of "I'll take my marbles and go home if you don't agree with me."

So we have a situation, a rather covert one as most role model learning is, where it appears that, in addition to learning some specific things, what was most important to the learner was the idea of being "classy." To put it in other words, one of the things that this person learned from his role model was the importance of bringing some grace to the practice of school administration. I suspect that bringing grace or "classiness" to one's practice is not something that is learned over night. I further suspect that some people can never learn it, and one of the things that affects whether or not a person will is if that person recognizes it when he or she sees it. The things one learns from role models tend to be those that one is predisposed to learn in the first place. Thus, for example, for a person who tends to devalue reading and studying as being helpful to a superintendent, the fact that "Frank is one of the few intellectual in the superintendency, one of the very few" would have little meaning for his or her subsequent behavior though, indeed, other parts of Frank's practice of his craft might have a great deal of meaning.

It is important to understand, then, that as we think about the part that role modeling plays in helping administrators learn their craft, each of us has screens that we use to sort out behaviors of the other that we want to make part of us. What is at issue is a sort of goodness-of-fit idea between what is modeled via the behavior of the other and the extent to which that behavior "feels comfortable" on the person who is trying to learn.

We have an interesting example of this screening and sorting process in operation. Recall from this chapter's section on learning through mistakes that we discussed a principal's bad experience at having followed his superintendent's advice (not exactly an example of role modeling, but close enough) "to jump down this person's throat and let her know who's boss." That behavior, it turned out, did not fit him well. It was at variance with the image he had of himself, made him feel uncomfortable, and was rejected by him as a way of dealing with similar situations in the future. However, at a later time in our interview, as he was talking about administrative techniques that were important to him, he said:

> So, seeding is important. I learned that from the man who gave the bad advice on jumping down the teacher's throat. He wasn't all bad. In fact, he was very good. I observed him a lot and learned a lot. He was a good reader of boards and an excellent reader of parents. He seeded all the time. Every time we met with the board, he would be seeding, and they would vote on it and it would be unanimous and he would turn around and look at me.

"If it fits, wear it." Perhaps that is as good a way as any of framing the idea of modeling. But implicit in that idea, as we have noted, is knowing whether and how well a particular way of thinking or behaving will, indeed, fit. That is not, though, as simple an idea as one might first think. As a starter, for example, what it implies is having a sense—perhaps a "sixth sense"—of how one looks "dressed up" in different types of ideas and behaviors. Although such a sense may start to get developed early on in one's career, it takes a while to mature. So what may indeed happen, and it seems reasonable that it should, is that a good bit of trial and error learning goes on as one tries to see how things fit.

As one might suspect, there were many examples of memories of models (sometimes referred to as *mentors*) that occurred through the discussions I held with administrators about how they learned to do the things they do. All of them contained the central themes noted in the two examples I have used—observing something in another that one found to be helpful, and perhaps even admirable, and trying that something out to see to what extent it would look good on oneself. There was also another theme that was subtler, but one I think is a basic ingredient to the whole process. It was obvious that there had to be a certain minimum compatibility between the model and the person who was doing the emulating. That is, the extent to which a learner gets along with a potential model will be related to the learner's willingness (1) to seek out something worth learning from that person, and (2) to try it out.

Much as a good bit of modeling occurs as people in the early years of their administrative career try to establish and be comfortable with their own ways of doing things, so, as well, do they come across negative models along the way. These negative models, ways of enacting administrative roles that people see as dysfunctional, seem to be encountered in one's teaching career rather than during the course of preparing to be or being an administrator. For example, a high school principal stated:

> Sure, I've observed what I thought to be some bad administrators and I've always said that if I became a principal I will not do what such-and-such did. For instance,

I once had a principal who practically never left his office. If you saw him on the second floor twice a year that was a lot, and I said, "That's bad." What brought the point home was one day he was up on our floor and one of my kids, who was out for a drink of water, came back in and said, "Who is that person?" I said, "Well, that was our principal." He said, "No, it's not." I said, "Yes, it is." The kid was a senior. He had been there three years and he did not know who the principal was. And I just thought that was terrible. So, I made a vow that if I ever became a principal that I would be very visible to teachers and students and to get to know them. It's tough to do.

This is the way an elementary school principal reflected on learning from negative role models:

I didn't have any principals after whom I wanted to model myself. In fact, it was usually the opposite, like "I don't like the way they're doing that and somebody could do it better." I felt then, and I still do, that there was a large element of administrators who did not treat teachers as human beings, adults, or intellectual creatures. I may have a lot to learn but I don't want to be told "You couldn't understand that" or "You can't know that." I still hear that stuff from principals about not being able to trust teachers. Not for me.

And from a superintendent who had been an assistant superintendent in a neighboring district:

My previous superintendent communicated with each board member individually and they started to feel very threatened by that. They were almost paranoid about it because they would never know what each had been told. And I made up my mind I wasn't going to do that. It was a question of dividing and conquering and I don't believe you need to do that.

In a way, it almost seems that the learning of what not to do from negative role models was a more powerful sort of thing than what was learned from positive models. Perhaps this is to be expected in the sense that throughout our lives, learning what not to do seems to have been accompanied by strong negative emotionality, usually via some form of punishment. For example, I have a more vivid memory for times when my behavior was negatively sanctioned by my parents than when the opposite was the case. And I doubt I am much different from most other people in that regard.

There is another interesting if possibly troubling thing about this. It is that it may well be that each of us, including school administrators, needs a negative role model who teaches us what not to be in order for us to decide what it is we should be. Regardless of whether or not that hypothesis would hold up on close examination, such role models do abound in the schools, it seems, and they may well have played an important baseline part in the way the people about whom I have written learned their craft.

In closing this chapter, I want to make it clear that I have not tried to write a treatise on the psychology of experiential learning. Rather, my effort has been to try to understand what it is the administrators who were part of this study said *they* understood about how they learned to do what they do.

Chapter Thirteen

The Administrator's "Baggage"

In a conversation I held with a high school principal about his work and how he approached it, there was continual reference to his need to make sure the emotionality inherent in situations with which he was dealing, particularly anger, was either drained or prevented from surfacing. Although behaving in a way to drain another's anger is usually a prerequisite to solving problems at work, and sometimes it may be wise to declare negative emotionality out-of-bounds (e.g., "I won't talk with you unless you are civil"), the pervasiveness of this concern of his apparent need to avoid becoming a contributing party to angry confrontations, suggested that this avoidance tendency was more than a matter of some approved administrative technique that he had learned somewhere along the line. And so we talked about it as I raised the question of how this central tendency of his interpersonal self came to be:

I'm pretty sure it goes back to my growing up time. My mother and dad split up when I was five so my mother and I went to live with my grandparents. They took us in with, I think, no questions asked. And I think my mother always felt that my grandparents had done so much for us that we had to behave in a manner that was not going to be a problem for them. I was there from the time I was five until after I graduated from college and then moved out to my job. Obviously, there are going to be times that as a young person growing up—you've got feelings of anger and there were times when I was angry. But my mother always made it clear to me that these kinds of feelings were not to be expressed because my grandmother and grandfather were not to be upset. So I think I never really learned how to deal with either expressing anger nor having it expressed to me.

I think that really influences the way I deal with people. I think that's why it bothers me when there's a lot of vehement anger around. I'm still trying to learn to deal with it. I have a hard time separating the fact that when people may seem to be yelling *at* me, they're really yelling *to* me.

This anecdote nicely sets the theme of this chapter. It is an exploration of the notion of the administrator's "baggage," those ways of thinking, feeling, behaving, and so forth, that are simply part of an administrator's concept of self and that are brought with him or her to the job of being a school administrator. That self is a combination of preferences and skills of relating to people—personal, interpersonal, or group styles, of attitudes and values about the work of the schools, and of attitudes about self in relation to work. The preceding anecdote is an example of the former—an orientation toward and preference for avoiding a particular kind of interpersonal situation.

Implicit in the idea of "baggage" is that, whatever its specific content, it has been carried by a person for a long time, perhaps from childhood or even infancy as far as matters of interpersonal relations are concerned. It takes no great flash of insight to understand this. With regard to that part of the self that has to do with work and the schools, that too has been carried for a long time but not as long as our interpersonally related baggage. It seems reasonable to think, for example, that notions about work and its meaning develop a bit later in life than comparable notions about how best to relate to others. And the same would certainly hold true about the meaning of school.

Two further thoughts need consideration as a sort of prologue to the body of our discussion. First, the idea of "baggage" emerged rather forcefully for me, although it was not dealt with forcefully, in the study and writing that William Greenfield and I did for our book, *The Effective Principal*. What was clearly apparent from our study was that the people with whom we were concerned were all different, had different styles, different interpersonal predispositions, and so on, and that these differences were not of recent vintage. To the contrary, as I wrote in reference to these people and their formal preparation for administration in that book, "They brought themselves with them to graduate school, so to speak—their visions, their security, their intuitions—and they took those same selves back to their schools, knowing some new things, but they were still basically themselves." And what I meant is that most of what a person will be as an administrator, he or she is long before that person ever thinks of being one. The point is that (1) the practice of the administrative craft involves at its roots the idiosyncratic use of self in interactive, work-oriented situations, and (2) all of us started to learn about using ourselves in human interactive situations not too long after we greeted the light of day in this world. So I think it is the case that our predispositions for understanding and dealing with problems of interpersonal, group, and organizational life have a long history, as do the perspectives we have on work and what it means to do a good job.

The second prefatory thought is this: As I listened as people talked about their work, the very talking seemed to serve as a sort of projective device for them to tell me something about themselves and about some of the themes of their life that they brought with them to the job. Themes concerning ways of work or ways of viewing schools kept on repeating themselves, almost inviting themselves to be talked about, which is what we did.

As might be expected, the great bulk of the conversation about the "baggage" that the administrators and I talked about centered around their early family life, though this was not true in all cases. The way I approached the topic was this: Toward the close of our discussion and after picking up what appeared to be the recurrent theme or themes, I would say something like, "Several times in our talk, you've made reference to X as a sort of central theme of the way you view you work. Can you reflect back into your own history and think about where that might have come from?" Indeed, they did and without too much difficulty, at that.

The purpose of what follows, as has been the case throughout the book, is to be illustrative of an idea and not definitive. In no way, that is, does my discussion in this chapter purport to cover the topic of "baggage." But it will suggest that the topic is one that must be considered if one would understand the work of administrators.

My last point before getting into the discussion is to note that I plan to structure it differently than I have previous chapters. In the latter, I used the ideas of people, irrespective of who they were, to explain the concept with which I was working. Here the people are important in themselves so that the balance of this chapter may be seen as a series of mini-case studies designed to illustrate, albeit briefly, the concept of administrative "baggage." Finally, the examples I provide are brief. I was not interested, nor would it have been appropriate, to conduct an in-depth interview on family history, for example. My aim was simply to tease out some close-to-the-surface thought about the idea of one's "baggage."

• "If Life Gives You Lemons, Make Lemonade"

Margie is an elementary school principal in a very rural area of her state. Though her school was not one in which rural poverty was dominant, the district could by no means be considered an affluent one, nor was the school board predisposed to providing much money for new programs. My impression of her was that she was a very good principal and highly concerned with instructional matters. But it also appeared to me that she had to "make do" a lot and that was often necessary for her to make things happen for herself rather than being able to depend on outside support. And she seemed to be most adept at doing precisely that. That is, she seemed to be most clever at making something out of a set of circumstances that other people might simply leave alone. I asked her about that, and this was her response:

I really don't know if you're born that way. I don't know if it goes way back when, although it very well might be the case. I'm one of seven kids. My own personal history had a lot of ups and downs, making lemonade out of lemons in some cases. I even think I can remember back in high school when I was president of the class two years in a row and it wasn't a popularity contest. I'm pretty sure I was elected because I got things done. So I think even as early as that I was learning to work either with or around other people. I can remember a senior high school English teacher who was our advisor. She was getting in the way of what the class wanted to do or what I saw the class wanting to do. I was thinking of all ways to work around her rather than with her. I'd call special meetings and she wouldn't know about them. Kid stuff, really, but we were able to pull it off.

The critical thing, if I understood Margie's "baggage," was to "pull it off," to make lemonade even when the circumstances were not propitious. Note how she saw herself as having learned, as a youngster, to work with people if they were willing to go in the direction she wanted but, if not, to work around them. There is no malicious intent here at all. In fact, she has a very firm and wholesome value base and simply wants to get things done "either with or around other people."

What I think is most interesting, though, is how, with simply the gentlest of my prodding, she was able to relate what appears to be a central part of her administrative style to some of her early life experiences. It was as though her story, brief though it was, was waiting to be told.

• The Practical Intellectual

George, a middle school principal in a working-class city neighborhood, presents an image of continual motion combined with continual thoughtfulness. His small office has bookcases that are crammed full of books about adolescents and about middle school administration and curriculum. To talk with him is to have the experience of opening up a can of question marks that all have to do with the application of one or the other theory of instruction or discipline or curriculum problems of the middle school. When I called this to his attention within the notion of his "baggage," he said:

The baggage, I guess, is that I see myself halfway between the idea of university and the idea of school. I adhere to a lot of the intellectual stuff, the research. It's all part of me and it's refreshing. The other part of me is that I need to be where it's possible to change things, where it happens. I've always enjoyed studying. I love learning new things. I read all the time yet a part of me says I wouldn't be satisfied with just study and research. I need to see what really works.

Where did all that come from? I really don't know. I guess probably my parents. My dad was on the school board. Books were valued. He had a real commitment to city schools, particularly to inner-city schools. And I grew up in the late sixties and early seventies. Those were times that made us really think about what we were after and I guess I've carried that with me.

So, once more, we have memories, though with not as clear images as "making lemonade," that seem to relate early life history to attitudes about work and, particularly, it seems about the schools. As well, though, there was reference to the period of the late sixties and early seventies as a time that made a powerful impact on his thinking. And though the memories were not as clear cut as in the previous case, it was interesting to note that in a discussion the two of us had about a year and a half after the one from which I quoted, the same themes came up, quite unprompted. Particularly the theme of "the middle school as the place to be" was prominent. And he said, "The frustration is my being unable to bring that which is intellectual together with that which is practical and to really get people to take a look at teaching as an intellectual, demanding kind of profession."

One can almost feel the energy generated by this frustration born of unrequited idealism, so to speak. As George talks what gets communicated, in a way, is the frustration of the sixties with things that were perceived to stand in the way of creating a more decent society. "We know how to create better schools," George seems to be saying, "but it's so hard to get the system to buy in." And it felt as though he had been saying similar things for a long time.

• Be Responsible and Listen

Frank is a superintendent in a large, sprawling suburban district. He laughs a lot, his eyes sparkle, and much of his talk is peppered with references to kids and what they can and should learn. It seemed to me that for a superintendent of a large district to use youngsters as his continual reference point (i.e., not program, not personnel, not budget, not the school board) was a matter of some interest. So I called that to his attention. He responded:

I was oldest of four boys and my parents both worked. I had the responsibility for taking care of my brothers when my Mom and Dad were working. And, boy, you know how badly my Mom would feel if anything happened to them. I had a great deal of empathy for her and I think I'm an empathetic guy now and that's where it came from. There was a lot of love and warmth in my family. And I remember my sixth-grade teacher writing on a report card that I really ought to consider teaching. And there was another thing. My grandparents ran a Mom and Pop store, one of those small corner grocery stores. I remember working with them every Saturday. I can still remember their idea that the customer was always right. They always said, "You've got to listen to people." That started when I could hardly see above the counter. In most cases that lesson has served me well.

Three separate relationships come into play in this excerpt—the superinten-dent's immediate family, school, and grandparents. The messages, which he ap-parently carries to this day, were concerned with the importance of being respon-sible for others, together with feelings of guilt if you weren't; the early-on focus of working in the schools as a career; and the idea that one must listen to others, particularly those people who, broadly interpreted, may be considered as customers. I also get the impression that an unspoken bit of "baggage" that this man carried with him came from the fact that both his parents worked as did both of his grandparents. That is, to work was of positive value. One can hardly be a superintendent without understanding this.

• Being the Best

Jill is a high school principal with boundless energy. As I followed her around one day, I frequently found myself running to keep up with her as we moved from one part of the school to the other. But it was more than just quickness that struck me as I observed and listened to her throughout the day. It was the number of times I heard her, in one way or another, tell another person that "we've got to be better than we are" and, in her discussion with me, her saying "I want to make this into the best high school in the country and I want people to know it." And so we talked about what she acknowledged was this drive to be best:

> Since the day I was born, I think I've sort of been a high achiever. First it was at school. I was the kind of child who my parents begged not to do so well. Like, "Relax, you don't have to be the first one. You don't have to have an A+." The first time I got an A instead of an A+, I was devastated. I still remember that. It was a social studies teacher and I thought the end of the world had come. The funny thing is my folks were not like that at all. I come from a working-class family and I was the first college graduate. I used to buy *Time Magazine* with my allowance when I was nine years old. Never read a comic. I think where the drive and the competitiveness comes from is my older sister. She was a genius. Really. And she never went to college. She was everything I wasn't. Looks, brains—everything. Everything came naturally for her but she didn't do much with her talent. My way out, I guess, was to be best at something and school was a natural. And I can see it today. I have to be damned near the best principal around and I'm not the best by a long shot. I think, sometimes, "Geez, I probably could be, maybe, if I had all the right ingredients." But so many factors are out of my control.

So, once more, we see very powerful lessons having been learned as a youngster that play a strong role in this principal's daily work life. The need to compete and to excel are with her all the time. And it is of some interest to note that both of these needs are highly approved of in our society—but they are usually deemed more appropriate to the makeup of men rather than women. Regardless, the "baggage" is there for this principal and it was of more than passing interest for me to note how vivid was her recall concerning some important events or circumstances in her childhood and the way they seemed to influence her adult work life.

• Know Your History

This case presents a different view of the idea of "baggage" than the previous ones. It involves a superintendent of an affluent suburban school district. We had been talking about a school closing operation that he had planned and supervised. It had been conducted successfully and its success had depended on accurate prediction of enrollments. "We were very much on target—like almost 100 percent," said he. Additionally, "I felt really good about that because for about eight or nine months, my figures had been challenged by some very vocal elements in the community, but I was right. Basically, what I did was to take an historical approach to things and, in effect, do a case study."

The use of the phrase "historical approach" is not one that is run into as a rule in the everyday talk that school administrators use to describe what they do. So I asked this man the "baggage" question, "How come you take an historical approach to things?" He replied:

> Basically, it's a perspective I guess I gained from having been a history major. Through my studies and my experience I've come to appreciate the historical progression of things as a means of looking into the future. The future tends not to change dramatically just because it's tomorrow, and it relies very much on those reciprocating events that have led up to tomorrow. In a sense, tomorrow is always with us at any given time. So, like closing a school is not something new. It's been written about in other situations. They become history and you read about it and tuck it away for future use. Basically, it's the whole idea of using past experiences to, in turn, anticipate what future experiences would be like. I rely on that very heavily. I think I learned to do that from my training as an historian. I tend to see myself as that.

Two things make the "baggage" that this superintendent carries with him somewhat different than the other examples. First, he seemed to be rather consciously aware of it being there. Being an historian who also happens to be a school administrator is, it seems, a substantial part of the way he sees himself, and this definition of self serves as a sort of rudder for him in deeply problematic situations. "Think historically," seems to be his methodological guide. Or, another way of putting it is, "Everything that happened today or will happen tomorrow had its genesis yesterday." And so the meaning of that historical rudder is that if you understand yesterday and the complex of events that made yesterday, you stand a better chance of understanding today, predicting tomorrow, and dealing better with both of them.

The second point of difference between this man's "baggage" as historian and the others that have been discussed is that it appears to have been "packed" (to continue the metaphor) much more recently than was the case of the other examples. That is, the "baggage" that I sensed in the others and about which we talked was most often traced to experiences and memories of one's early years. This situation, though, was different in that the superintendent's training as an historian, as a person who found it helpful to think historically about the meaning of work of a school superintendent, began in college when he was about to enter adulthood. (For whatever it's worth, part of the "baggage" of another superintendent was that of an historian, as well, though the references were not as clear cut as those in the case described.)

• People Not in the Front Lines Don't Know What It's Like

The final mini-case of administrative "baggage" also involves a set of attitudes that found their genesis in late adolescence and early adulthood. The person with whom it is concerned, Jim, works out of the central office of a small city school district. He is primarily responsible for the development and maintenance of the district's programs of special education, the gifted, and so forth. We were talking about how he saw his work and particularly how he saw the relationship between the central office and the school buildings where the program operated, because the manner in which he conceived this relationship would have a strong influence on the way he practiced his craft. The way it turned out was he saw that relationship in consultative terms, not in terms of management-worker. That theme seemed to run through our entire conversation, almost irrespective of the particular topic discussed. And this is not to say that he was not capable of issuing directives when the need was obvious. Rather, the focus of his thoughts and actions seemed continually to derive from the notion that in order to produce the best educational programs you had to counsel and support the people who were involved in the action. They were the ones who knew what was going on and what was needed. This is how his comment started:

> I have a basic belief about my work. It's that people in the front lines know what it's like in the front lines. People not in the front lines don't know what it's like. I started to think about that when I was a teacher and I knew my principal didn't know what it was like in the classroom. And then working in a junior high office and realizing that the downtown supervisor had no idea what was going on in the school.

And he reflected further back in his experience to when he was just out of high school:

> But even before that, during the summer I graduated from high school, I worked cleaning animal cages in a zoo. The white, college-bound kids get summer work there and the blacks worked there all year round. I was full of liberal ideas of equality and suddenly realized that I knew nothing of the black experience, except what I began learning from the folks I worked with. And then that came home clear to me—more clear to me—because I talked to some of my white, middle-class friends and they told me what blacks were like. But I knew different. I knew they didn't know and couldn't know. And so I think that maybe that was the start of my beginning to understand that being there is a lot different than thinking you know where "there" is.

Again, we have the development of an important piece of administrative "baggage" from what might be thought of as memories of relatively recent experience rather than those of childhood and family life. But one also must suspect that there were characteristics of this man's early socialization that enabled him to start to understand that "being there is a lot different from thinking you know where 'there' is," which, as a matter of fact, is a rather eloquent definition of what experiential learning is all about. That point aside, the case is an interesting example of the way that we might define as the "baggage" of a politically liberal philosophy being transferred into a pervasive action orientation toward one's job. But what was required was an open and possibly deliberate decision to let that happen. That is, it looks as though this man made a conscious decision to take that orientation with him, not only on-the-job but in the larger arena of life.

These several cases concerning the way some school administrators sense how some part of their own personal history plays a continuing though subtle role in their day-to-day work give a flavor of the idea of administrative "baggage" as I have used it. There were numerous other examples of this idea among the people with whom I talked. Briefly, to cite some of the others, there was an elementary school principal who could reflect quite easily on her mother's influence on the way she worked with her staff and on the way her experience as a 4H'er—"make your best better"—was part of her view of her job; a high school principal who was very much concerned that her faculty feel a part of things and who had a strong memory of her parents always being inclusive of her and her sister in family matter; a superintendent bent on building a sense of community in his fairly small district who vividly recalled his own family sense of community; and another superintendent, thinking about how his father had stressed the need to be honest to oneself and one's ideals, who said, "It may sound crazy, but it has really guided my whole life."

The fact of comments like these and of the mini-cases that were presented in this chapter should come as no surprise to us. If anything, given our psychologized society in which the jargon of one or more psychologists or therapies is common to the everyday language and thought of most of us in the field of education, what may be surprising is that we don't attend to that fact more than we do. But then, it may be another example of our taking the commonplace for granted. If we are to understand, and thus be able to explain better, the differences in the way administrators work at their craft, we probably need to give more attention to the "baggage" idea. I think, for example, that the chances of a school with a principal who grew up in a family that emphasized the need "to walk in the other person's moccasins" being different from one in which the ethos of the principal's family was "the survival of the fittest" are very good indeed. And this is not to posit that one will be a better school than the other—only that they will be different and that it might be well to understand the differences before making judgments concerning the value of one or the other.

What follows are some summary thoughts, deriving from data that have been presented in this chapter (and my own interpretative baggage), with which the person interested in a more elegant understanding of administrators at work might well be concerned. The character of that highly particularistic history that is brought to the task of leading and administering schools certainly influences the following:

- The types of behavioral cues to which an administrator attends and the interpretation one makes of them. If I grew up in family whose view of the world was conspiratorial, I would definitely view and interpret the events of school life in a manner different from you whose early socialization taught the lesson that the basic concern of humankind was the welfare of others.

- The tendencies that an administrator may have to shape relationships with others as well as the goals of these relationships. Are other people to be used by oneself to further one's own ends or are other people and their work thought of as ends in themselves? Or, are other people thought of as simply another cog in the machine and to be treated as just that? Our "baggage" contributes mightily to whichever perspective is taken.

- The analytic and interpretive stance one takes toward the problems or predicaments with which one is confronted. I am utterly sure that my students who, like the superintendent of our earlier discussion, have backgrounds in history and other social sciences see things differently than my students whose training was in biology or child development.

- The perspectives that an administrator has on the school world and on the world at large. I think one's particularistic history, for instance and perhaps too simplistically, helps answer the question that all of us ask in one form or another: Is the world basically a frightening, cruel place with some aberrant examples of safety and benignness occurring or is it quite the opposite—basically safe and benign with some aberrant examples of fright and cruelty? Or is it some place in between?

- The goal-setting tendencies of administrators. It all comes together there, I believe. What is finally at issue is to understand that the "baggage" that an administrator brings with herself or himself is observed, in some fashion, in how she or he defines what the schools are all about.

Chapter Fourteen

A Conscience of Craft: Being the Judge of One's Own Work at One's Own Craft Show

This final chapter of Part Two focuses attention on the question of how an administrator knows when he or she has done a good job or a poor one. In this connection, my reason for the use of the phrase "conscience of craft" will soon become clear. It is not related to anything having to do with an administrative code of ethics or to a discussion of the nature of a universal morality that may underpin the practice of administration. Rather, our concern will be with how the notion of craft seems to generate its own criteria for making judgments about the efficacy of one's work and how these criteria get applied.

I noted in an earlier chapter that one place where the administration-as-craft analogy broke down had to do with the difference between the tangibleness of what is produced by, for example, a woodcarver and the intangibleness of what is produced by a school administrator. Another difference, of course, has to do with the manner in which the product is put on display. In the case of the woodcarver, or any other traditional craft, we have the institution of craft shows where one's work is submitted to the judgment of experts, where prizes are awarded, and where the prize is considered to be an accolade from one's fellows.

There is no parallel to these processes and events where the craft of administration is concerned. There are no shows where what one has made is put on display and there are no blue ribbons for first place. In fact, there is no first place. And though I am aware of some very informal inquiries about the matter of competition among school administrators, it appears to be the case that this competition is almost always a private matter. It's almost as though a principal, for example, desiring to be the best one around, scans his or her competition (who don't know about this at all) and gives himself or herself awards in the privacy of the principal's office, or at home in conversation with one's spouse, or possibly quasi-publicly in the superintendent's office or in a written annual report.

In addition to this private type of competition in which awards are given to oneself by oneself and which, strictly defined, may not be competition at all because of its privateness, a school administrator may learn of how well she or he has performed via an occasional pat on the back by a superior, a parent, and so on. But pats on the back are just that—praise that tends to be short-lived—and, as administrators will tell you if asked, many times given for the wrong thing. Further, as you may well be told if you ask the right question, administrators are sometimes praised for being skillful when, in fact, they were lucky that certain things happened at just the right time and they emerged from a situation appearing masterful—having done in the eyes of observers just the right thing—when, in fact, they were just plain lucky. Indeed, given what I think is the global uncertainty that attaches to school administrative life, it seems clear to me that a cogent argument can be made that one needs to be a bit lucky in order to survive, let alone excel.

Regardless of the private awards that one receives from oneself or the public or quasi-public praise that may be received, we are still left with the question of how a superintendent or a principal knows when he or she has done a good job or a poor one. (This is not the same question that was addressed in Chapter Ten, "Knowing the Right Thing to Do." The concern there was with predicting what would work to help resolve a problem. Here we are concerned with assessing whether or not what one has done was, indeed, the right thing to do.) The essential question that this chapter deals with is contained in its title: What is it that enables an administrator to be "the judge of one's own work at one's own craft show"?

My approach to dealing with this question leans very heavily on the thoughts contained in the 1984 John Dewey Society lecture by Thomas Green, *The Formation of Conscience in an Age of Technology*. Green's concern is that of the education of the conscience and the manner in which the various "voices" of conscience speak to us when we are confronted with alternate choices of action and need to produce a prudent decision. And prudence, the use of good judgment and skill with a focus on one's own self-interest, may be the key to it all.

In a general way, Green sets the tone for our discussion in the following way:

> It is a simple fact that each of us has the capacity to judge our own conduct. . . .
> The point I want to stress . . . is not that it involves judgment of moral approval
> or disapproval, but simply that it is judgment that *each of us makes in our own
> case*. In short, it is reflexive judgment. Furthermore, it is judgment always accompanied by certain emotions which, if not exactly the same, are nevertheless like
> the moral emotions. I can feel guilt, shame or embarrassment at a job poorly done
> and these are the same feelings I have when viewing some moral failure of mine.

This capacity of ours to be judge, each in our own case, is all that I mean by conscience. Conscience, as St. Thomas put it, is simply reason commenting on conduct. And this capacity . . . can extend to self-judgment even in such matters as washing the car, planting the garden, getting dressed, or crafting a good sentence. These are all things that can be done well or badly in our own eyes. They are all activities that are subject to the commentary of conscience (Green, 1984, pp. 2–3).

Several points critical to this chapter's argument are imbedded in Green's position. Note, for the example, the stress on the following ideas:

- Each of us has the capacity to judge our own conduct.
- These judgments need not involve moral (normative) approval or disapproval, but are pertinent to us as individuals and our own work.
- The emotionality attached to how well or poorly we do our work is similar to that attached to behavior we consider highly moral or that associated with a moral failing.
- By the exercise of one's conscience is meant the reflexive judgment that each of us places on our behavior as we subject that behavior to criterion measures that we have established for ourselves.

Thus, it should be clear that administrators have the understandings required to pass judgment on themselves and the efficacy of their work. This does not assume that they are immune from external judgments. An administrative embezzler is an administrative embezzler and, if apprehended, is subject to all the legal and moral sanctions that would accompany being caught. Nevertheless, if we follow Green's argument, it becomes clear that one may award oneself a first place prize in the administrative craft show; award no prize at all and feel uncomfortable at the shoddy workmanship of whatever it is one has done; or perhaps award oneself an "A" for effort.

The capacity to make these or other judgments is what is meant by conscience. But, recall our use of the phrase, the "voices" of conscience. That is, when we use the term *conscience* as capacity to judge ourselves, we are not referring to some undifferentiated whole that simply emerged life-size into the self-concept of mature adults. Rather, Green would have us think, that each of us carries with us several types of conscience (another type of "baggage," I might add), each of which may speak to us in somewhat of a different "voice," depending on the character of the judgment to be made, I suspect. These voices act in a way so that we may speak of conscience as many voices, such as:

- *membership,* because part of our capacity to make judgments about ourselves and our work is related to the work standards and values of the various groups in which we hold or have held membership.

- *sacrifice,* because part of our capacity to make judgments about ourselves and our work is related to our ability to act prudently, to balance our self-interest against the interest of others.
- *memory,* because part of our capacity to make judgments about ourselves and our work is related to our memory, our "rootedness," our social inheritance of the way things should be and the way whatever we create should look.
- *imagination,* because much as our capacity to make judgments about ourselves and our work is, in part, related to our memory, it is also in part related to the image we have of the future. In fact, I know of no other group of people who are so consistently concerned with the future and the nature of the world they are helping to create than school people. And many of the things a principal, for example, might do I think are related to his or her imagination of the world the day after tomorrow.
- *craft,* because part of our capacity to make judgments about ourselves and our work is related to how well we understand what is meant by the criterion of excellence in our "craft guild."

Obviously, though, I felt obliged to take brief note of the several "voices" of conscience to which Green refers, the one that has overriding importance for us here is the last, craft as conscience. (Incidentally, the text on which this discussion is based listed "craft" as the first of the "voices.") Here is how he elaborates on the idea:

There is such a thing as conscience of craft. We see it whenever the expert or the novice in any craft adopts the standards of that craft as his own. That is to say, it is displayed whenever we become judge in our own case saying that our performance is good, bad, skillful, fitting, and the like. Whether one is a writer, a cook, a gardener, or a mechanic, there will be standards for the practice of one's craft. Becoming a musician is not simply becoming able to perform on an instrument. It is also becoming able to judge one's performance by the standards of musical taste and judgment as to what is good, what might be better and what is downright unacceptable. Thus, to possess a conscience of craft is to have acquired the capacity for self-congratulation or deep self-satisfaction at something well done, shame at slovenly work, and even embarrassment at carelessness (p. 4).

Green then goes on to make these comments: "It is this sense of craft, moreover, that underlies our concern for excellence. It is what impels us to lay aside slovenly and sloppy work simply because of what it is—slovenly and sloppy" (p. 4).

My reading of the idea of our conscience speaking to us in different "voices," and particularly of the notion of conscience as craft, suggests immediate relevance to the experience of anyone reading this book as well as he who is writing it. With regard to the latter, for example, picturing myself as someone who writes well and who has a deep and abiding affection for the English language, I know how good it feels to have crafted a good sentence or paragraph. I also know how uncomfortable it feels when the words link together in an awkward fashion so that a reader might have to wonder aloud at whatever it was I had in mind when I wrote such a jumble. As another example, I consider myself (as, I suppose, do just about all college professors) as a good, a very good, teacher. I have vivid recollections of having performed poorly in a classroom, of having not been too well prepared, of having taken my skills too much for granted and, thus, failing to get my students interested. And accompanying these recollections was my tendency, first, to blame my students as unworthy of my time and then my feeling of embarrassment on being forced to assume the blame myself. Mostly, though, I recall the privacy of my judgments about myself and my performance. I simply said nothing to anybody about my failures but, for sure, *I* knew I had failed.

Interestingly, relative to my practice of teaching as a craft, though I do recall having an occasional class in which I did something that caused me to judge myself as excellent—and even talk with others about what I had done—most of what I think are very successful classroom experiences fade away. So I judge myself as competent and skilled—but I say little about my successes to any of my colleagues.

Perhaps, then, the conceptual case for "conscience as craft" has been well made. But for our purposes, it is important to understand that it involves the capacity to make judgments about one's performance only to the extent that, for the most part, the judgments are made in private. And there is a bit of curiosity to this point, too, in as much as the huge part of what a school administrator does is open to public scrutiny. It's almost as though the "craft show" itself is a public one but that both the awarding of prizes and the criticism of some products is largely a private affair. Perhaps, in a sense, we have two different "shows," one that is seen by others and one that may only be seen through the eyes of the administrator.

In many of the discussions I held with school administrators, we talked about things they had done that they considered to be highly successful and also about things they had done that had been considered by them as much less than successful, if not a clear case of ineptness on their part. Things that were thought to be successful typically involved a drawn-out series of events with no particular one of them being seen as critical to the success of the whole venture. The reader may recall, for example, the earlier story of the elementary school principal having been able to get a computer literacy program going in her school and the computer lab along with it. Her feelings about her work were expressed in a sort of quiet satisfaction with her accomplishment, though there seemed to be no single thing crucial to her success that had occurred. She knew she had done well, and that the time and energy devoted to the project were well justified by the result. Indeed, she took pride in what she had done and her reactions, I think, were rather prototypical of others. These judgments and the positive emotionality that accompanied them, though, were privatized. I almost had the feeling that she was holding on to them to use as possible consolation when something didn't go well.

All this is not to suggest that administrators do not have successful experiences on a daily basis. Indeed they do, but it is more, I think, like my success at being a good teacher. That is, by and large, on a class-by-class basis, nothing outstanding seems to happen, at least nothing I can recall. I suspect a similar type of thing takes place on a daily basis with school administrators. They have their successes but outstanding successes seem to occur only occasionally.

Recalling experiences in which they judged themselves to have been inept if not downright failures was not a difficult task for any of the people with whom I talked. It was almost as though they were waiting for the opportunity to remember them aloud, and this they did, it seemed, in exquisite detail. What follows are some samples of episodes in the work life of school administrators in which they saw and judged themselves to be inept by their own standards of good administrative craftwork.

First, a new elementary school principal:

> I was the new principal in this school. I had worked as a teacher in another school in the district, but it was a completely different place. I brought the staff together a couple of times those first few months and attempted to talk with them, give them an idea who I was as principal and what I expected, and create an atmosphere of support. What happened was that I found myself constantly referring to "the other school."
>
> It was a big mistake. I was terribly naive. I had a very positive impression of this other school. It was a nontraditional place and I am now principal of one that was very traditional. And, in my naivete, I found myself pushing for the other place and they heard it, too. I'm standing there like a dummy trying to tell these people what I hope they will do, what I hope they will feel free to do—some of these wonderful things I had been doing at this other school—under my glorious administration. I was a terrific veteran of education with all of five years of experience under my belt. I stood up in front of a group of old, entrenched, well-established, and very successful classroom educators and told them how it was done successfully up the street.
>
> Boy, I could see it right on their faces. A couple of them, because I had been there for five months, were friendly enough with me to tell me point blank, "Don't tell us how they do it at. . . ."
>
> I felt stupid, overwhelmingly so, and embarrassed. I made these wonderful speeches thinking I was drumming up enthusiasm. I could have died afterward. I meant well, but nothing happened until I learned to say it all differently.

Another elementary school principal:

- I was a new principal and after doing very routine teacher evaluations, in writing, I put them in the teachers' mailboxes. They got very upset. They expected a chat about them, even though they were routine. I was embarrassed. I felt I should have known better and as if I was not on top of things. It was as though I violated the image I had of myself as a competent administrator.

A high school principal:

- I've always been fairly adept at understanding and diagnosing things. And when I was working with a group of other administrators or teachers, I would typically sketch out a rather elaborate scenario of how this "thing" would be addressed. And more often than not, I would insinuate myself as the key player and give the others only a small slice. But what happened is that I would consistently overcommit myself.

  I remember one time I was scrambling to keep up with things. And I was late with my work or reassigning work to others. It was the old pattern. I felt enraged with myself. Stupid! I got some feedback and I started to understand the pattern, but it took me a long time to learn not to do it and I'm not sure I ever really learned it. It was an ego trip.

  What would happen was that I would become annoyed with myself, disappointed, embarrassed. Then I would compensate with my personal charm. I'd muddy the waters so that I'd get off the hook. But I couldn't deal with it in public. I wasn't up front and I was embarrassed. But no one else knew it.

A superintendent:

- One time, at a board meeting, a board member started to discuss the possibility of changing the name of the high school. He wanted to change it from the town's name to that of a particular person. I remained silent. The more they talked, the more enthusiastic they became. I still was silent and this was a big mistake because right out of the blue a motion was made to change the name. It passed unanimously. Afterward, when I went home, I was thinking: "Changing the name of a school? That touches people's hearts and it shouldn't be done after an hour's discussion." I should have slowed it down. But I remained silent. Stupid? Even when I knew the board president was looking to me for help.

  So at the next board meeting a couple of weeks later, 500 people showed up. We had to change rooms to the school auditorium. They had an attorney with them. They were up in arms. I sat there again, totally embarrassed because it was all caused by my silence. I knew better. I should have slowed it down. I was stupid. And I only mentioned it to my wife. I violated my own sense of being skillful and I really didn't want to talk about it too much.

What is important about these anecdotes, of course, is not the uniqueness of their substance. These are examples of everyday, commonplace ineptness.

Most of us, for example, have had the experience of saying things in front of a group that, in retrospect, turned out to be foolish, if well-intentioned; of over-committing ourselves, discovering it, and then creating one or the other set of circumstances to remove ourselves from responsibility; or of remaining silent when our reflection on a situation told us we knew better and should have said something. So, though the stories themselves are of little consequence for our purposes, the reactions of the storytellers are. They define the theme of this chapter. Notice, in particular, the way that these people described themselves and their reactions—"stupid," "embarrassed," "annoyed with myself," "disappointed," "terribly naive," "dummy," "violated my own sense of being skillful," "should have known better," "was not on top of things," "violated the image I had of myself as a competent administrator."

In a sense, then, we are observers of the "conscience of craft," in operation. Or, going back to the elaboration of this chapter's title, we are privy to the judgments of one's work being made at one's own private craft show. But in order to make these judgments, one has to have evaluative criteria at hand. These criteria may stem from the practice of the craft itself or, as I think is more likely the case for the problem being addressed here, criteria that derive from each person's image of self as skilled administrator, leader, or what have you. The point that I believe becomes crucially important in all this is that the judgments placed on self tend to be more important relative to one's conscience of craft than any that might come from external sources. That is, it is an individual feeling embarrassed by her or his behavior that is important and not being told by someone that "you should feel embarrassed." Likewise, it is the individual's sense of ill-feeling after having judged that he or she "should have known better" that is important rather than being told that by someone else. As a matter of fact, it is probably a rare circumstance in which a "someone else" tells a superintendent or a principal that she or he "should have known better."

There is more to it all, though, than the mere observations of the manner in which the "conscience of craft" works. That is, what we are interested in is active practice, not simply passive observation. And so, much as everything else that has been discussed related to one or another facet of the practice of administrative craftwork, here, too, there is a relationship. It has to do with learning what to do, or with reinforcing what one already knows. That is, we have discussed the development of one's memory as the central meaning of the phrase "to learn by experience." But memory fades, of course, and what we have observed as a result of these "private craft shows," I think, are individuals relearning something important that they alredy knew. This is no small matter, in my judgment, as we try to subject the craft of administration to a kind of inquiry that goes beyond passing the lore of the craft from one generation of administrators to another. I think it may be true that the relearning of something that a person already knows but has forgotten probably takes place more as a result of one's self-judgment of ineptness than of a successfully utilized skill. We tend to pass off success lightly, or pass off the way we created a success lightly—but we remember, frequently with pain, our failures.

It makes sense to suppose that the more highly skilled an administrator is, the more highly developed and sensitive will be that person's conscience of craft. What this suggests is that this person will have more things to look for and to be concerned about in the performance of his or her work than will the novice administrator or the one who simply has reached a level of ability that enables him or her to produce passable work, satisfactory to both the administrator and the school system—but not more than that. It also means that for the highly skilled administrative craftsperson, there is potentially a wider spectrum of events or behaviors over which he or she might become embarrassed or feel "I should have known better." Curiously, we might say, that through the operation of a conscience of craft, the highly skilled principal, for example, has more to learn than one who is not so skilled. And this may be so, it seems to me, because this person has a more highly refined sense of "knowing the right thing to do."

In summary, the several chapters in this part of the book elaborated on and illustrated the idea of the "idiosyncratic use of self" as the base point of understanding what is meant by working at the administrative craft. To understand this idea means much more than to mouth the platitudinous "administration is getting things done through people." Rather, it means the ability to conceive of one's "self" as a tool, and the most important tool, of the craft.

This idea may also be seen as somewhat of a platitude so I elaborate a bit more. The character of the metaphoric tool I have in mind is much more complex than a screwdriver, for example, which has one primary function, that of turning screws, and a couple of ancillary ones for which it was not consciously designed, prying off lids, gouging out a hole, and so on. Rather, the character of the self-as-tool is much more like the most elaborate Swiss army knife that one can buy, one that has a multitude of different implements embedded in a quite compact and sturdy structure. If a person would make good use of such a knife, he or she must understand what its capabilities and limitations are, as well as knowing how skilled he or she may be in its varieties of usage.

So, too, is the case of thinking of oneself as a tool to be used by oneself. Put quite simply, but with an acknowledgment of its extremely fine complexity, the "idiosyncratic use of self" means, first, that one must understand one's capacities and limitations; one must have a sense of these situations where one feels comfortable, capable, skillful, clumsy, "in over one's head," and so on. Second, what is implied by all this is the making of judgments. To think deliberately of one's work as the use of oneself means to be able to make judgments based on what one knows about what one can or cannot do; or, about which one can do well or not so well; or about environments in which one operates well or not well, and so forth. For me, at least, as I think back on what I have written, these kinds of ideas become a central message, the message being that essence of the craft of administration involves a uniqueness of ways of doing things within a centrality of purpose. That purpose, of course, is ultimately concerned with creating the best learning conditions for youngsters and the best working conditions for adults. How this is done, how one is best able to use oneself, is a matter that cannot be prescribed by another. But, in the final analysis, I think it is this nonprescriptability that provides the argument for deliberately encouraging the development of a fine conscience of craft.

Part Three

Beyond the
Craft

Metaphorically speaking, with the completion of Part Two the first page has just been turned on the study of administration as craft. It revealed two things. First, it is important to understand, though I have not mentioned it previously, that not once in my discussions with any administrator about his or her work was there any mention of "administrative research." Administrators simply don't seem to spend any time thinking about what professors spend their time researching about in the hopes that they can influence the behavior of administrators. (Quite personally, I add, "Nor should they.")

Second, it should be obvious that what we are dealing with is the exercise of a highly individuated way of thinking about problems and about skills needed to accomplish generally common purposes. On any number of occasions throughout the book, for example, I have remarked on the essential idiosyncrasy that attaches to the way each administrator practices his or her craft. I make this point over and again not to suggest that there is no structure to that craft for, as we have seen, indeed there is. That is, it is clear that though each person interprets events and does things differently, the character of the things they do and the way they think about those things revolve around elements of the craft that have a certain commonality. This observation suggests that there is a type of generalizability of thought and action that emerges from idiosyncrasy of thought and action. Carl Rogers (1961) in his book, *On Becoming a Person*, noted a similar idea as he wrote about "a learning which has been most rewarding" that came from his practice of psychotherapy. He said:

> I can word it this way. *What is most personal is most general.* There have been times when in talking with students or staff, or in my writing, when I have expressed myself in ways so personal that I have felt I was expressing an attitude which it was probable no one else could understand, because it was so uniquely my own. . . . In these instances I have almost invariably found that the very feeling which seemed to me most private, most personal, and hence most incomprehensible to others, has turned out to be an expression for which there was resonance in many other people. It has led me to believe that what is most personal and unique in each one of us is probably the very element which would, if it were shared or expressed, speak most deeply to others (p. 21).

I was unaware of this particular comment of Rogers as I went about studying and writing about what school administrators do and how they think about it. Yet, in my own way and in retrospect, I was able to confirm his idea that "what is most personal is most general." As I shared what I was starting to learn with my students and administrative and professional colleagues, there seemed to be a collective nodding of heads. I was not dealing with the highly personal expressions of self as was Rogers, of course. But, for sure, I was dealing with some very highly individualized ways of looking at the administrative work world in the schools. It was, though, no figment of my imagination that all these people, different as they were, were able to think about what they did in terms that were easily understood by others. There is a common and generalized language of craft and it is this point I want to make. I hasten to add, however, that even though I think that this language as it is spoken in this book is the *lingua franca* of school administrators—they all understood it—they seem not to use it. Instead, they seem to use the language of technology—"give me your input" (a phrase that almost makes me ill) or "we have to engage in strategic planning" (a way, I think, of mystifying the public). So much the pity because this language of craft communicates so easily.

All this notwithstanding, it does seem as though that which is thought to be idiosyncratic is quite generalizable relative to what it is that school administrators both do and think. That which is generalized, though, is an idea, a way of thinking about and explaining administrative work and not prescriptions about that work. And so, because the data and their interpretation as they appear in the preceding chapters speak for themselves about this way of thinking and explaining, I want to start to bring closure to this book by raising and dealing with a series of questions that have occurred to me as I made my way through it all. And so the title of Chapter Fifteen is, quite simply, "Questions." Chapter Sixteen is also concerned with a question. In it, I want to bring the book full circle by returning to an issue I dispensed with in a rather offhanded fashion in Chapter Two and which I still have occasion to wonder about: Is there a way we can talk about administration as art? Is it even a viable idea?

Chapter Fifteen

Questions

In the March 1987 issue of *Harpers,* its editor, Lewis H. Lapham, wrote, "I seldom know what I think about anything (not even the weather or Burt Reynolds' wig) until I am obligated to write something on the subject . . ." (p. 10). A similar process seems to work with me. As I write, I start to understand and clarify for myself whatever it is that I'm thinking about. As well, the process of writing seems to force me to reflect and raise questions about the very ideas about which I am writing.

These two outcomes of writing—clarifying and raising questions—seemed very much in evidence for me as I went from chapter to chapter. I found myself understanding better the craft of administration as I wrote about it and I also found myself raising questions that derived from what I had written. In this chapter, I will note these questions—at least those I consider to be major ones—and discuss my own reactions to them. There is no particular hierarchy of importance attached to the order in which the questions are presented. I simply note them as they occurred to me. They are all premised, of course, on the notion that the most valid metaphor for the practice of administration is that of the practice of craft—of people putting their interpersonal, group, and organizationally related skills to work in the service of some school-oriented end. And this is to say, to come back to a position I took earlier, that the science and applied science metaphor of school administration are myths that exist in the minds of professors, for whom they serve university career purposes (not an ignoble aim). Here are some questions, then, premised on the validity of the metaphor of administration-as-craft. The one caveat I offer with regard to these questions is that though I raise them, I do not answer them in any detailed sort of way. And the reason is that I only have hunches about the direction in which one may find the answers—if they exist.

- *Is there a body of knowledge which, if learned by a school administrator, would make that person better at his or her craft?* I have queried administrators about this and the general answer is "No." And I think I can make a case for that being the correct answer. As a matter of fact when the question is raised, one usually is greeted by a puzzled look that almost communicates "The body of knowledge that one needs to know cannot be put into writing for public consumption." Further, I have talked with any number of principals or superintendents who would be considered quite good ones and would suggest that what one principal "knows" is only distantly related, if at all, to what his or her colleague "knows."

  I think I can make this point clear by moving away, for the moment, from the field of public education to higher education. I think of my own university, for example, and several top administrative officers. Their graduate training, thus the body of knowledge they "know," was in such fields as geology, chemistry, economics, history, philosophy, mental retardation, religion, political science, engineering, and so forth. Surely, they don't "know" a common body of knowledge related to administration. This would still be true if they have studied any so-called administrative theory and research at all.

  Still, I must say, my own answer that there is no body of knowledge which, if learned by a school administrator, would be helpful is not one that makes me very comfortable. We need not—we ought not—be simply a group of pragmatic doers whose theme song is "Whatever Works Rules the Day" because in that case another theme song, "Que Sera Sera" (what will be, will be) will become what schooling is all about. So it seems to me that at least those administrative craftspeople who would be thought of as educational leaders should become experts on matters educational. I have in mind here a comment I heard Ralph Tyler make to a group of professors of instructional supervision. He said that his view of supervisors was was that they should be experts on knowledge about how children learn. I think that, minimally, school administrators should know that body of knowledge. That is, the enterprise of schooling is concerned with establishing a base upon which youngsters can learn and grow into intellectually, socially, and vocationally skilled adults. At minimum, then, it seems reasonable that those whose job it is to lead that enterprise possess substantial knowledge of matters concerned with learning. Though, of course, they need to be able to use what they know when they encounter problems of instruction and curriculum development, they must, first of all, know something.

- *Is there a language of administrative craft work?* I asked the traditional craftspeople with whom I talked if there was a special language associated with their craft. Were there words or phrases that had special meaning to them and their colleagues and that could be understood no matter where they went? The answer was in the affirmative. Potters, no matter where they are, can understand each other when they talk about centering clay on the wheel, about "throwing," or about what is meant by "porcelain wants to do what it wants to do."

Does the same sort of thing hold true for administrative craftwork? It was more difficult for me to get at this, but I believe the answer is, again, in the affirmative. For example, when a superintendent says that he or she has a "4-3" board, his or her colleagues know just what that means in terms of the kind of conflict among board members and the political acumen it may take to maintain a semblance of civility in discourse about the schools. These colleagues may also have a sense of the tenuousness of the "4-3" superintendent's tenure. Similarly, most principals can communicate readily about "screamers" (parents who have tantrums in their office) and the "slack" necessary to maintain in class schedules that are built for high schools. As well, great numbers of principals, particularly in larger school districts, are familiar with the game of "pass the lemon" as they refer to meetings with fellow principals in which they try to get them to accept as teachers on their faculty people who are considered less than desirable.

The essential point in all this is that every craft does, indeed, develop a language of its own and this language is based on experience that somehow gets shared. Most importantly, I think, it enables even strangers to share the emotionality of a particular experience he or she has not had. Thus, although I can understand intellectually having a screamer in my office, I can't really "know" that experience and be able to talk about it with an emotional memory as most of the principals I know are able to do.

Another point about a special language of craft that I believe attaches to school administration is that this language is the stuff of which the lore of craft is made. Its tradition, that is, stemming from and existing alongside its language, gets transmitted to new generations of craftspeople. Indeed, it is very much true that an interested person can study old books on school administration, particularly if they are written by school administrators and not professors, and find himself or herself understanding rather precisely what the conditions of the craft were at the time of writing.

- *Are there certain types of people who are more "cut out" to be school administrators than others?* This is a curious question because within very broad limits, practically anyone can be a school administrator. And the same holds for most other crafts, I believe. Even I, with little sense of physical perspective, could learn to be a potter though what I would pot would not win first place in a craft show. And I also need to say that within narrower limits, but wide just the same, anyone can learn to be a physician or dentist or lawyer. It is true, though, that just as I would not win first prize with my pottery in a craft show, all of us have known or heard of physicians, dentists, or lawyers who would not be awarded a blue ribbon for their craftwork.

Back to the question, though. I'm not at all sure that practically anyone can *not* be a school administrator as far as the intellectual complexity of the job is concerned, or its physical and emotional demands. I do not mean, though, that the position places no demands on the person for particular skills. Obviously, it does, but these can be learned. Nor do I mean that everyone can be equally good at the job. One has only to visit different schools to understand in short order that, in some rather ill-defined and nonmeasureable ways, their administrators exhibit different degrees of skill and different degrees of intelligence—in working with youngsters, teachers, or parents. And one certainly senses different types of emotionality and interests associated with different administrators. It is one thing to spend a day with an excited and exciting superintendent or principal and quite another to spend a day with a bore.

Nevertheless, the point still holds. I believe that practically anyone can be a school administrator. There is nothing special about the job that says, "Only X can become Y." And this is not to say that everyone who wants to be a principal, for example, will or should get to be one. Some control is exercised over hiring but the criteria used are rather vague, to the best of my knowledge.

There is a thought, though, that takes perhaps a half-step toward answering the question posed. It has to do with the notion of "goodness-of-fit" between what the school or school systems says it needs and what a prospective administrator can supply. For example, there are some districts that sense themselves to have a quite satisfactory program and require above all from their superintendent the ability to keep the budget stable, not to "rock the boat," and to be able to "work the crowd." A school board intent on hiring a new superintendent will sense in fairly short order, or so I have been told, the extent to which a candidate meets those criteria. Or, as another example, I know of a high school principal whose primary job in his suburban high school is to keep the parents happy. Again, a "goodness of fit" problem in the sense that there are principals who are not good at that but who at good are curriculum development.

Things work both ways, of course, as I have just implied. That is, it certainly can come as no surprise that an individual makes the same type of "goodness of fit" judgments about a system as the system makes about him or her. A student of mine visited a middle school in a very heterogeneous city neighborhood and another in a quite homogeneous suburb. His judgment was that he would not like to be in the former but would be quite comfortable in the latter. The present urban principal, incidentally, loves and has a commitment to that school or one like it.

Let me go back once more, though, to the initial question. The skills of the craft that are necessary to one's being able to carry out an administrative job in education are neither arcane nor so intellectually demanding that their acquisition acts as a barrier to shut out anyone who wants to be a school principal, for example. Any teacher can probably qualify after some type of experiential training, although this does not mean that any teacher can be a beyond-the-ordinary administrator. I also think that as far as matters of skill are concerned, almost any reasonably intelligent person with no experience in school work could also learn to be a principal or a superintendent. We are not, after all, dealing with theoretical physics that, I am told, demands the type of intellectual capacity that is the province of a relatively few of us.

- *Is there a particular type of value base that attaches uniquely to the craft of administration?* Or, is there anything singularly unique about school administration that affects the worth we place on certain goals or actions? This question has bothered me a bit. I found myself wondering whether or not there was anything more to being a highly respected high school principal, for example, than being highly skilled at "keeping the peace." Or, I asked myself whether or not all there was to being considered an excellent superintendent was to be politically skillful enough never to lose a school budget vote or to be able to avoid conflict with the teachers' union? These questions may be put in the context of our discussion of a conscience of craft in Chapter Fourteen. That is, is excellence in school administration to be judged by one's skill to produce an excellent product regardless of the nature of that product? Or are there other rudders besides doing a good job at something that tell us, for example, whether that something ought to have been done at all?

Perhaps the question will become clearer if it is taken out of the field of education and put into the sphere of war and peace. This country apparently did a very good job of creating the conditions and the technology through which we were able to make the world's first atomic bomb which was, of course, then dropped on Hiroshima. But should we have done it? Is there nothing beyond the meaning of the conscience of craft besides being skillful? Or, as one may mistakenly infer from Green's discussion of that type of conscience, is all that we have to be concerned about is that one's work not be "slovenly and sloppy"?

Obviously, I think the answer to these questions is in the negative. There is some type of ethical or moral system operating in the field of school administration but I don't believe it to be well-thought out, articulated, or agreed upon. This is most certainly true in individual situations in which there are ethical conflicts or conflicts among the various voices of our conscience. Another way of putting it is to suggest that there appears to be no single set of criteria for goodness. What one administrator judges to be the ethically correct thing to do, another, after weighing all the conflicting alternatives, judges to be the ethically wrong thing.

"Well," you say, "that's what life is all about. There are at least two sides to every argument. Who's to say who is right?" I am forced to agree, of course, and yet there is something that nags me about my agreement. Let me provide a few examples.

- A school superintendent is confronted with the problem of whether or not a youngster should be permanently expelled from school. It is not that the youngster has committed a crime, but that he, in this case, has been a constant source of irritation to teachers because he seems not to want to be in school and behaves accordingly. The superintendent must make a decision that may well have life-long consequences for the youngster. What to do? The platitudinous response to the question is, Do what is best for the youngster. Of course!! But that response is not only platitudinous. It is stupid.

What we must end up doing, of course, is deciding *what* is right; *who* makes that decision; and *how* that decision is made. And for those of us who have an interest in problems such as this, as I do, there are still left-over questions about the nature of those value-oriented positions that affected the decision.

- A school principal, on careful observation, conversation, and thought, has decided to recommend to the superintendent that dismissal proceedings be instituted against a tenured teacher. All the evidence necessary to be successful in these proceedings, the principal believes, is at hand. The superintendent must make the decision whether or not to go ahead.

A simple decision, it would appear. Not so, at least if we can judge by the relatively small number of such proceedings that are instituted each year and weigh that number against the fact that practically every principal has about one or more tenured teachers on his or her faculty that have been judged less than fully competent. There are competing values, again, and money is not the least of them. In the local newspaper I read on the morning that I wrote this, it was noted that dismissal proceedings can cost, minimally, $45,000 in legal fees to say nothing of the time and emotional cost involved. Can we say, then, that whatever it takes to get rid of an incompetent teacher is worth it? I would like to take that position, but there are some very fine, skillful, and thoughtful superintendents who might make a different decision. Their analysis and judgment of the conflict of value involved would be different from mine. But I "know" I am right and they "know" they are right.

We can think similarly about cases that, on the face of it, are quite benign and seemingly devoid of value conflicts of any sort. Take the situation described in Chapter Four of the elementary school principal who established a computer literacy program and a computer laboratory in her school. No one could argue with that accomplishment. Or could one? Might she, her faculty, and the students have been better off had she devoted her time and energy to other parts of the school program— reading, science, math? Certainly, I don't know the answer to that question, but I also know that the question can legitimately be raised; that there can be contending views; and that whatever answer one finally arrives at will be based on some sort of analysis and weighing of the educational worth of one alternative compared with another.

Obviously, the situations that can be considered under the question are of an infinite number. Even decisions about how one uses one's time have a value component attached to them. Were I a principal, for example, my values would lead me to ignore my correspondence and telephone messages in favor of spending my time talking with teachers and students. At least, I think that would be the case. To do so, though, might make for sloppy administration. But who is to say what is more important to do?

So we come back to the original question concerning the value-base of the craft of administration. It does seem to me, despite some lingering doubts I have, that question gets resolved largely in favor of a situation ethics type of thing. There is no single standard of goodness or rightness of decision, except perhaps in cases where the law is involved. And even there, I am aware of the law having been violated in secrecy in favor of what an individual has judged to be a higher standard of what is the moral thing to do.

What we have called the "conscience of craft" comes into play with regard to how well we judge we have used our understandings and our skills to accomplish certain ends. Judgments about the worth of the ends are subject to a different array of factors and ultimately involve an individual's assessment of what is right, moral, and of value.

• *What does using the craft metaphor of school administration imply for thinking about how school administrators can become better at their work?* In the case of teachers, the granting of tenure is much like the immigration official stamping a passport when one goes to a foreign country. It grants access to particular territory, grants certain privileges, and implies certain responsibilities. One must have one's passport renewed from time to time though, whereas tenure for a teacher is for a lifetime. Competence is assumed and it is also assumed that teachers will seek opportunities, on their own volition, to become more skilled. My sense is that school systems and their administrators really don't believe this latter point. They continue to develop and frequently mandate teacher attendance at in-service programs of one sort or another as though if they didn't mandate attendance, teachers would stay away. And they may, indeed, be correct in that prophecy. If they are, I suspect it's more a comment on the content of in-service programs and how they are developed than it is a comment on the motivation of teachers to become more skilled.

Curiously, though, we have a similar set of employment conditions holding for administrators. They are presumed to be competent upon being hired. Some states tenure school principals (but not superintendents). My sense of the administrative employment situation is that there is some vague assumption that superintendents and principals, like teachers and in the name of some ill-defined notion of professionalism, will also seek opportunities to become more skilled. The similarity between teachers and administrators stops there, though, as practically no systematic attempts are made to upgrade an administrator's skills. It is true, of course, that national and state organizations conduct workshops and institute programs for administrators. Yet attendance at them is purely optional (as I think it should be) in contrast to the frequently mandated attendance case with teachers. It is a situation in which administrators are thought to be and treated like adults whereas teachers are seen as and treated like children. "Go get trained," we say to teachers, "It will be good for you." To administrators we say, "Make those decisions for yourself about the further training you need. We trust you." There is another interesting point about all this. It is that at the instant a teacher, certified to be an administrator, receives a first administrative appointment, he or she becomes a "professional" administrator and is trusted to make those decisions for self. (As an aside, these conditions seem to have held ever since our system of common schools was developed. At least, that is my reading of some early books having to do with public education.)

A reason, and one that makes sense to me, why we seem to have neglected the continuing education and training of administrators, is that we have really not known what that meant. Nor have we known (or do we know) what might be anticipated as a result of administrative training efforts. Will we have more efficiently run schools? Will teachers be happier? Parents? Will youngsters learn more? I must confess I would be hard pressed to answer these questions but, in a way, they may be the wrong ones to ask. And by this point, I want to suggest that a more appropriate question to ask, using the second half of the title of Chapter Fourteen is, How can school administrators learn to be better judges at their own private craft show?

I don't use the phrasing of this question to be flip. Quite the contrary, I think it is a succinct way of putting the question of the meaning of what we now call professional development for administrators. First, it is based on the notion that the concept of administration-as-craft provides people with an understandable way of reflecting on their work in a way they had not had previously. Using the administration-as-craft notion, as well, enables principals, for example, to review a day's or a week's work in clinical terms. That is, they can ask themselves if their understanding of the "material" they were working with was adequate. Or, what more is needed for them to be able to get a more refined "nose for things." Or, what kinds of experiences are needed to give them a more extensive memory for "knowing the right thing to do."

There are other reasons for using the craft and craft show ideas as vehicles for professional development programming for administrators. First, the image it conjures up seems to have a definite appeal for administrators. At least, that was the case with every person with whom I talked. It made sense; it was not arcane; it could be used. It was an idea on which they could "hang their hat." I think this was so because it is a work-oriented idea. It has to do with a way of viewing and understanding what they do, daily. And this leads to a second reason for using the craft and craft show ideas. It is that most administrators simply seem to enjoy very much talking about their work with someone who is interested in their work.

It seems clear to me, then, that thinking about ways to enable administrators to be better at their craft should be premised, first of all, on the notion that they enjoy talking about their work. This thought may appear as too simple a one to base any serious administrative craft improvement efforts on, but I don't think so. That is, I am convinced that the huge majority of school administrators (1) are interested in doing their work better, (2) already have the intellectual and behavioral resources within themselves that may be needed to become better, (3) need some concepts around which to organize their thinking about themselves, and (4) need deliberately to provide time for themselves that is devoted to becoming better. Our focus will be on the third of those four items, the one that deals with organizing concepts.

I suppose that any number of conceptual orientations may be advanced to organize one's thinking about the problem of becoming a better administrator craftsperson. In the context of this discussion, what makes sense to me is to start with the question, How can one become a better judge of one's work? The point here is not to suggest that others do not see and make judgments about how well a principal, for example, has done his or her job. It would be ridiculous to think that such "other group" judgments do not get made. But I do think it's true, except in cases of blatant incompetence which do periodically occur, that the judgments that count, the ones that our principal attends to, are the ones that he or she ultimately makes. And so the question becomes, In what ways can we organize our thinking so that more refined judgments can be made?

Two concepts feed directly into this question and both of them reflect my own bias. The first has to do with the sensitive and possibly soon to be overworked ideas implicit in Donald Schon's (1983) *The Reflective Practitioner*. Rejecting the rational-technical-scientific approach to enhancing professional competence, Schon calls for conditions under which professional problems may be thought about, analyzed, discussed, and critiqued—mostly with the aid of a colleague or teacher—so that a person, in the language of this book, can become a better judge of the craft work or the craft thinking that he or she has produced.

The second idea that feeds into the question of learning to make more refined judgments about one's work relates to the concepts of connoisseurship and criticism as they have been developed by Elliot Eisner (1985). Building on the art critic function as it is enacted in the art world, Eisner (himself an art educator by training) speaks first to the idea of educational connoisseurship, to be able to *appreciate,* in the case of which he writes, the "performance" that is the classroom. And by appreciation, he means to be sensitive to and take note of the metaphorical drama or symphony that is being played out in classroom life—its plot, its mood swings, its softness, its hardness, and so on. Similar "performances," of course, are a way of looking at the daily work life of administrators, and the problem with which we are dealing here is that of helping an administrator become his or her own connoisseur. Put another way, the problem is how to help administrators learn to reflect on their work in ways that enable them to be sensitive to its plot, mood swings, and so forth.

The concept of criticism, as Eisner discusses it, refers to "going public" with one's appreciation. In our case, though, "going public" is not the issue. We have noted how judgments are made in private and, despite plans for more openness in the system, I suspect the ultimate judgments about an administrator's work will continue to be made in relative private. The problem raised by the idea of criticism as it is used here, then, is how to help administrators learn a more functional craft language with which they can talk to trusted colleagues and, much more often, to themselves.

I do not know how all this is to be done. The problem, in fact, probably deserves study and a book of its own. But I do remain convinced that the most potent resource for enabling administrators to become better at their craft and to learn the skills of administrative connoisseurship and criticism presently exists among the ranks of already practicing administrators. Professors can assist in all this, I think, but their assistance has potentially much less power than that of the practitioner. My guess is that the best way a professor can help is through acting as an administrative alter ego.

- *Can there be something called a theory of school administration-as-craft?*
  What has been called the theory movement in educational administration is generally considered to have had its birth in the mid-1950s. This
  birth was coincident with that of the University Council on Educational
  Administration (UCEA), an organization of departments of educational
  administration in major research universities throughout the country (a
  condition of membership which, given the financial problems of many
  universities and of the UCEA itself, no longer holds). The predominant
  character of the professoriate in these departments is that they were either
  bona fide social or behavioral scientists by training or they grafted
  themselves on to that branch of learning.

    Thus, the direction that the thinking of influential thinkers about
  school administration took should come as no surprise. It was in the
  direction of theory-building based on scientific models borrowed from
  the physical sciences. I have already noted in the early chapters of this
  book that I think the results of all this have been unproductive as far
  as the practitioner is concerned and that the scientific metaphor is inappropriate for the field of administration and administrative practice. I
  hasten to add, however, that though I take that position, I don't consider the last thirty years of the "scientific" study and writing about administration to have been wasted. Primarily I think they have been of
  value because they have raised the level of thought that was devoted
  to the field. As well, though I reject the scientism that accompanied all
  this, I must say that proponents of the theory movement have introduced
  concepts into the field that I take to be of value. Such ideas as organizational culture, norms, and influence patterns, I believe, are important
  for a school administrator to think about. They form that part of his or
  her experiential memory which may well help to make an action
  decision.

    All this notwithstanding, it does seem clear to me that no scien-
  tific theory of administrative practice can be developed. And so, seeking an alternative because I think that administering a school district or
  a school need not be a random affair, the question gets raised as to
  whether or not there can be a theory of administration-as-craft. The
  answer to this question depends, in my judgment, on what is meant by
  the term *theory*. For example, a rather commonly used statement of the
  meaning of theory is found in Kerlinger (1964, p. 11): "A theory is a
  set of interrelated constructs (concepts), definitions, and propositions that
  presents a systematic view of phenomena by specifying relations among
  variables, with the purpose of explaining and predicting the
  phenomena." For all the reasons that have been discussed in this book,
  and probably some more, this statement is of little value when it comes
  to understanding the practice of school administration. Like it or not,
  the social and behavioral science cadre of professors of educational

administration have to accept the fact that the practice of administration—by which I mean what it is that administrators do—is not a matter related to scientific theory.

Where, then, can we turn for a meaning of the term *theory* that will, in turn, have meaning for practice? A comment of Lawrence Cremin's (1976) in the preface of his book, *Public Education,* very simple as it is, sets the context for thought about administrative theory very well. He wrote that it was his intention "to sketch a theory of public education . . . , using theory in its commonsense meaning as a systematic description or general statement of a field" (p. x). If the reader will substitute the words "school administration" for "public education" in Cremin's definition, we would then have what I think is a sense-making statement of what form a theory of administration-as-craft make take. It would be, in nonscientific fashion, a systematic description or general statement of the field. And the field of interest, school administration, is a field of practice. Further, the position here is that that practice may best be conceived of as a craft in the sense that the way school principals and superintendents think about what it is they do and how they do it, as the reader may well be tired of hearing, bears a very close resemblance to the way practitioners of traditional crafts think about what they do.

What would be the substance of this craft theory of administrative practice, this "systematic description or general statement of a field"? In a way, but I am not sure how thorough a way, this book may be thought of as a start on that substance. And this is by way of saying that the substance of this theory would deal with the actions and thoughts of organizational leaders as they endeavor to make prudential decisions about dealing with the endless human predicaments they encounter, both their own and those that involve others. Further, I suspect the theory would include subtheories that are situationally specific as far as categories of work are concerned. That is, the systematic description of craftwork in administration is probably different when the problem being dealt with is concerned with the work (see Chapter Four) of "keeping things running as peacefully as possible" than when it focuses on "implementing or reinforcing educational ideas."

A final point is in order relative to any theory of craftwork in administration that might be developed. It is that I think it would include statements about the traditions or lore of the field. And it would probably include numbers of "rules of thumb" that are used by administrators to guide behavior. Truly, it would not be a scientific theory and, so, probably all the more useful to practice in the field.

- *What type of inquiry would be most helpful in efforts to try to understand the nature of administration-as-craft?* Before starting to deal with this question, I need to make something very clear. I am not, on principle, anti-social or -behavioral science nor am I anti-scientific method anymore than I am anti-word processor, a machine I do not know how nor want to learn to use. However, and as should be plain, for our concerns with trying to understand the practice of school administration,I think the "scientific" approach has been tried, found wanting and not terribly useful. This does not mean I reject the notion of social or behavioral science or the scientific method *in toto,* but I do for those things for which their use seems to be inappropriate. From my point of view, one of the things for which the scientific metaphor seems to have been inappropriate is learning anything really important about the practice of school administration. So we have in this book the proposition of administration-as-craft put forth as a more productive way to think about the work of school administrators.

Given an assumption of the validity of the idea that the practice of administration fits most closely the metaphor of craft, the question still remains of how and about what should systematic inquiry be conducted so that (1) we will learn more about it, and (2) what we do learn will be of use to practitioners. Most emphatically, I do not have a clear-cut answer to this question nor am I sure a clear-cut answer exists. But for a starter, here are some thoughts:

- An umbrella theme under which most if not all administrative craft inquiry could be conducted would be "people at work." There is a large literature concerned with work and it should be taken advantage of. In addition, a literature that should not be ignored is fiction. A colleague of mine (Pajak, 1985) has made some studies of teachers as they are portrayed in fiction, but to my knowledge no similar studies have been conducted with principals as their target, if indeed, such fiction exists. But we do know that principals have been portrayed, usually in humorous fashion, on television.

- Under this theme, most anything concerned with what administrators do and how they think and feel about it becomes grist for the inquiry mill. But I think the primary issue is concept development and elaboration rather than trying to make broad-based statements of statistically significant relationships, whatever they may happen to be. The point is that superintendents and principals will remember concepts related to their work but most certainly could not care less about standard deviations, variances, and so forth. It is not so much that it is evil to conduct inquiry that yields findings that must be expressed in those terms as much as it is meaningless as far as practice is concerned.

- Following this point, it is probably true that the methodologies that will yield findings that will have potentially the most impact on practice will be found in the qualitative, not quantitative, tradition.

Participant observations, case studies, interview studies, and oral histories fall under this heading. Superintendents and principals, I think, are eager to learn about and from the experience of their colleagues. Studies that yield a $p < .05$ are rather less than likely to communicate that experience. And so, for the most part, they have little meaning for practice.

- Critically important, I think, is the need to help school administrators learn to be their own inquirers of their practice. That is, there needs to be found a way so that a principal or a superintendent may study systematically and learn from his or her practice. The outlines of how this is to be done are not clear to me. But I can visualize the formation of collegial inquiry pairs, triads, or larger sized groups whose task it would be to inquire, that is, to learn, about the practice of each other and, in the process, help that other to develop the ways and means to conduct his or her own study.

A final thought related to the type of inquiry one might imagine necessary for the systematic study of practice of administration-as-craft, but not a content or methodological concern, is this: The demands on the reporter of such inquiry, as far as writing is concerned, are different than than the demands on the writer of "science" or scientific findings. That is, the writing of the results of the type of inquiry I have in mind mandates readability. By this I do not mean simplicity of thought but the ability to write a narrative—almost a story—that will attract and hold a reader.

- *If the concept of administration-as-craft is taken seriously, what might be some implications for the preparation of administrators?* We must understand something at the outset of this discussion of preparation programs for school administrators. It is that, in my judgment, we do not train people to be school administrators. And to repeat again, recall my comment in Chapter Two: "They brought themselves with them to graduate school, so to speak—their visions, their security, their intuitions—and they took themselves back to their schools knowing some new things, but they were still basically themselves." In a very real way, the implication of this statement is that these people knew how to be school administrators before they became one and certainly before they took part in a graduate administration program.

Of course, this last sentence is a bit of an exaggeration. Most certainly there were things these people didn't know about being a school administrator. They must have had to learn certain nuts and bolts of school operation and more than likely they had to learn some new skills or some add-on ones to those they already possessed. But for the most part, I think, they had learned, at its most basic level, what is customarily involved in administering a school through the normal process of grow-ing to be an adult together, quite probably but not absolutely necessary, with having been a teacher. And by this I mean that I think a very pro-ductive way to view the activity of the human system that is the school or the school district is that it is a daily reenactment of everything that people—adults and children—have learned about relating to and deal-ing with authority, peer groups, group and organizational standards, political intrigue, censure, praise, good behavior, bad behavior, rewards, punishments, and so on. At its most basic level, dealing with and in-fluencing this reenactment is what being a school administrator is very largely about. In other words, it is the techniques and skills associated with this reenactment that constitutes the major part of the exercise of the administrative craft. Further, I maintain that, on some level, idiosyn-cratic to themselves, most adults have learned the rudimentary skills necessary to managing this daily drama through the very process of becoming an adult. But I also think that schools, the adults who work in them and the youngsters who attend them, deserve more than effi-cient and effective management of the daily kaleidoscope of events that occur in them. In the context of our problem, that is, it becomes impor-tant to think through the way in which thinking of administration-as-craft might enable us, as well, to think about administering as leading. And this, too, is very much involved with the craft of administration.

A detour is necessary here because we must ask what it is that graduate programs prepare people to do now if it is not, at the very least, to create images of what it might mean to be a school leader. To be quite blunt about it, their orientation seems largely to be a technicist-management one. Helping would-be administrators develop imagina-tions of what might be and helping them think through how that "might be" might indeed "be" seems to have a low priority. Further, this orien-tation to management, which has a history to it (Callahan, 1962) that goes back to the early years of this century, seems clearly to be in the process of perpetuating itself if we agree with Gibboney's (1987, p. 28) assessment of the report of the National Commission on Excellence in Educational Administration. He wrote:

> The report of the National Commission on Excellence in Educational Ad-ministration, "Leaders for America's Schools," is deficient and inadequate. How can it speak seriously about reform when it resurrects and builds on the same trivial courses in management and administration that have been taught for several decades? This is not even old wine in new bottles; it is more like Mississippi river water in tin cans.

Gibboney's article, more properly called a polemic, may be somewhat hyperbolic but his points are well taken, I believe. It does seem that an increasingly popular role model for both administrators in the field and educational administration professors has been the industrial manager. Indeed, I have heard countless school principals refer to themselves and be referred to by others as middle managers. It is as though (1) the term *principal* which derived from "principal teacher" is somehow distasteful or demeaning or, perhaps, not professionally sounding enough, or (2) managing schools has simply become a higher priority than thinking about them in educational terms.

Much as the professoriate may wish to avoid the thought that most graduate preparation programs seem to focus their course work on what it means to be a manager of an institution that has the learning of youngsters as its "most important product" and not the leader, the mover and shaker of that institution, I think it is a conclusion that eventually needs to be confronted. And so I agree rather generally with Gibboney's final comment in this reaction to the Commission's report. Noting (1) that the curriculum it proposed stems from the scientific management thinking of Ellwood P. Cubberley and his colleagues in the early decades of this century and, (2) agreeing with Callahan who called the education of administrators an American tragedy, he says:

> Two generations of administrators have been trained in this tradition. Management served no larger end than itself. Efficiency was extolled. School law and finance replaced philosophy, history, learning and children. This was the foundation and this was the sand. The commission's report reiterates the essence of Cubberley's curriculum. This *is* an American tragedy (p. 28).

- The administration-as-craft idea suggests that most of what people need to know about managing a school they already know. It is not that taking a course in educational finance and the like is worthless, but it and others like it—personnel administration, school-community relations, for example—deal with those parts of an administrator's job that can be learned rather easily on the job. Recall in one of our early illustrations a superintendent saying, ". . . . you learn to do a budget by doing a budget." That is, it is in the process of doing, which is a craft, that one learns to make judgments of educational worth—if, that is, one is inclined to think more educationally than managerially. The point that needs to be made is that although there are types of know-how associated with school management that are not commonly held by prospective administrators, they tend not to be esoteric or highly difficult to learn. Even I, who have difficulty balancing my checkbook, could probably learn to construct a school budget. The difficult part would be learning to make the appropriate judgments— another part of the craft.

- The administration-as-craft idea permits a type of curricular freedom that we don't currently have. That is, it provides a direct entree into what I think might be the first question that should be asked of a prospective administrator, "What is it, when you become a principal (or whatever) that you want to make?" If we ask and then build a student's curriculum around the answer and subsequently revised answer to this question we may well develop a different look to our graduate programs. No longer would we have a cafeteria of management-oriented courses. Instead, we would have programs that would reflect the knowledge and skills needed to plan and make, as it were, an educational happening. That is, that very simple question, "What is it you want to make?" quite possibly has the most complex and intellectually elegant implications for learning as any I can image.

- The administration-as-craft idea mandates a focus on the value-set (recall my earlier question about values) that accompanies the decision-making process of each individual. My colleague, William Greenfield, wrote about this most eloquently, I think, in the second edition of *The Effective Principal* (Blumberg and Greenfield, 1986). Linking the idea of "making something" to decisions that involve competing values, I quote him as follows:

> We note the centrality of values to making decisions not only because it is a work-world reality that has been ignored by educators and researchers; even though making decisions is so central to the work of principals and teachers—decisions regarding curricula, methods of instruction, school goals and objectives, and policies and practices regarding student conduct and development. The list could go on *ad infinitum*. Making judgments about alternatives introduces a moral component to action, to the activities of teaching and to the activities of leading and managing a school. Values held by individuals therefore not only reflect but also sustain and sometimes change school culture.
>
> The moral component to action and decision-making requires that a judgment be made. It thus carries with it the possibility, often a high probability, that one standard of goodness may be sacrificed for another. We cannot always have our cake and eat it too, so to speak. The work of the school principal, as illustrated in the examples given by those we revisited, and others as well, is characterized by many a moral dilemma—that is, the necessity to make a judgment that one set of valued alternatives is to be preferred over another. In one instance, for example, a principal had to decide whether to support a teacher against a student—and thus validate and reinforce a criterion of goodness central to the ethos of teachers as a group ("principals support teachers, right or wrong")—or to subscribe to a criterion of goodness held central by the normative community of educators as to what constitutes good teaching or good educational practice; and by this standard support the child against the teacher, knowing in the particular instance that, by the standards of good teaching, this teacher did not behave appropriately (p. 226).

- The administration-as-craft idea encourages us when we think about "making something" to think in terms of what Greenfield called our "moral imagination." Again, as he said it better than I could, I quote him from the same source:

> So when we speak . . . of "moral imagination," we refer to that quality of character that distinguishes the morally educated person, that gives that individual the ability to see that the world need not remain as it is—that it is possible for it to be otherwise, and to be better. It is this quality that differentiates the school principal who leads from those who do not; and, while it is a quality found in other persons as well, it is especially critical for principals, because principals must bear the greatest responsibility for, and hold the greatest potential for, determining what sort of school a school is or is to become. . . .
>
> Vision, the capacity to exercise moral imagination, is the foundation upon the moral authority of the principal rests. It is what enables the principal to lead a school well. While authority of position provides the principal with an institutionalized base for influence, this is not sufficient to lead a school; yet too often it appears to be the only basis used by principals, and thus many attempts to improve the school (by "somebody's" standard) are resisted or aborted. Thus, in order to lead a school well, one must have a vision of what is desirable and possible in that school's context; one must be knowledgeable about and believe in the standards of good educational practice, which are the gift of a normative community of educators extending throughout history. Finally, one must have the ability to communicate those possibilities to others and to move others to action to realize those possibilities (p. 228).

What, indeed, would a curriculum for the preparation of administrators look like if it was based on the idea of developing one's moral imagination? Perhaps we should attend to that idea.

As I indicated earlier, there is a final question that I needed to address and I do so in the next chapter. It deals with the notion of artistry in administration, if there is such a thing.

Chapter Sixteen

Beyond the Craft—
Administrative Artistry

In Chapter Two, along with rejecting the science metaphor of administration, I also put aside as unhelpful the idea of administration-as-art. I did this not because I think there is no such thing as an artistic administrator, but because the use of the art metaphor is not helpful in understanding the work of administrators or in constructing any kind of model of that work. Collingwood's (1938) definition of art as the exercise of creative imagination or Croce's (1976) notion of art as lyrical intuition, for example, leave us little to work on as far as making sense of administrative work. Likewise, Howard's (1982) suggestion that the boundary line between art and craft is a fuzzy one, though of interest to those who wish to argue the philosophy of art, proves not to be helpful if one wishes to know how a school principal or superintendent approaches and thinks about his or her work.

Yet my own experience and that of every reader of this book I suspect, has put me in touch with administrators who seem able, for whatever reason, to work with people, to solve problems, to create a school environment, and so forth, in ways that leave the rest of us with comments such as, "How in the world was he or she able to pull that off?" On the occasions when we are moved to such comments, I think we have a sense of having experienced something unusual. We don't forget it.

The best parallel I can draw from the real world of art was my sense of myself when, some twenty years ago, I was in Amsterdam and saw both up close and from a distance, Rembrandt's *The Night Watch*. Evidence of my not forgetting was in a note to the first paper I wrote (Blumberg, 1984, p. 40) about administration-as-craft, where I said the following, "I was awestruck and, as I think about it now, wished I could have been part of Rembrandt's imagination and taken my place in the painting as he himself did." My suggestion here is that we develop feelings about these very unusual administrator-craftsperson-artists that are analogical to those I had about *The Night Watch*.

My intent in this last brief chapter, then, is to explore the idea of administration-as-art. And I do this knowing that the chapter will end with no definitive point being made except one that suggests that to deal with that idea is to deal with a bit of mystery. The mystery, I think, cannot be unraveled but its nature can, perhaps, be clarified. We start by picking up on the paper referred to in the previous paragraph. After making my case for administration-as-craft, I wrote (pp. 33–35):

> There is another side to the whole business. It is that the idea of administration-as-craft leaves room for those circumstances—rare though they may be—in which the administrator as craftsperson somehow is able to do things with such an exquisite sense of the human condition that such terms as "a work of art" or "the work of a master" can only be applied to his or her work.
>
> This thought led me to seek a person who was skilled in a traditional craft. Another colleague was such a person in the bona fide sense that he did indeed build things out of wood. The essence of our conversation went something like this:
>
>> I: You see lots of things that people build. Tables, chairs, and so forth. Every once in a while I know you see something that in some way stands out from everything else. It almost makes you gasp at its loveliness. What is it?
>>
>> He: You're right, of course. I really don't know. I think it's a sort of grace about the work that can't be copied. It's like things fitting together and flowing in an elegant way. And it works so well.
>
> The idea of things fitting together and flowing in a graceful and elegant manner and, at the same time, working well was attractive to me, as was the thought that the work could not be copied. The "noncopyability" represented, for me, that idiosyncratic expression of creative imagination about which Collingwood wrote. It was kin to my idea that whatever an administrator will be, he or she already is long before becoming one. It is not so much that visions do not change or that one cannot alter ways of relating to people as it is that the basis for what one becomes as an adult is, as I see it, almost unknowable, uncopyable. It certainly is unchangeable. In a somewhat deterministic, but not pessimistic, sense, "Whatever will be, already was."
>
> What my craftsman-colleague had in mind, of all things, was a particular corkscrew that he owned. But corkscrews or tables are not human organizations, and that part of the metaphor that involves "things fitting together and flowing in an elegant way" is bound to break down in the day-to-day-life of a school, college, or university. Life in those situations tends to get messy, if not sloppy. School faculties react in ways that are much less predictable than does wood in the hands of a woodcarver, although sometimes wood does "talk back." At times, though, one can spot an organization that is able to deal with its messy and sloppy self in ways that convey to an observer that graceful sense of things fitting together that links a work

of craft with a work of art. It reflects, somehow, the exquisite understandings and skills of the administrator.

I know of one such organization and decided to talk with several of its members about their administrator. Did they have a sense of his doing his craft with the lyrical intuition of an artist? Or was I all wet? Was there anything that could properly be conceived of as craft-artistry in human affairs? Or was that just nonsense?

I found out that what was on my mind was not nonsense and that I was not all wet—at least from the perspective of the several people with whom I talked. The administrator in question was good at his craft, which he had learned without formal training. He handled his budget well, seemed to make wise personnel decisions, knew how to bargain and compromise, and had a finse sense of the political side of organizational life. Beyond these things, though, were the following remarks made by members of his organization that spoke to that part of him—I think the most important part—that seemed to set him apart from most others who practice the same craft:

- He has an exquisite sense of timing.
- He has a passion about his own life.
- He defines himself rather than being defined by others.
- He believes he can shape the world.
- His humor works as glue. It pulls people together.
- He has a sense of the absurd and the ability to treat absurdity as just that.
- He has a vision like the Biblical prophets.
- He has a ready-made image of a world that doesn't exist, but could. And he speaks this image all the time.
- He is patient and knows perfectly well his vision will come in its own time.
- He has an authentic compassion.
- He has an elegant sense of history.
- His sense of optimism is such that the cup is always half full, never half empty.

Is what I am writing about simply charisma—a personal magic of leadership arousing special popular loyalty or enthusiasm? I think not. For one thing, I do not believe in magic. Second, from Katz and Kahn (1978), "Charisma derives from people's emotional needs and from the dramatic events associated with the exercise of leadership." It is related to the dependency needs of followers, and "it is a means by which people abdicate responsibility for any consistent, tough-minded evaluation of the outcome of specific policies." Being a charismatic leader, then, is more a function of the needs of the followers interacting with some personal characteristics of the leader than those characteristics acting alone. When there are no followers in need of a charismatic leader, then one will not be so labeled regardless of his or her personal qualities. And, although it may be true that the characteristics of this school administrator about which people remarked may well be those that are typically associated with charisma, the state of the organization in question and the needs of its members suggest that charisma is not the issue. For example, there has been no member abdication of responsibility. Quite the opposite seems to be the case.

What I think enables the craft-behavior of this administrator also to be artful in his believability. He seems to live the imaginative vision he talks about. All of us have had the experience of smirking with a cynicism born of previous experience with visionaries who spoke, it seemed, more for effect than anything else. There is little, if any, smirking in the present case, although sometimes there is a lot of laughter when the administrator I described seems to go overboard on one issue or another. Further, when these occasions occur, he joins in the laughter, perhaps realizing that he has stretched things beyond the point of believeability.

My purpose in discussing this particular school administrator has not been to extol him. (I am not preparing a speech for his retirement dinner.) Rather, the points have been made to reinforce the idea of administration-as-craft and to suggest that, in those rare circumstances in which it also appears artful, it is a function of some thing or things about the person involved and not just the degree of skill with which the craft is practiced. As Collingwood noted, the technique or skill is always considered in the service of the art and is never the art itself.

There is a second purpose to this discussion. It is to suggest that those things that are better understood in the practices of a skilled craftsperson or an administrator as the work of an artist are not trainable and are not copyable. It is not so much that a person is born with them as it is that somehow, and, in some way, he or she acquires them through his or her particularistic life experience. What, how, or why I am not prepared to say, nor, I think, can anyone else. That is the mystery of it; I believe it defies empirical study. And, since I think that part of the beauty and joy of life involves its mysteries, I am perfectly content to leave it that way.

As I read back over what I wrote about the idea of an administrator who was, by almost total agreement of his faculty, an artist, I find myself thinking that the thoughts I expressed then would be the same ones I would express today. This sameness is perhaps a way of validating the notion of the mystery. That is, though I have thought about it often, my thinking has not clarified anything except to make me feel reinforced for what I already have said. But there are two points that need to be emphasized. The first has to do with Howard's idea that the work of artists is craftwork. They simply must be very good at the craft upon which their art depends before being able to produce a painting, for example, about which people might marvel. The same holds true of administrators. They simply must be very good at their craft before others could even begin to think of them as administrative artists.

The second point is that whatever attributes administrators have that influences others to think of their work in artistic terms are uncopyable. One cannot copy "an exquisite sense of timing" or "an elegant sense of history," for example. And, to take this a step further, it becomes obvious that one cannot learn to be an administrative artist. What is implied by that idea is probably a learned but unteachable ability to view schools—the adults who work in them, the youngsters who attend them, the parents and community who support them—in ways of grace and compassion that are given to only a few of us to possess as our own.

All this is by way of saying that if you happen to cross paths with a principal or superintendent to whose work the notion of artistry is attributed, treasure the experience. It is not apt to happen again soon.

Finally, I want to end this book with a story told to me by a colleague. Though it is about the work of a sculptor, it has a lesson for those of us who would lead or teach about leading a school. My colleague said:

When I was in college I was taking a course in art and artists. Our professor brought as a guest a man who was a famous sculptor. Everyone, it seemed, came to learn from him. His specialty was to carve animals out of stone. He had several of his pieces with him. They were of dark stone, I remember, and they were beautiful.

After his lecture, we were standing around, feeling embarrassed because we didn't know what to say. So, to relieve my tension, I guess, I asked him how he thought about what he was going to do, and, then, how he went about doing it. He said that when he was younger he used to plan things out very carefully. After years of experience and many struggles he discovered something. It was that what he wanted to carve was in the rock somewhere and that "My job is to chip away till it comes out. It's in there and I'll know it when I see it."

I didn't know why at the time, and I'm really not sure I do now, but I had a sense of his comment being incredibly important. It's as though for every school building, there's a beautiful school in there somewhere and, if you keep on chipping away, you'll find it. But you have to know what you're looking for.

Bibliography

Administrative Science Quarterly. 1956. Ithaca, N.Y.: Graduate School of Business and Public Affairs, Cornell University, p. 1.

Alexander, C. 1927. *Educational research: Suggestions and sources of data with specific reference to educational administration.* New York: Bureau of Publications, Teachers College, Columbia University.

Allen, W. 1907. *Efficiency democracy.* New York: Dodd, Mead.

Barnes, O. 1845. In *Annual report of the superintendent of common schools of the State of New York.* Albany: Carroll and Cook, pp. 258–262.

Blanchard, K., and Johnson, S. 1982. *The one minute manager.* New York: William Morrow.

Blumberg, A. 1980. *Supervisors and teachers.* 2nd ed. Berkeley, Calif.: McCutchan.

Blumberg, A. 1984. The craft of school administration and some other rambling thoughts. *Educational Administration Quarterly* 20:24–40.

Blumberg, A. 1985. A superintendent must read the board's unwritten job description. *American School Board Journal* (September):44–45.

Blumberg, A. 1987. The work of principals: A touch of craft. In W. Greenfield (ed.), *Instructional leadership.* Boston: Allyn and Bacon, pp. 38–55.

Blumberg, A., and Greenfield, W. 1986. *The effective principal.* 2nd ed. Boston: Allyn and Bacon.

Blumberg, A., and Wood, B. 1986. The principalship as a craft. Syracuse, N.Y.: Syracuse University. Unpublished paper.

Bogue, E., and Saunders, L. 1976. *The educational manager: Artist and practitioner.* Belmont, Calif.: Wadsworth.

Bolster, A. Toward. 1983. A more effective model of research on teaching. *Harvard Educational Review* 53:294–308.

Cubberley, E. 1947. *Public education in the United States*. Rev. ed. New York: Houghton Mifflin.

Curtis, E. 1845. In *Annual report of the superintendent of common schools of the State of New York*. Albany: Carroll and Cook, pp. 253–258.

Educational Administration Quarterly. 1967. Columbus: University Council on Educational Administration, Ohio State University, p. 1.

Educational Administration Quarterly. 1982. Columbus: University Council on Educational Administration, Ohio State University, p. 18.

Educational Literature, 1907–1932. 1979. New York: Garland.

Eisner, E. 1985. *The educational imagination*. 2nd ed. New York: Macmillan.

Gibboney, R. 1987. Education of administrators: An American tragedy. *Education Week* (April 15, 1987):28.

Green, T. 1968. *Work, leisure, and the American schools*. New York: Random House.

Green, T. 1984. *The formation of conscience in an age of technology*. Syracuse, N.Y.: Syracuse University and the John Dewey Society.

Greene, M. 1984. How do we think about our crat? *Teachers College Record* 86:55–67.

Griffiths, D. 1979. Another look at research on the behavior of administrators. In G. Immegart and W. Boyd (eds.), *Problem-finding in educational administration*. Lexington, Mass.: D.C. Heath.

Hines, W. 1987. Rules of thumb: An inquiry into the acquisition of professional knowledge. Syracuse, N.Y.: School of Education, Syracuse University. Unpublished paper.

Howard, V. 1982. *Artistry: The Work of Artists*. Indianapolis: Hackett.

Howsam, R.; Corrigan, D.; Denemark, G.; and Nash, R. 1976. *Education as a profession*. Washington, D.C.: American Association of Colleges for Teacher Education.

Katz, D., and Kahn, R. 1978. *The social psychology of organizations*. 2nd ed. New York: John Wiley and Sons.

Kerlinger, F. 1964. *Foundation of behavioral research: Educational and psychological inquiry*. 2nd ed. New York: Holt, Rinehart and Winston.

Kmetz, T., and Willower, D. 1982. Elementary school principals' work behavior. *Educational Administration Quarterly* 18:62–78.

Lapham, L. 1987. Notebook. *Harpers* 274:10–11.

Levine, A. 1917. Better schools through scientific management. *Educational Foundations* 28:535–540; 29, 20–23.

Magnus, P. 1907. The application of the scientific method to education. *Nature* 22: 434–439.

March, J., and Simon, H. 1958. *Organizations*. New York: Wiley.

Martin, W., and Willower, D. 1981. The managerial behavior of high school principals. *Educational Administration Quarterly* 17:69–90.

Mintzberg, H. 1973. *The nature of managerial work*. New York: Harper and Row.

Needleman, C. 1979. *The work of craft*. London: Routledge and Kegan Paul.

Pajak, E. 1985. The changing image of the teacher in 19th century American fiction. *Journal of Psychoanalytic Anthropology* 8:135–150.

Payne, W. 1875. *School supervision*. Cincinnati: American Book.

Pelz, D. 1952. Influence: A key to effective leadership in the first line supervisor. *Personnel* 3:3–11.

Reeves, C., and Ganders, H. 1928. *School building management: The operation and care of school plants*. New York: Teachers College.

Rogers, C. 1961. *On becoming a person*. Boston: Houghton Mifflin.

Rosenberg, A. 1983. The human sciences: Obstacles and opportunities. *Syracuse Scholar* 4:63–80.

Ruesch, J., and Bateson. 1951. *Communication, the social matrix of psychiatry*. New York: Norton.

Scheffler, I. 1960. *The language of education*. Springfield, Ill.: Charles Thomas.

Schein, E. 1985. *Organizational culture and leadership*. San Francisco: Jossey-Bass.

Schon, D. 1983. *The reflective practitioner*. New York: Basic Books.

Schon, D. 1987. *Educating the reflective practitioner*. San Francisco: Jossey-Bass.

Shulman, L. 1986. Those who understand: A conception of teacher knowledge. *American Educator* 10:8–15, 43–44.

Stallings, J., and Nelson, D. 1978. *Nuts and bolts in school administration*. Washington, D.C.: University Press.

Strayer, G., and Thorndike, E. 1913. *Educational administration: Quantitative studies*. New York: Macmillan.

Taylor, F. 1911. *The principles of scientific management*. New York: Harper.

Tead, O. 1935. *The art of leadership*. New York: McGraw-Hill.

Tead, O. 1951. *The art of administration*. New York: McGraw-Hill.

Tom, A. 1984. *Teaching as a moral craft*. New York: Longman.

Weick, K. 1980. Loose coupling: An unconventional view of educational bureaucracy. Paper presented at the convention of the American Educational Research Association, at Boston.

Wittgenstein, L. 1958. *Philosophical investigations*. 2nd ed. Oxford: B. Blackwell.

Zurner, R. 1986. Illusions maintained by principals. Syracuse, N.Y.: School of Education, Syracuse University. Unpublished paper.

Index